ORPHIC CANTOS

IVAN ARGÜELLES

With an Introduction by
John M. Bennett

LBP

LUNA BISONTE PRODS
2016

LUNA BISONTE PRODS
137 Leland Ave.
Columbus, OH 43214-7505 USA

www.johnmbennett.net
https://www.lulu.com/lunabisonteprods

This book is dedicated above all to
the Spirit and Memory of my Twin Brother
Joseph Anthony Argüelles

si potuit manis arcessere coniugis Orpheus
Threica fretus cithara fidibusque canoris
Aeneid, VI, 119-120

LBP

Other titles by Ivan Argüelles that
were published by Luna Bisonte Prods:

DUO POEMATA [2015]

FIAT LUX [2014]

A DAY IN THE SUN [2012]

ULTERIOR VISION(S) [2011]

Additional copies of this book and
above listed titles are available at:
https://www.lulu.com/lunabisonteprods

THE CHAOCOSMIC POETRY OF IVAN ARGÜELLES

Introduction by Dr. John M. Bennett

PART ONE

Ivan Argüelles begins his book, *Orphic Cantos*, with a question: "how does language work", and the lines that follow make it very clear that this is, and has always been, one of the fundamental themes or concerns of his work and voice as a poet. For starters, the poem begins with no upper case, just a lower case "h", as if the poem were the continuation of a discussion that had been on-going for years. Which in fact it has. It is a question with no single answer but which is at the very center of human consciousness.

When I asked Argüelles about this, part of his reply was:

" ....a major theme in Orphic cantos, indeed in much of if not all of my work from *MADONNA SEPTET* on is language and the destruction of syntax in order to get at the *ultimate* meaning of things, that is, to unravel from the many ruses of language and descriptive grammar to get at the core of what humanness is, perhaps an articulated silence. We do lots of things without language, principally making observations with our eyes, such as staring with awe at a summer night sky. We call this activity the *ineffable.* There are also unspeakable acts etc. Language is THE distinguishing characteristic that supposedly sets man off from other living entities. It is a labyrinth that creates the ego-self and ensnares that self into delusion and illusion and often madness. It is capable of logical constructions and arguments as well as Dada and nonsense."

In the poem, Argüelles refers to language as being inextricable from our consciousness of death, and that in a way it *is* death. I suggested to him that if language is consciousness, if it is the container of civilization, the form in which we are aware of time, if all that; then could we think of his writing as comprising a kind of "quantum poetics". A quantum poetics would suggest that the concept of THE is illusory, and that, as William Burroughs repeatedly suggested, it is the root of all our problems and delusions. In Canto 9 of this work, Argüelles says "to articulate / *the* behind the vowels a messy scene". His reply to these issues:

"I've always been fascinated with the definite article and its use. It seems that only languages in the western part of the large Eurasian ecumene (e.g. Arabic, Greek, English etc) employ a definite article, while those on the eastern side of some invisible language border do not have a definite article (e.g. Russian, Farsi, Hindi, Chinese, etc). What is "the"? what is "a"? How can some languages do without something that seems so essential: not just dog any dog but THE dog! Why don't we just point and say "Woof! woof!" The fact is billions of people get along quite well without having to "articulate" a specific canine. Ancient Greek is replete with the definite article, classical Latin does not have it. Greek seems the more supple for it, while Latin seems marmoreal without it. Just an observation. Yes, THE is an illusory concept. As for "quantum poetics", are we talking metalanguage, images beyond the pale, syntax unbound by the rules of relativity (which is no syntax at all)? Language is at the root of all our problems. How many times a day do we say to someone else "What do you *mean?*" We never fully understand what the *other* is really saying. Sometimes that drives us crazy. As for Orpheus, he created song and music, and some say also writing. Writing is precisely the effort to record in some sort of symbolic form and/or combinations of letters that are supposed to interpret in a *meaningful* way what we have heard and keep hearing."

Ivan Argüelles is not a poet who mines the general Anglo-American vein of poetry that is supposed to be *of use* in some way. That poetry is basically didactic, prescriptive, or therapeutic, and could not be further from what this poet has achieved. Argüelles writes from the same psychic urging as someone like José María Heredia writing about Niagara Falls or the temple at Cholula, for example: it is a romantic expansive summoning of an entire multiple and swarming world and history. In Argüelles' case this romantic and epic tendency has been filtered, originally, through a fascination with surrealism. His early writings, from the 1960's, in fact, contain some of the very best surrealist poetry ever written in English. That work is very much in the line of Breton and others, and in some ways is superior to it, in that Argüelles' work seems more felt, more urgent, more expansive. His later work, in fact, can be seen as an expansion of that surrealist phase: as if it, the later work, were an attempt to fill in the blanks, and to truly fulfill the vision his earlier work implies.

So where did this poet come from? His story is a unique one, and many details of it can be found in the sources listed at the end of this essay. Argüelles provided some further clarifications, however. When I asked him if he could talk a bit about how his particular upbringing might have given rise to his approach to poetry, which in so many essential ways is outside the mainstream of Anglo-American poetry, he replied:

"I think the best way to answer that question is by this little anecdote. We had just moved from Los Angeles to Rochester, Minnesota. Mom was diagnosed with TB and her brother, my Uncle Wally, had our family move to that parochial small Minnesota town, home of the Mayo Clinic, in order to get my mother into a sanitarium (a word I mistook for *"cemetery"*). [In Spanish, the words "cemeterio" and "sanitario" sound somewhat similar – *JMB note.*] My father, my sister, my brother, and I moved into the cramped quarters of my maternal grandparents' rooming house. Dark days those. My brother and I had been in the first grade in LA, it was winter, the middle of the school year and after some tests, instead of finishing the 1st grade they put us into the 2nd half of the 2nd grade. Our first day of school there some boys approached us in the lavatory and quite bluntly said this to us: You're not Americans, you're Indians. Well that settled it: *Others* from the start. From that moment until the day I graduated from Rochester High School in 1956 I never rid myself of the sense of being other, different, a foreigner, someone who didn't meet the norm and didn't fit into the community.

This was a predominantly white, German and Norwegian Lutheran town. We were Mexicans! Dark foreigner, my father spoke with a very heavy Mexican accent and looked every bit the Latino, black wavy hair and mustache, rather romantic and handsome, but still a Mexican, a wetback. We were unique. Walk into the living room of our new home at 904 7th Av SW and what do you see on the living room walls: silver Aztec masks! On top of that I was an *identical twin.* Unless you're a twin, you don't know how odd it is, because you're, let's face it, peculiar. Kids all razzing us because we look alike. The teachers seated us at opposite ends of the class room in order to tell us apart. And we were odd, bright and dark at the same time. There were times when I wished my name were *Argyle* and not *Argüelles,* a name nobody could pronounce! Our father was not only an Outsider but an artist, a painter, to boot. And he gave us art lessons, wanted us to be painters. So we had this aesthetic upbringing, as it were, that also marked us. By the time we were in high school, though somewhat integrated into the community, there were parents who did not want their kids to hang out with the *twins.* And they had some cause to do so, as, in addition to being gifted and talented, we were also wild, and formed part of the "wilder" group of kids who smoked, drank and listened to rock 'n roll and rhythm and blues.

By the ninth grade I had decided I did not want to be a painter because then my brother and I would be in fierce competition. I told my father I was going to be a poet instead. This disappointed my father, and I felt slightly rejected. But I went on nevertheless to devour what poetry and literature I could find in the public library. Instinctively I was drawn to "experimental" stuff: e e cummings, Eliot and Pound, Djuna Barnes' *Nightwood*, William Faulkner's *As I lay Dying* and especially James Joyce's *Finnegans Wake*. I clearly stayed away from more formal paradigms of literature. Clearly these authors and their works, exemplified by broken syntax, lack of ordinary punctuation, a stream of consciousness that broke the rules, etc., had a profound influence on me. They didn't write like O. Henry or Charles Dickens, or Alfred Tennyson. Nor would I!

The relief I felt, and at the same time an anxiety, upon graduating from high school was enormous. I was free to leave the wretched stifling small town atmosphere and fly, like Stephan Daedalus at the conclusion of *Portrait of the Artist ... "*

Argüelles' twin brother is José Argüelles, the New Age artist/writer and activist. Although the two brothers worked in very different fields, it has seemed to me that there were some real similarities between their quests for a fuller or broader meaning or understanding of *everything*. Argüelles said, in response to my question about this:

"You're absolutely right. Identical twins! At about the 4th grade we saw a map of Los Angeles, big sprawling thing, which just fascinated us. We then began collecting maps of large American Cities, as many as we could find. Our favorites were the Thomas Brothers Street atlases of the California Metro areas (LA and San Francisco). And of course there were the Twin Cities (Minneapolis and Saint Paul). We divided the world between us: I was Los Angeles, he was San Francisco; I was Minneapolis, he was Saint Paul; I was London, he was Paris, etc. We then started making our own maps on large brown sheets of x-ray (?) paper of imaginary cities. We began mapping the cosmos in our own way with our collective imagination. Believe me we were never more identical than in our creating these maps. We would listen to radio programs and project the adventures of these shows on maps spread out in front of us. To the end of our days, as far apart as we had become (apparently) the maps remained with us. He traveled and lived in various places far more than I did, and whenever he settled in a new place, he'd send me the map of that place (e.g. Auckland, NZ). This omnivorous collection of maps, I believe, led to an omnivorous sense of taking in the world, the galaxy and the universe in our burgeoning adolescent minds. In high school we consciously divided the creative worlds before us: he would be a painter, and I a poet. His painting turned into Mandalas and then into his New Age Mayan projections of the Universe, as he saw it. My poetry similarly has never been concerned with the trivial or the quotidian aspects of human life but has always taken on mythographic extra-historical dimensions. We mean or meant in our endeavors to be all inclusive, "to take it all in". The part doesn't have a meaning without the Whole."

I would say, however, that the quotidian aspects of life *are* present in his work, but that they are recontextualized within a much broader picture, as parts of the whole universe. He agreed with this, saying that the things of everyday life are "all part of the large endless mythology of my life."

I then asked him when he started reading stuff in Spanish and what did he think of it? His answer:

"My linguistic (dis)orientation is an odd one. I was bilingual from the time I started talking (living in Mexico City then) until a point when I must have willfully ceased speaking Spanish probably when we went to live in Minnesota (although I don't remember *not* speaking Spanish). My parents conversed in Spanish maybe 50 per cent of the time so I kept hearing it. The first day of Latin in the 9th grade was a revelation to me, because the budding historical linguist in me immediately saw the parent/child relationship of Latin and Spanish (e.g. mensa/mesa). This fact so amazed me that I at once rounded up all the Romance languages in that parent/child relationship and throughout high school I became a linguistic auto-didact, teaching myself what I could of French, Italian and Portuguese from grammars I found in the public library. My prize was Romanian, as I finally got my hands on a Romanian grammar in the summer of 1955 on a trip to Chicago. (Drove my mother nuts rattling off sentences in Romanian). So I obviously was reviving my Spanish, but this time by reading it (to compare it with the other romance languages). For a while I was in interested in Spanish texts only as documents of interest to a comparative or historical linguist, that is to say snatches of poetry and prose in Old Spanish. I did read *Don Quixote* in the original for the first time around 1968. When I seriously started writing poetry, in the early '70's in New York City I had recourse to Italian and troubadour poetry at first, but then I started reading real Spanish literature. I believe the novels of Miguel Angel Asturias were the first I read, *Mulata de Tal* and *Leyendas de Guatemala* made a special impact on me. Then I discovered the poetry of Lorca, Vallejo and Neruda, and after that I went back and forth between the Siglo de

Oro (Góngora and *La Celestina*) and the 20th cent. (*Cien años de Soledad* or Octavio Paz). I always felt that reading Spanish kept me in touch with my roots. Period. In fact I feel that way about all the romance literatures (they're all one dialect spectrum) and Latin. No translations for me. "

As Argüelles indicates above, the deep background of his work is a grounding in the classics – the classics of avant-garde modernism, especially surrealism, the classics of Romance literatures, and the classics of the ancient world. Yet he is sometimes described as a Chicano writer. I have also noticed, in speaking to him, a bit of that particular Mexican-American slang in his speech. When I asked him about this, he discussed his relationship with that world:

"Chicano Spanish: Don't really know what that is, presumably Mexican Spanish spoken by Mexicans living and working in USA. My father qualifies as a someone of that group. Though not a migrant laborer like César Chavez, he nevertheless suffered great humiliation trying to find work in Rochester, starting as dishwasher in the hospital where I was born and working up to being a popular bartender in a so-so hotel downtown. I get most of my colloquialisms from his speech habits, including the wonderful violent cursing he was wont to vent ("me cago en la madre de dios!"). I became aware of the movement founded by Chavez and this sent an electric cue to my identity: ah, I guess I'm a Chicano!. Ironically my father refused to identify with the movement. I was very much influenced at the time and found myself writing lots of poems about my Mexican identity. Many of my earliest poems were published in "chicano" magazines, such as *Revista Chicano-Riqueña*, *De Colores*, *Aztlan* etc. I was quite flattered when Ishmael Reed's Before Columbus Foundation anthology chose a poem of mine, previously published in *Revista Chicano-Riqueña*, as representative of Chicano poetry. When I was a librarian at the University of California Berkeley I had strong ties with the Chicano Studies Library. Now all that is a thing of the past for me. The Chicano thing blurred into the Vallejoesque poetry, characteristic of my 2nd book, *The Invention of Spain*. The rest is Surrealism and beyond. Ándale pues!"

One of the great strengths of Argüelles' writing is that his use of Spanish, as well as his English (most of his work is in English) is neither Chicanoesque nor Vallejoesque, nor Golden Age nor Elizabethan nor Graeco-Latin, but completely unique. It's Argüellesesque, and full of an exciting and ever-changing mix of profane slang, elegant diction, and everything in between.

The issue of being bilingual is one that will become more and more pertinent as our cultures diversify and writers and poets increasingly use more than one language to express themselves. I asked Argüelles how writing in Spanish differed from writing in English:

"My Spanish must be as idiosyncratically Argüelles as my English is. That is, whether expressing myself in either language, it is from the dark root of the unconscious whence the words or expressions and images spring. Still the Spanish does seem different, but I am not sure how to say why it is so. In my Spanish I feel a much quicker easier flow of absurd juxtapositions than in my English. Somehow it feels more unfettered ... cannot explain why. It's as if I am sleep talking in Spanish. Whereas the English comes roaring out of all kinds of books of poetry philosophy history myth and my own personal experiences. Then the Spanish is all free form nonsense and pure automatic writing. Why the division I don't know. Does that make sense?"

To me, (also a bilingual poet), this makes a lot of sense; my first language was English, and I mostly live in an English-speaking environment, so that when I write in Spanish there are fewer constraints due to there being less conditioning through the everyday usages I make of English. The kind of linguistic freedom this creates bleeds over into my use of English to some extent, and thus has an effect on everything I write. At the heart of Argüelles' diction one experiences this same kind of freedom, a joyful and at times ecstatic playfulness with language. It is a kind of language that can sustain itself, that never gets tired, and that tends toward what I think is one of this poet's major goals, a goal that arises out of the very linguistic environment he has created. That goal is to recreate or invoke the universe in its entirety. I think it is also true that there is something in the way words are formed in Spanish that makes word-play easier. There is more consistency in how words are constructed than there is in English and this makes it easier – and more obvious – to take them apart and recombine them, to make outrageous puns, and so on. There is also a strong cultural practice, especially in México, of word play, broadly documented, as for example in the many volumes of *Picardía Mexicana* by Armando Jiménez.

Obviously, this is not the aesthetic of most Anglo-American poetry today, or perhaps ever – (except perhaps in the 17th century with a poet like Milton). I asked Argüelles how he would describe the differences between his own world and that of some of the kinds of writing being produced in the US today ("creative writing"/academic, Language, Beat, Slam, etc.):

"First of all I feel my work, when it is received, is perceived somehow as "outside" from the start, not worthy of serious attention. In the so-called poetry scene of the Bay Area to this day, although I have been widely published and received two major awards, plus a lifetime achievement award, my work has never received any real critical attention. I focus on the Bay Area because it has a rich poetry/literary tradition that includes Rexroth, Duncan, the Beats and Language poetry, and because I have lived here some 35+ plus years, the period of almost all my poetry output. I should add that currently the scene is dominated by the academic/workshop poetry best exemplified by Robert Haas. For me the feeling is a duplication of the feeling I had living in Rochester when I was not invited to the County Club dance for achieving high school seniors going on to college. That aside, I *know* my poetry is different, because it is more complex, more lyrical, more experimental and draws on more intellectual sources and traditions than does most poetry written today. It may be puzzling or infuriating at times, but it is also more interesting for the same reasons, and read aloud often packs a punch. Finally, on this note, my poetry from the beginning, was considered to be surrealistic, which it was, and there was a distinct hostility towards surrealism, which was another strike against my work.

Insofar as the differences between my work and other Anglo-American poetries, there are many, but also some similarities. The Beat influence has an undercurrent in my work, especially when I touch upon themes of topical interest, where the influence of Ginsberg may be noticed. I think the Beat influence was more noticeable in my earlier work, and has probably disappeared. The Language poets are a self-congratulatory and self-perpetuating group, who are also basically rooted in the academy. Similarities have been pointed out between Language and Surrealism, I guess in the *use* of language as the predominant factor. But Language poetry for me has never seemed like "poetry", it has no lyricism, unless by chance, and flatly lives in a contradiction with what poetry has traditionally been about. Like early surrealism, as championed by Breton, Language poetry has become very dogmatic and more about post-modernist theory than about poetry. On the other hand my poetry is quite the opposite of the predominant school today, the workshop/academic school. It seems that in order to be published by any major publisher or university presses, a poet first of all has to have a degree in writing. Time was when a poet lived outside the academy and its rules. This poetry focuses on the quotidian experience, and fills the page in neat lines of really ordinary language which might as well be prose. The ego functions as the main determinant in a banal narrative description of an event and the feelings aroused by it. That there is so much of it, and that it is so much alike that it is difficult to distinguish between authors, and that it is accepted by the NEA and public radio and television as *poetry per se* is appalling. By contrast my work is informed with rich imagery and lyric flights as well as the consciousness of poetic traditions both modern and ancient. It is also experimental in a tradition set by Pound and furthered by Olson, though having little to do with these poets. My poetry is distinctly not about the quotidian world, but includes the whole muddled elements of history and myth, and concerns that may well be galactic at times. It may be seen as a fusion of surrealism and mysticism, employing a multiplicity of voices and linguistic orientations that have little to do with accepted syntax and in fact often destroy it. My poetry definitely works at levels of consciousness ranging from acute perceptions of the real to the deliberately confused states of the unconscious and dreams."

One of the striking characteristics of Argüelles' work, present in the work of a very few others in English (such as Olchar E. Lindsann to name just one, and my own work), as well as in work from Latin America and Europe, is a presence of, and a dialogue with a universe of *literature*: other authors, classic works, pulp writing, all kinds of things from the present, and the near and distant past. This dimension seems largely lacking from most US poetry - at least the poetry published by university presses, small presses, etc. It's as if there were a conscious avoidance of any reference to literature. As if history didn't exist, as if culture (in the anthropological sense) didn't exist. This, in my view, is part of what makes so much of such work shallow and of little real interest. I asked Argüelles about this:

"I couldn't agree more with your observations about the absence of any notion or concept of literature and history in contemporary American poetry. Perhaps it's because when they teach poetry they focus on teaching how *to write (sic!)* poetry. They are not interested in teaching the history of poetry, only how to write down one's emotional tangents in this very prosaic version of "poetry". I have long bemoaned the lack of a sense of historicity, be it literary or political, in the turgid stuff that passes itself off as verse nowadays. I have always felt infused by the books and poets I have read, by the history that surrounds the writing of poetry in various eras, be it Homeric, Vergilian, Dante-esque, Siglo de Oro, Elizabethan etc. Poetry is not written in a vacuum, or at least until now it hasn't been. Vergil wrote conscious of the Augustan period and its apparent greatness, just as Dante wrote informed of the violent politics of his Florence, the *bianchi* and *neri* factions. But more than that, great poets have always written acknowledging a literary tradition to which they are heirs. Ezra Pound is perhaps exemplary in this matter. As for my poetry, it is obvious I feel heir to the ancient classical traditions, as well as to modern schools such as Surrealism. For me history is the myth from which I draw my poetical themes, and myth itself is as real as history. Images from all periods of time and space swarm in one vast poetical *present tense* for me. You might say it is the very *stuff* of my poetry.

I should add that it's no accident that my career choice for a profession was librarianship, and prior to my 20+ years as a catalog librarian at the Library of UC Berkeley I had the fortune of working for 10 years at the New York Public Library, a monument of a building housing a fantastic collection. My relationship to books has been very much like that of Don Quixote's: the world which they open up to me is quite often far more real than the world in which I wake daily."

As a result of all this, Argüelles' poetry demonstrates an enormous erudition, but it is an erudition that leads to and expresses a vivid sense of what life, and the universe it inhabits, is: his work occurs as a consciousness within a vast panorama of human history and cultures, of civilizations and languages. But, and this is important, it is never just in some misty zone of other worlds and times, but is a consciousness of those other worlds as being in the background of, or surrounding, a person very much in the here and now, who walks in the street, who engages with a family, who sees in the dolled-up girl in a record store the ghost of Beatrice, who hears the voice of Krishna in the raucous sounds of rock and roll.

The consciousness of these other worlds and cultures is, at least in Argüelles' work, in language. Language, in fact, is in the marrow of this book, as it is in so many of his. *Orphic Cantos* opens:

> how does language work
> by subterfuge and shadow
> by echo play of the vast Unknown
> or is it because we are on death row
> playing with substitutes for the word *mother*
> employing enormous syllables of sand at day's end

Note again that the poem, and the book, opens in lower case, as if the poem were the continuation of a canto or a discussion begun long ago, implying that there is no beginning to this song, which thus suggests that it has no end, either. That is, there is no answer to the question.

Argüelles commented on this issue:

" "How does language work?" is la pregunta misma ... for me furthermore it's a matter of breaking syntax down, which I started doing in a big way with *MADONNA SEPTET* ... Noam Chomsky once said that if you came to earth from Mars you would think all the languages were the same language! Syntactically they are ... it's kind of like saying that life is the same as death etc; it's fascinating to me how you can learn a totally different language and can get so good at it that when reading a text in that language "translating" from the "mother" tongue ceases altogether ... you're actually *being* in that other language ... I notice this most when I read texts in Hindi (my favorite really other language)."

In other words, for Argüelles, the major way of striving to understand or perceive in some way, the everything that is, the universe of life and death and consciousness and motion and memory, is through language, or better said, *languages.* The more languages one knows, the greater one's knowledge of these vast issues of human life.

The first lines of *Orphic Cantos* quoted above also refer to one other major theme of this book, as well as so many of his others, which is the theme of a female presence or presences that seems to represent something like the entire universe and/or the context in which everything, including oneself, seems to exist. Canto 61, for example, consists of a kind of mantra on "her name":

her name is cloud
her name is absence
her name is the thing you keep hidden
    between books no one ever looks at
her name is Lala the free-for-all
her name is not what you think it is
.....

I asked him to discuss what this über-female means to him:

"I was wondering when you'd get to this question. Indeed the *Ewig-Weibliche* has been a dominant, and at times *the* dominant theme in my poetry. It stirred in me first upon reading Robert Graves' *White Goddess*, in which he demonstrates the real mythos in our ancient and now unconscious culture is based on a matriarchical system and not a patriarchy. Zeus and his Indo-European Olympian male deities are usurpers uncomfortably trying to replace the deep rooted female deities, etc. My first "epic poem", *"That" Goddess*, is essentially a neo-Vergilian working of this theme. Prior to that in my dense surrealist phase I was always aware of the adulatory semi-mystical role the surrealists accorded to the feminine. My poetry has always had a heavy erotic dose to it, and as time went on that eroticism became more and more embodied specifically in the feminine. For me the feminine, in Platonic terms, is simply the other half of the man. As an identical twin, it was easy to incorporate this sense of being a half of something or someone. I was always aware of the critical role Beatrice or Laura played in the poetry of Dante and Petrarch. In the late 90's I became obsessed with Madonna, the pop singer, or more specifically the image or images she radiated, changing swiftly in fashion and mood, and she fit neatly into my poetics, evolving into the dominant work *MADONNA SEPTET* in which she becomes the cosmos in all its (female) aspects: temple whore, street slut, idealized star, mystical goddess, etc. My poetry since then has always included a heavy dose of the eroticism I explored in that work. I should add that this eroticism was also infused with the Hindu Bhakti (devotional) poetry usually centered around the love of Radha and Krishna. Finally, the feminine is for me the ultimate in mystical exploration and expression, approaching the ineffable. In the constellation of medieval Hindi saint poets, the woman Mira Bai stands out. To her we owe the dictum: In the whole world there is only one man, Krishna. Everyone else is a *woman.*

As an afterthought this "psychoanalytical" footnote came to mind: when I was 6 my mother had to be placed in a Sanitarium for TB. For one thing I heard the word as "cemetery" and for another we were *separated* from her a good 2 years, being allowed a rare visit from which we had to look at her across this big room, pale distant wasting figure she was. Hence the (for me) feminine attributes of loss, longing and Echo.

That was a really bleak period ... we were basically uprooted, living happily in Culver City, California when the diagnosis came in about the TB (a real scourge in them days) ... my mother's brother, a doctor at the Mayo Clinic, moved us up in the winter of 45/46 to Rochester MN ... for two years we lived with my maternal grandparents, stern German Lutheran no nonsense types ... My father, a virtual Mejicano got the worst of it ... broken English, had to get a job doing dishes in a hospital ... that's when on our first day at school there some kids approached my brother and me in the lavatory and told us "You're not Americans, you're Indians" ... and so forth ... "

Argüelles' comment about Mira Bai above and there being only one man with everyone else a woman could be applied to his work in general, in that there is a center of some kind – usually represented by a female presence – around which not just everyone but everything else is swirling. I asked him if this seemed accurate, and if so could one say that his work represents an attempt to control, or understand, or to describe, the universe he experiences:

"There seems to be something to that. I think I recall someone saying "Socrates was a woman" as well. Yes, there is for me this indefinable but feminine presence around which the cosmos, however plural it may be, swirls like mad, taking in its composition all the elements of history and myth, making a riddle of the whole. In the end both as substratum and superstratum is this "woman", or at least the female pronoun very much in evidence: she, her. My work definitely is not an effort to control anything. It is at best a chaos out of control, with a longing for the center. Nor is my work meant to be understood, explained away, made coherent by various rationalizations. My work however *is* an attempt to *describe* what I perceive as the universe, my (?) universe, the one that came into being when I was born, though it probably was there before, I just didn't know it. It might be better to say my work is an attempt to *remember* my universe and the feminine presence that animated it, knowing some day it will be utterly forgotten."

Memory, of course, is fundamental to poetry – and to human life as we know it – but I thought I would ask Argüelles how his personal memories function in his poetry. Is there such a thing as a purely "personal" memory? Or is memory to some extent a social construct that is constantly changing? Is there such a thing as a memory in his work that maybe isn't something literally from his own direct experience? He replied at length:

"Memory. Memory works on several planes for me. The first is the purely personal, and of course my poetry to a large extent depends upon so-called "personal" memories. There are a few salient memories that have determined the course of my life and poetry. But rather than dwell on such memories in detail or in a "confessional" way, I mythologize these memories, integrate them into a larger fabric mixed up with history and mythology. I do not place these personal memories in the context of their own historical reality, but abstract them, poeticize them, remove them from their narrative or autobiographical environment. For example: I never tell the reader about the exact moment in time when I was with my twin brother and out of curiosity he stuck his finger into a moving lawn mower and all but lost it somewhere in the grass. I have mythologized that memory, placing that missing finger into a grass that constantly symbolizes some sort of arcadian loss ... Again the memories I have of a short lived first marriage to Claire Birnbaum frequently occur but again are mythologized. In *COMEDY , DIVINE , THE* those memories are a principle leit motif, but it would take a Sherlock Holmes to deduce that. Again when I do take a personal memory and overtly make a poem out of it, that memory takes place on a mythological plane becoming confused with apparently unrelated historical phenomena. My collection *Looking for Mary Lou* is based on a mythological search for the original Mary Lou, a girl I went steady with in high school. Here Mary Lou is disseminated over a litter of surrealistic landscapes, more often despised than not. I probably invent memories as well, who doesn't? But are there such things as "personal" memories? I am not sure how to answer that, and in a sense all of life is a memory constantly shifting from instant to instant, until we get to the point when there is nothing left to remember. Death. A few minutes ago is already a memory, and sometimes yesterday seems like years ago, and then we start forgetting all about it, details blur, oblivion takes over, leaving only a few choice moments which themselves become altered perhaps by *how* we want to remember them. Finally Memory itself is a grand subject, the nymph and muse MNEMOSYNE."

I replied that this very instant is really a memory of it:

"and who is to say that the future is not a memory already? What can I say about the countless evocations of my identical twin dead now four years to the day? Here it is something more than memory, more like a genetic riddle, as often I cannot be precise that between him and me which of the two it was that did and said what?"

Orphic Cantos focuses on all the major themes of Argüelles' work through the lens of language or song, the vehicle through which we are human and somehow *more* than human. The Mexica called poetry *in xochitl in cuicatl* ("the flower the song") and it was the means of creating a contact between the transitoriness of life and consciousness and the eternal. This is what has motivated poets throughout history, even, perhaps, in a small way, those pallid domestic whimperers Argüelles refers to above (their poetry being "...a banal narrative description of an event and the feelings aroused by it.")

In contrast, Argüelles' conception of poetry is that it is an Orphic song; ie, an emission that feels like it comes *through* him: "...who am I but a

bearer of unknown letters/signal of noise in the arcane galactic silence"
(Canto 7). Earlier in the same canto, he speaks (or *sings*) of language as
the self:

> itching to touch *skin* once more the song
> ....
> mmm I could have been the alphabet
> the roaming siege of letters scribbled in air
> sandstone amorphous dwindling script
> yellowish bracken misread ungiven vowels
> the coiled reference to the unending snake
> which is You my obsession and destruction

This passage and others suggest that there is a close association between
language/song and woman/the other, as well as between language/song
and the corporeal self.

In Canto 9, he speaks of language as the "braid" of human culture and
consciousness, the thing that makes us human:

> the uniform of the text
> the braid that wraps around the long unwinding column
> ....
> a thing that makes human sounds darkening
> the boots of the text make no sense
> each time it starts *they* get excited
> to learn a new language to shape the lips

But all this is framed in the human awareness of death, of our own death:

> removing the tongue to articulate
> *the* behind the vowels a messy scene
> murdered the word every time
> the lingerie of the text flimsy
> ....
> *"Orpheus!"* they call *"Orpheus!"*
> the purple buskins of the text
> inveterate byzantine symbols ornate and useless
> tumultuously shining in the nowhere
> narcolepsy of the fifth tone pure music
> this is failure of Athenian statecraft
> an entire history of phonetic decay
> shrouded in a text of indecipherable hieroglyphs

man is a two-timing worm...

In this passage one can see how various themes are conflated into the context of language: "consciousness, woman, history, song." One could say that language is *the* theme of Argüelles' work, around which all the others cluster and swarm: consciousness, love, woman, life and death, memory, motion in time, history and literature, culture (in the anthropological sense).

One can certainly see all these themes in his earliest work, and – as we have seen above – they seem to swirl around the central theme of language. For example, *The Structure of Hell,* 1986, opens with these lines:

> the ocean in my ear has turned off its siren
> a gypsum foam gathers rushing
> to erase the dark alphabets of my knees

In the poem "Milk", he says

> a drop of ink has been buried in the milk
> and the light of the first door filters through the mask
> of one drinking the milk trying to taste the words

In the background of this one might sense the experience of his mother in the hospital. It is an experience contextualized as something written, which is emphasized by the aural associations between the words ink/milk/drink. In other words (so to speak), consciousness and even the world in general, occurs in language. "Was it a metaphor when I fell?" he says in the poem "Fear of Falling".

There are a number of references to music in *The Structure of Hell.* Music/song is, of course a major theme, associated with language and poetry. But it is worth noting that Argüelles has had a long interest in music, especially early music, as is perhaps suggested by his reference to "Luneberg" ("I am going to Luneberg to study the signs") in the poem "The Great Fish of Exile and My Father". Lüneberg is one of the towns where Johann Sebastian Bach lived and worked. The poem "Gleich wie der Regen und Schnee von Himmel Fallt" which is the title of Bach's Cantata BWV 18, has its themes and topics all framed in the context of music, "for the doctor whose cunning prescription is death itself/ descending on the minor key bass chord backwards in the mirror". These early books, rich with swirling metaphors and images with a strong surrealist flavor (I have said that Argüelles' early work is probably the best surrealist poetry ever written in English), are still very much in the unique voice of Ivan Argüelles, and contain all the themes and contextualizations that run through his entire work.

PART TWO

At this point I want to step back and look at how Argüelles' work has evolved over the past few decades. My comments will necessarily be incomplete, because this is a poet who has not slowed down in his output, and is still turning out vast and evolving tomes of ground-breaking work.

The question of "influences" in a writer's work is a slippery one, and is often misunderstood to mean where an artist or poet "got" something. In a recently written but at this writing unpublished article about his own influences, Argüelles makes some very astute observations about some of what opened his eyes to the possibilities of poetry. This happened when he was in a 9th grade Latin class when he encountered Vergil's *Aeneid*. Argüelles speaks of finding in the opening lines of the *Aeneid* a "...marmoreal terseness and evocation of a totally mythical but *real* world..." which was"...the origin of poetry...: majestic, yet cryptic, difficult to truly translate, yet full of awe and distance, ultimately imbued with *longing*." It would seem that Argüelles saw in Vergil the poetry he would create himself, for he also realized something very important: "...that Vergil's great poem was an imitation, and that almost all works of poetry and art are basically imitations..." In the same article, he talks about James Joyce's *Ulysses* and *Finnegan's Wake* as further confirmation of this understanding of what literature is, as well as the great Sanskrit classics of India, which have figured so prominently in his later work. As Argüelles' work evolved, these ideas or aspirations were first filtered through his fascination with early 20th-century French and Spanish surrealism, and of some of its manifestations in English, such as in the work of Philip Lamantia.

Although Argüelles refers to works of poetry as basically "imitations", it is important to contextualize that comment for what it does *not* mean. It does not mean something like Borges' creation of Pierre Menard rewriting *Don Quixote* exactly as Cervantes wrote it. There is no way in which one could confuse Argüelles' *Madonna Septet* with the *Mahabhrata* or the *Ramayana*, just as one cannot confuse Joyce's *Ulysses* with Homer's. In fact, what Argüelles does, as all real poets do, is overlay his own unique experience of his own time and place, his own history and personality, on top of, or mixed in with, the forms, the psychic structures, the rhetoric and emotionality, of the earlier work. Earlier work which, in his view, is itself a mixture of a present and a past.

Argüelles' work has moved steadily through full-page "poems" of strong and authentic surrealist consciousness, toward the epic. These shorter early texts are in fact mini-epics, and the expansive texts to come are present in kernel form in them. This impulse, so strong in Argüelles' work, to create a full work, to somehow include and make present all that is and was and that is hurtling at a future, is one of the foundational tendencies or "purposes" of poetry, and is perhaps one of the activities that language itself makes possible (unlike visual art, which is much more static and atemporal). Because a language artifact can be extended through time, it is an ideal vehicle for an attempt to contain or encompass that time; thus the epic impulse in poetry, which Ivan Argüelles has fomented so extensively in his work. It is an impulse that has been suppressed in most Anglo-American poetry today, and that has made that poetry seem pallid and irrelevant to the human condition or possibility. It has, however, been present in contemporary poetry in all kinds of ways: think of Vicente Huidobro's *Altazor*, or the *Cantos* of Ezra Pound as only two examples. Not just poetry, either: there is the example of Joyce mentioned above, and works such as José Lezama Lima's *Paradiso*, Roberto Bolaño's *2666*, or even the novels of William S. Burroughs, someone whose writing Argüelles read and worked with extensively, (he compiled *An Annotated Bibliography of the Works of William S. Burroughs*, 1968, for his Master's degree in Library Science from Vanderbilt University). It has always seemed to me that the references to popular culture in Argüelles' writing is similar to the same phenomenon in Burroughs', especially in *Naked Lunch* and in the "cut-up" trilogy: for both authors, current popular culture topics and memes are incorporated into larger mythic structures.

As I discuss the various stages of Argüelles' development, it is good to keep in mind that his work can be seen as one long poem, with no "beginning" and no "end". It's a cycle or spiral, evolving, but coming back again and again to the same almost obsessive world-view. This is emphasized by the fact that there is little in the way of normal punctuation to impede the flow, and many works have no capitalization at the start of sentences, the sentences are continuations, not startings. There is, then, a kind of atemporality in this most temporal of artistic genres, literature. This implies that, in a sense, Argüelles writes to us from the future, and thus his work provides a perspective from which to see and evaluate everything else that is being written today.

Argüelles' earliest publications clearly show his attraction to classic surrealism, as discussed above. For example, from the title poem of *The Invention of Spain*, 1978:

> the archbishop and the talking coffins
> are loaded into airplanes made of sperm
> while the ships of taxonomic regression
> adjust their television antennas...

And from "ode to miguel hernández":

> I pound my fists into shoes
> and walk parallel to myself
> in a dream that consists entirely of stone

From "vencer juntos":

> at dusk they take the moon
> turn it upside down letting all the sand
> run out for the ants to eat
> then nail it empty to the wind

If these poems are reminiscent of anybody, it would be César Vallejo, especially of his *España, aparta de mí este cáliz* (because of the title and recurrent topic) but Argüelles' poems are not like Vallejo's at all, except perhaps in their mixture of intelligence and passion. In this book, as in so many of the places in his work, "Spain" is basically an imaginary space, as it was in part for Vallejo, (and as it has so often been for artists and writers since the 17th century). For Argüelles it is also a literary space, populated with voices from Lorca, Cervantes, Fernando de Rojas, Ramón Llull, Josep Vicenç Foix, Miguel Hernández, Pablo Neruda, and the Peruvian Vallejo himself. It is an imaginary space into which to project one's own passions and obsessions, which in Argüelles' case are couched in his unique driving style, as if he were trying to say every-thing in one vast expostulation, in one breath, without the pauses of punctuation. It is the voice of "this unnamed soul abandons his furious planet/to its own unmitigated design".

That voice starts to grow larger and more expansive within a very few years, and by 1983, when he publishes *The Tattooed Heart of the*

Drunken Sailor, we can see a channeling of his surrealist vision through a style reminiscent of Allen Ginsberg's *HOWL* (and through that of Whitman and Poe). From the poem "Mechanical Pianos":

> MARY LOU lives with disembodied monkeys
> in a jungle of septic tanks and automobile parts
> MARY LOU is dead she is more dead than Israel
> the angel who fornicated with the city of Chicago
> the teeth of the clouds the fingernails
> and what is written beneath them in permanent mud !

Another example is the title poem from this collection, in which Argüelles' intense relentless voice is fully developed, to become a central characteristic of his work, and which will become the heart of the long "epic" book-length poems – or anti-poems – of his maturity. The title poem opens "and water is the only element", proceeds on a journey through the "waters" of existence, and ends "and I wake in the endless ruin of water/pleading with the Poet to let me be !" Note the exclamation marks, set out after a space (as in the previous quotation). This is a characteristic device of Argüelles, which suggests that there is no end to the poem, or to any poem of his.

In 1984, he published *Nailed to the Coffin of Life*, which was subtitled "Automatic Poems". The subtitle, a term from surrealist theory, can easily be misinterpreted to mean a kind of mechanical writing process that is thoughtless and impersonal. But in this case it is anything but. In part it refers to the extensive use of anaphore, which functions to crank up the intensity of his voice, to make it more emotional, not more mechanical. From "Hiroshima Poem":

> shadow of a hundred million killing macromolecular seconds
> shadow the weight of a universe of blazing steel
> shadow the congress of human biological terror
> shadow the shadow of the fire of all the shadows

In *Pieces of the Bone-Text Still There*, 1987, the poems are getting longer than in preceding books though they still fit on a single page. The lines are also getting longer and, in Argüelles' intensely emotional surrealist diction, his later voice is becoming clear. From "Tenochtitlan Freeway Blues":

> they have stolen my hair and given it to the WOMAN of sand
> my hands they have given to [the] poisoner in the tower

they have stolen my arms and tied them to water
a single piece of bread is watching me turn blue
a demon with door-knobs for eyes is wearing my BODY
I am shivering in the hottest day in Los Angeles
It is every day in Los Angeles I am in all automobiles

These poems look forward to his prize-winning work, *Looking for Mary Lou*, 1989.

In 1988 he published *Baudelaire's Brain* in which the surrealism has a dense, rich quality, similar in some ways to the poetry of Dan Raphael from this period, no fluff or looseness:

here in full view I shall put a sky with its mirror
behind the view a pair of keys made of flesh
with the patina of angels shall hang freely
but which of the two shall I choose to open heaven's wardrobe?
cloud substance of words at the threshold of thought

These lines, from the poem "Which shall I choose?", illustrate the syntactical condensation, the elliptical diction characteristic of this book. The book explores specific topics in some of the poems – the Manitou (Algonquin great spirit), sport hunting, an eye exam – but these seem to be stops in a single long canto. The overall thrust of the book is the creation and voicing (creation and voicing being the same thing here), of the mythologizing of Argüelles' life, his life in the context of his reading: Baudelaire, Calderón, the Beats, etc. But although there are shadows and echoes of these and other literary voices, the voice and the themes are very much Ivan Argüelles', as they have been from the earliest things he published. In this book, the poem "What Is a Poet?" opens "up all those stairs and without a solution" and ends "she is there shining in the midst of shifting !" The poem is written, like most in this and other books, as a single sentence, or as a single expostulation, with no punctuation. Although it "ends" with a sort of punch-line, it doesn't really end at all, but continues in the next poem "Alone Drowned I Talk with the Submerged Corpse of Mary Lou", a poem focusing on that central Argüelles topic, the female presence/idea/other.

This book, as noted above, can be read as a single long poem, divided into "cantos", which has come to be the dominant form of Argüelles' output. In fact, his entire oeuvre can be read as a single long work, an observation he agreed with when I suggested it to him. After describing how he read James Joyce's entire work straight through as if it were a single long work, he observed:

"...in a way I see my work as a continuum developing from the simpler pieces first published in 1978 until the works in progress online today as a whole ... we can refer to it as a dialect continuum perhaps ... but I have always felt this sense of developing, not turning back, pushing outward in my writing ... I consider the high points to have been some of the early chaps such as *The Structure of Hell* or *Tattooed Heart of the Drunken Sailor*; *"That" Goddess*; *Madonna Septet*; *Comedy, Divine, The*; *FIAT LUX*; and possibly *Duo Poemata* ... "

In 1989 Argüelles' book *Looking for Mary Lou: Illegal Syntax*, which included some stunning photos by Craig Stockfleth, won the Poetry Society of America's William Carlos Williams Award. The book represents a culmination of the poet's early "surrealist/beat" style, with individual poems of long lines mostly confined to one page; a few extending to two pages. Many of the poems ring changes on his Madonna/woman/other theme, as well as current events and topics such as the Vietnam war, the H-bomb, Hollywood, geo-politics, and so on. But these are always placed in the context of universal history. From the poem "Vietnam War Memorial":

> they will not bring the mechanism to bear upon the source of light
> empty casks of body withering in the unkempt lawns of matter
> things going out one by one mouths tongues lips eyelids shattered nerve
> looking for the heroes in their wayward ditch abstemious & solemn
> the bleak absence from life broken promises from the surgeon general's
> notebook
> I am indented in the clause of impossible reunion nostalgia for
> unbearable horror!

After publishing *Looking for Mary Lou*, Argüelles made a decision to change direction, to stop writing "short" poems and "get to work on what I had always wanted to do, write epics"[email to author]. So he began a series of long poems he called "*Pantograph*". Some volumes of this monumental work have been published, three of them through his own Pantograph Press: *"That" Goddess*, *Hapax Legomenon*, and *Enigma & Variations*. *The Tragedy of Momus* and *The Second Book* were published elsewhere, but the "bulk resides handwritten in spiral bound notebooks".

"That" Goddess, 1992, opens in the middle of a sentence, and is set as a retelling or *redreaming* of a swarm of mythologies and ancient literatures, told as if they were all one story. Yet it is presented with

breaks in the text blocks and in the lineation as if these were nothing but fragments of a much much larger story, far too long and ancient to fully encompass or understand, especially within the limitations of a work of literature, or writing. The themes are the essential ones in Argüelles' work: woman as focus of consciousness and meaning, death, language and text, time, etc. From the opening "Urtext":

> ...Virgil in a light blue cassock
> holding in his right hand a burning copy of his Great Work
>   then dust the immense density of dust

which is a stand-in for Argüelles' own book, or the whole book of his entire work, held in his own hand.

Hapax Legomenon, 1993, opens, unusually for Argüelles, with a word beginning with upper case - "Shining and not shining"- a phrase exemplifying another constant in his work, the embrace of paradox, or the perception that "opposites" are the same thing, are not really oppositional, but are parts of a much larger whole thing. The book continues essentially as a single sentence until the end, with a question mark: "where is the light/that opens the palms?"

The themes in *Hapax Legomenon* are basically the same as in *"That" Goddess*, but the tone is very different. It is much more subdued and meditative, reflected in the scattered-down-the-page lineation, as if the speaker had to constantly pause to find (or remember) the next words. This more introspective, less expansive tone is spoken as if from on high, from a distance:

> personally
>   it is a strange thing
>   to be
>   alone
> to keep the mind on
>   its eye
>   sinking

Enigma & Variations was published in 1995, the third volume to appear of *Pantograph* through the author's own press. Running through this book is the shadow of the 1991 American invasion of Iraq: there are numerous references to "president bush", "the gulf", "no blood for oil", etc. But this is not a poem "about" that war. It is "about" the constant themes and topics of Ivan Argüelles experienced through a scrim of social consciousness of a specific war, or with the smoke of war drifting in and out of the window. The book is ultimately about itself, or about the need for itself to be written, which could be said about all great books. The war in this book is not just the Iraq war of 1991, but is all war, which is another example of how in Argüelles' work mythic or historical events are all such events, all happening, in a sense, at once:

it was in Dresden of a cruel
winterwar night
when agamemnon got it
where agamemnon got it

. . . .

how does a war? who works the wealth?
who wears the wealth also works the war
who builds the tension prepares to weave the war
almalisa lisasoma almasoma alive?
lissome somatic but why the war telegram?

The Tragedy of Momus was published in 1993 in the anthology *Terminal Velocities*, edited by Andrew Joron. It is the fourth book of *Pantograph*, and is in the form of a play. A rather Elizabethan style play, it is a serio-comic work in which the character Momus is portrayed as both tragic and ridiculous, in spite of his representations to "'that' goddess" (yes, the book by Argüelles himself) and "despite his having written such semi-anonymous works as the Celestina". Momus consorts with a huge cast of mythical, literary, historical and pop-culture characters from across cultures and history before meeting his end. Once again we see Argüelles' perspective of history as all occurring at once, this time couched in a dramatic and sometimes farcical context showing considerable skill at theatrical speech and stagecraft. The work would make for a lively and fascinating production if it were ever staged as live theater.

In 2012, Peter Ganick published *The Second Book*, which, according to Argüelles, "is really the 2nd book of [*Pantograph*] (Hapax I think is really the 8th or 9th)". *The Second Book* consists of two poems, "The Gaoler's Dream" and "Aida". The *Pantograph* books clearly stand on their own as major works, but they can also be seen as a preparation and build-up for the author's next great project, *Madonna Septet*. The themes are spelled out, various styles and dictions developed, and the reach and length of the poems is extended and stretched. As he says in "The

Gaoler's Dream":

> each page separated from the order of its style
> unnumbered to the third degree and released
> into that leafy bower unconscious of all stimulus

Although most or nearly all of Argüelles' books cycle around a consistent set of themes (time, consciousness, "woman", language, and the overlapping of these), each book has its own unique tone and style. An example of this is *La Interrupción Conversacional*, written in 2000 but as of this date unpublished (forthcoming in 2015 or 2016). Much of this book, or long poem, is in lines of approximately five stresses each, there are no periods or commas. Some question marks are the closest thing to stopped sentence endings or pauses, although there are sections indicated by double spacing between them, and the occasional uppercase header, such as "RED KIMONO". The typescript's 158 pages are a seemingly single outpouring of speech: "...tick tick tick/head plodes neatly in parenthetical squads..." as if the whole poem were an opening into, an opening up, of what were in the head/consciousness/unconsciousness in a single instant, in a brief pause in the "conversation" indicated by the title: "never more I wrote it once/and not the same step twice..." The tone of this work is rather more meditative or "thoughtful" ("thinking" is a better way to put it) than much of his work, which is surprising if one considers that it purports to be what passes in the mind in a very short few seconds: "phrases shift subtly in a sleep".

The massive two volume "poem", *Madonna Septet*, was published in 2000 and is a major step in an extraordinary literary odyssey. It is certainly his most ambitious work to date, although "ambition" is a concept that perhaps cannot apply to a work written with such urgency and such a need to "get it out". It is more like a vast exorcism or orgasm, an explosion contained in a shape of epic poetry. In an email exchange, he said "*Madonna Septet* is in a category of its own … writing it was as obsessive a thing as the obsession that triggered the writing … from the opening lines I was already at work deconstructing syntax skipping sentence/phrase endings and putting them elsewhere etc it was written in a fury and passion to get 'it all out'. " In earlier work the syntax deconstruction and ellipses, the cut-up-like techniques, were present from time to time, but in this work they emerge full bloom as a major component of the work's style and flavor. Argüelles, familiar with the cut-up techniques of William S. Burroughs, has taken the deliberate actual cutting-up of text that Burroughs and Brion Gysin did, and incorporated it into his voice without the use of scissors. (This is something I have done in my own work, having also read Burroughs in my youth.) Cut-up has become a form of expression, not a deliberative literary technique.

Madonna Septet, then, perhaps Argüelles' "major work" (864 pages in two volumes), is far from the Anglo-American preference for "slim volumes of verse" as it is possible to be. It is a validation of the enormous real power of poetry to create a textual – and permanent – consciousness of human experience of the universe. The work is complete and thus paradoxical: epic and lyric, joyful and despairing, frenetic and meditative, thoughtful and delusional, expository and nonsensically babbling, discursive and "cut up", prosaic and visionary, profane and divine:

> mitochondria bundles
> the world's ever a
> enigma &   versions later
> night

The book, mostly in English, with bits of Spanish, Latin, Hindi, is divided into eight large sections, each with several sub-sections or cantos using a great variety of forms and styles, making use of all the techniques and styles he developed through his prior work. All of these styles are aimed at the single goal of trying to Say It All, All at Once, with an urgency that at times breaks apart the limitations of language – this is what the deconstructions and the cut-ups communicate; it's what they *mean*. The urgency is also what drives the shifts in style and form among the sections; it's as if the poet were starting over, trying again and again to do or say something impossible: to say it all, to comprehend it all, in a single "thing"; i.e., the other, the female presence, which stands in for, or *is* how humans perceive the possibility of a universe.

Jack Foley, in his introduction to the book, quotes from it:
> other than naming the Other
> what is there
> to say

Madonna Septet is clearly a major work, which probably belongs on the shelf with history's other great long poems – *La Divina Commedia, Primero Sueño, Odissea, Las Soledades, Bahgavad Gita, Paradise Lost* – though it is unlike any of these, as none of these are like each other. The richness, variability, and pure beauty of the language, never "poetic" but always poetry, makes the reading of this book an unable-to-put-it-down pleasure, if "pleasure" consists of the effort to embrace a constant revelation. It is completely unpretentious, yet proposes something enormous and unattainable, while at the same time affirming that the attempt *is* the unattainable itself. The goal is the reaching for the goal.

    Hazard   Peligro

    young thing strolling down aile
    with big book called Suicide

    knew her from somewhere there
    was a before aching for a love

    barefoot in the part incandescent to the
    core naked from the   up

    and down below a union of Minds
    if that is still possible Sex

This is a book which uses all the techniques and themes of Argüelles' previous work, pulls out all the stops, tightens them up to a new level of intensity and focus, and in the process opens the gates to a vaster and more teeming panorama of human history and striving, a panorama in which everything seems to be happening at once.

Jack Foley, in a 2006 review posted on *Contemporary Poetry Review*, discusses surrealism and "readability" in *Madonna Septet*: "The length of *Madonna Septet* alone would qualify it as problematic, but the book is also in some senses an attack on the reader, challenging his/her ability to read it at all. The intense hostility, the fury that was part of the early impetus of Surrealism is definitely present here. Fundamental questions arise. Is there a single person speaking or are there many? Why are sentences broken off? Worse: Argüelles' subject matter is anything but politically correct, and the poem is shot through with the author's immense and often daunting learning. At one point the female figure is explicitly identified with 'Durga,' the name given to the fierce, murderous form of Devi or Mahadevi (Great Goddess). One of Argüelles' motifs is stated early on: the Goddess's mouth – the source of her singing – will 'swallow the god that created her.' The woman is 'Lady Death ringing her worm around the rosy hold...and ShivJi shudders.' The poet is supposedly 'in love with' the pop star – an 'amour fou' if ever there was one. But he is also in the realm of the 'devouring' vagina/mouth. These days, even the newspapers and television talk casually of 'oral sex.' In *Madonna Septet* oral sex has cosmic consequences – and they are proportionately disturbing: 'the way she took the god in her mouth/as if it were just a bottle of coca cola.' 'So who are the saints we rever [*sic*],' ['rever' in Spanish means 'to resee', or 'see again'; and in French 'rêver' means 'to dream' - *JMB note*] asks Argüelles, 'I mean the women.' (There is a later reference to 'the women we rever abhor adore.')"

In *Madonna Septet*, Argüelles has arrived at a point where the techniques and voices and themes he uses are pressured to the point of breaking, pressured up to the edge of incomprehensibility by an urgent need to say it all before it gets away, before it's forgotten. In a blurb on the cover of Argüelles' post-*Madonna* book *Tri Loka*, 2001, Jack Foley says that the author's poetry "...continually deconstructs the very guideposts to which we cling – in vain..." to understand the world we think we live in. He says that Argüelles' work is finally "...an amazing language which simultaneously attracts and betrays us at every possible moment," and that there is an "...infinite nothingness which saturates language, as words mean and fail to mean in an endlessly repeated dance." *Tri Loka*, written after *Madonna Septet*, is a volume with three long poems, using many of the same stylistic devices and processes, but with a much calmer, more meditative tone.

In an interview published in *vormals: perspeckive*, 43, 2002, Argüelles gave his own take on this issue: "...I understand my chaos, that is I understand it is chaos that I am creating when I 'write'... I know that when undertaking my large 2 vol. poem MADONNA SEPTET, I was very very conscious of deliberately breaking up syntax. I wanted to destroy the conventional English syntax while at the same time rendering a text that respected the continuum of texts of repetitive discourse alluded to above. [ie, 'the 'traditional' works of poetry that preceded them, such as the *Iliad*, the *Aeneid*, or the *Canterbury Tales* etc.'] As for rapture, the language I employ is in a constant state of rapture. It is not a simulation of madness, but the very process of orgasmic madness at work."

In 2005, Argüelles published *Inferno*, the first of a three-part work the whole of which appeared in 2009: *Comedy , Divine , The*. As the title suggests, the work is modeled on the great work by Dante Alighieri, *La Divina Commedia,* but Argüelles'work is in some ways more ambitious. Dante's work basically focuses on a single myth, deriving from a single culture, the Judeo-Xtian myth of the afterlife, although, as in Argüelles' work, that afterlife is a reflection of human life, society, and history on earth. What is different in Argüelles' *Comedy* is that it includes all cultures and times: Western, Eastern, New World, Ancient, Contemporary, personal, universal; all of it. All of human history and culture is a single swarming myth in this book, which means that underlying Argüelles' work is a question about what is real, and what the "real" is, and if it is possible to ever *know* what is "real".

Inferno opens with a quote from Simone de Beauvoir: "J'ai écrit pendant vingt ans. Et un jour je me suis aperçu que c'etait toujours le même livre." This, of course, is true to some extent for many writers and poets. In the case of Argüelles, one could say that all his books are not just rewritings of the others, rather that they are all parts of one single long book. But this applies to only certain aspects of the work: the topics or obsessions, the relentless driving voice, and the irrepressible need to say it all; to say it all at the same time. There are, however, differences throughout the books and within them: these consist of forms, diction, clusters of lexical elements, mood and tone. *Inferno*, like the *Comedy* as a whole, for example, is written in stanzas of six lines each. Each line appears to be about the same length, but varies in syllabic or stress count. Each of the three books has 33 cantos consisting of 22 of the six-line stanzas. In Canto xxxii, Argüelles addresses this issue:

> while not a formalist poem , it has the appearance of
> formalism , or in other words it is an imitation , of
> "inferno" , a circularity , going around itself into the
> depths , or it is an appeal to the dead who have written
> this poem before...

We have previously seen this idea expressed by Argüelles: the book is a kind of invocation, or "imitation" as he puts it here; a re-living/re-saying of Dante's *Inferno*, but focusing on Argüelles' persistent cluster of topics. In my introduction to *Inferno*, I discuss in more detail how the temporal perspective of this work, in which everything somehow occurs at once, is related to, and juxtaposed against, the work of which this is an "imitation". The paradox is that time in *Comedy , Divine , The* is at the same "time" circular, linear, and instantaneous. Circular in its retelling of Dante; basically linear in that any literary text exists to be read or perceived in linear time, front to back, or hopping around in it; and instantaneous in its thematic swirling in which any and all topics can and do appear over and over in different contexts in every occurrence.

Perhaps somewhat more than in other works of Argüelles, *Inferno*, *Purgatorio*, and *Paradiso – Comedy , Divine , The –* repeat words and parts of phrases throughout. On first consideration that might be considered as a kind of being "stuck" in a single "place", but in fact, due to the different contexts in which each occurrence of a word appears, the repeated word is different each time. The river is the same river but always with different water. It also creates the sense that the poem is endlessly self-reflective, so that in effect it is "about" itself. It is a self that includes, or moves toward including, everything that is. This tautology suggests that the poem has no end and no beginning, a concept that certainly is in keeping with the poet's idea of poetry as "imitation", a continual going-around of the same poems through history. This is what the lack of any upper case letters indicates, and the lack of periods or other end-stops, and the presence of many many commas, each with equal blank spaces around them (as in the book's title: *Comedy , Divine , The*).

Considering this book, or indeed Argüelles' work as a whole, as a kind of tautology suggests that it is complete and incomplete simultaneously, and that it has to be approached as existing outside of linear time as we usually conceive of it in our daily lives. It is outside of the flow of time, but, at the same time, it is a constant, swirling flow, "forward" and "backward". This, which requires of the reader a different mind-set, is a paradox, along with the paradox of topic/theme being always the same but always different, is one of the signature characteristics of Ivan Argüelles' work. It is what makes his work, again paradoxically, truly innovative, and truly revolutionary in the art of poetry. It is what makes his work fundamentally different from the mainstream of Anglo-American poetry, for which paradox is a kind of heresy, a big no-no. Mainstream poetries want to "solve" problems, make things "clear"; address social issues, be didactic and of "use" in various social, moral, or therapeutic ways. Ivan Argüelles want to create the universe, again.

In an unpublished review of *Comedy , Divine , The* I said the book is "Less 'poetry' than a kind of mandala or calendar of the universe", an idea that also describes numerous Meso-American representations of the universe, such as the Aztecs' "Piedra de Sol", now in the Museo de Antropología in México. I also said,

> That the title is "backward" (with commas, in the manner of American military supply designations) suggests that the book's motion is at least bi-directional forward and backward, "in a narrative of utter disconnections", everything connected because it's all disconnected (those commas with equal spaces around them), everything moving in all directions because it's a "greyhound bus

stopped in the middle of the corn field". So the book's consciousness – it is more of a mind, rather than a story told by a mind - "illusory meat/assigned to the disappearing text" holds all the fragments of what seems to be a multitude of lives or selves and this wealth of detail, ranging from the very concrete ("crunching of gravel", "grass and aspirin") to the ineffable ("lush when verbs have no use", "the word for 'fog' becomes recondite and useless").

Ars Poetica, 2013, is a book similar in length to *Comedy , Divine , The*, and focuses a bit more directly, as the title indicates, on the processes/meanings/functions and place of poetry. The book opens "how it matters doesn't end/it where syntax glides obfuscated" in which the idea of "purpose" (the quoted phrase suggests its "normal" structure of "how it ends doesn't matter"), *as an idea* alone is what is important, not so much *what* that purpose or mattering might be. In other words, poetry is a process, not an artifact with a fixed meaning. This implies that this work has no "end", no "beginning" (certainly no neat moral lesson), much like life as we actually experience it:

> ...what is lingering along the
> way, what is longing, what is
> ++++++++++++++++++++++++++++++++++++++
> mystery, lunar, what eclipsed
> brain can "see"?...

In a section or "canto" titled "(literature)", he says

> from the unknown to the enigmatic
> each hand is a struggle to "know"
> what is not   ever white
> the outside gleaming for a moment
> in the mist...

The "outside" referred to here would be that whole quotidian world "SE corner of Haste and Telegraph" which is nevertheless framed in mythic terms:

> goddess in a white t-shirt, echoes
> nameless across silent, pay for nothing
> at the end of the world, pink lipstick
> of surprise...

It is a world at once timeless and eternal, and fleeting and already over:

...a hissing on the anvil distant
whenever that was a second or two
before everything else goes out quiet
remorse dank sections falling off
into the water somewhere below
presentiment of meat and conscience
however that comes about a brief
wasn't that long ago...

The language in this passage illustrates an important aspect of Argüelles'
style. On the one hand it appears "cut up" ("...comes about a brief/wasn't
that long ago...") but at the same time it appears not cut up from two
separate phrases, but a complete phrase in which the word "brief"
modifies the nounal structure of the phrase that follows it. This is one of
the characteristics that keep these long poems moving forward. That and
the luminous imagery and language hold on to the reader, making it
difficult to stop, as there is no "natural" stopping place in the diction:

wet jungle from a silver plane
to speak with a tom-tom
a battering ram language
it is blacker now this night
all us becoming dead this
wonderful going around and
exorably   eyes
wet the magic show
each window has taking us
into the vortex here shake
my hand a fly plane silver
round a dizzying her
thread leading us in and out
no more alive than dead
with rain   if could speak

Although Argüelles, like many poets, myself included, much prefers
printed books to ebooks, the intersection of great productivity with
restricted resources (and low sales) of poetry, especially of innovative
poetry, makes the temptation to release at least some materials in
electronic form. Argüelles has published at least two books this way:
Secret Poem, Chalk Editions, 2009, and *What Are Probably My
Memoirs*, Chalk Editions, 2010. *Secret Poem* includes two long poems,
the title poem and a shorter one, "[another secret poem]". The first is a
series of meditations on the self and the other, or on anything and the

other, as being fundamentally identical:

> each is the who of the other
> .....
> an infrequent narration
> in first-person-other
> denied and doubled at once

This is at the same time a way of meditating about poetry: "a poem darker than its self":

> or just a narration in thought
> a time sundered over and over
> by the fuse that lit it, a section
> disappears into the dark another
> regarded as intrinsic lingers
> is the void a pattern...

The poem is written in cantos, with lines running together through various kinds of ellipses, a diction, very often of great beauty, which embodies these ideas of the identity of things:

> a likeness to japan or some such
> sentence, red is equal to the
> most followed by an azure point
> which is as always the horizon
> indistinguishable from the heaven
> that surrounds distance the ineffable
> a reason for childhood for the many
> similarities in grass or lying
> there unable to remember the lesson
> incapable of turning the next page
> a history of darkened armies
> running across like silent thunder
> no mind,

There are also references to various of the literary voices that echo throughout Argüelles' work; for example, one can hear the voices of Shakespeare, Whitman, and Ginsberg in the canto "for Philip Lamantia":

> who storm the egyptian pentacle
> to no avail within a work
> destroyed do rave stoned on the

delphic leaf in swoon denied

and Philip Sydney's in the canto "[in defence of poesy]", with its echos
of Elizabethan diction and vocabulary:

uninhibited the raging voice out
that fills the paragraph of still
cenotaph and sepulcher the dissent
-ing worm eats the spoken phrase
alive 'neath such discomfort...

What Are Probably My Memoirs, 2010, also consists of two long cantos,
the first an extremely wide block of text, prose-like in their appearance
on the page. The first canto is a long, somewhat agitated outburst:
"Listen, dog-ear!" about the relentless "thunder" of the poet's need to
write:

begin at the end of old supposed to be , waters running
through thought and thread, a section , hyphenated,
gives us the collusion between flesh and blank
so much trying to sleep, so little left to wake,
so I , nevertheless in old bookstores rummaging,
is that mine? chunks of rhyme and throw them
into the bay , listen carefully to kerouac reading
of ginsberg's "America" , what is it I am doing
reading writing taking walks and thinking , no,
"reflecting", when I am not getting dizzy...

It is a kind of exasperation at how difficult, confusing, and perhaps futile
it is to write, even as it is something that has to be done:

whatever, the ink drains to the left, while topright
utter sections delve into the half that cannot be
discovered, ignored the template where it says "right
thinking" goes away, we are, left alone, to the right a
portion of sky where Mummy Nut in her spangles blooms
starbright, what approbation there is flickers, a wrong
purpose, a passage into the tantric episode with, the
mere idea heads drift a realization that this is life's
exceptional moment the, horizon where Cipango stammers
its backname shifting syllables...

The second canto is calmer, more dreamlike at times, a canto in which the poet is *in* the poem, rather than writing *about* the poem and its need to come into being:

art of breath   is light so utter?
sub ended in appropriately and green
waves code switching in denial\after
birth I came to (be) a likeness
to either side of the smoking portal
snaps hawsers and slips anchor
deep a gore the depths unfounded
will I set sail, a ? whitened a
wisp entails section by section
the vivid reminiscence of obvilion'
a discharge   that vast anterior
yawning and while I look to other
side a watery mass with spume buried
planets hurks a   maze with codes
locked forever as enigmas are

In the interest of full disclosure, I want to discuss here some of the books and chapbooks published by Luna Bisonte Prods, a press run by myself and C. Mehrl Bennett. A couple of them will be considered in the section of Argüelles' collaborations with other writers. Argüelles was also a regular contributor to *The Lost and Found Times*, a journal I edited and published from 1975 to 2005.

Orientalia, 2003, is unusual in that it is one of Argüelles' few, if only, ventures into prose (leaving aside articles, reviews, etc.). It is a kind of "analysis" of the dream of writing, of the "functions" of "ineffable poesy", of the "Carniceria ilusion" of fiction:

The trick is to keep up the prose without letting the dynamite out. But in the end, ennui, a heartless disposition towards the frail whose hands intricately bound in the invisible can no longer be reached. No equation holds like the one without balance. By day's finish the uncountable losses ache in a small rumpled pull over. In either one a section tends towards red...The mind invents pornography. The few thoughts that get out get tangled in the ivy opposite the reflecting pool. Dive in and see. This will ultimately go nowhere.

The chapbook, 18 dense pages, addresses the central Argüelles concerns from a slightly more "prosaic" voice, a more analytic, less ecstatic diction:

Who will then these words give meaning? Why not give rope to the hanging of intention? Who fuse to particles of relativity the force of destiny. Then is this to be the fiction? A giving before the altar, fires a drive to understand.

It is important to note, however, that this more prose-like appearance is a kind of dodge; that is, it is really another of the many voices in which Argüelles speaks poetry, and speaks about poetry. The result here is to create the illusion of a kind of distancing, which is a multiplying of the point of view or "selves" that simultaneously come together and scatter in the lifelong canto that is his work.

Ulterior Vision(s), 2012 (written in 2001, which means that it follows closely on *Madonna Septet*), is a book without punctuation except for some ellipses, and question and quotation marks. The work, perhaps more than any other of his, appears to represent the chaotic totality of a single moment of total consciousness. It opens:

impressive instant over the
bliss edges re run in trial
of error symbology (other is
brahma is "real") poetic scape
nuance in orange fleece with
white hotel awning tripled for
gunfire in reverse as century's
ultimatum BANG s shut on finger
s of repose garlands of blank
…
…a vision in
whatever mirror the eye focuses
to end the fix of inches into
cycle rewind and start over
this was supposed to happen "later"

It ends with what seems to be a kind of conclusion, somewhat unusual for Argüelles:

as is to be done
so will it ever follow
that nothing = nothing

Jake Berry, in his blurb for the book's cover, says: "The boundaries of time and form do not exist for this poet – they never have. While we have been occupied by the single idea, the tight focus, trapped in a moment, Agüelles has refused to play by the rules or even accept the need for the game. His poetry exposes that idea as the provisional, phony construct that it is. Where most find chaos he discovers and sings sublime music."

A Day in the Sun, 2012, was written in the wake of, and as a response to the death, in 2011, of Ivan Argüelles' identical twin, José Argüelles, the New Age writer, artist, and activist. (For an interesting account of their youthful life together, cf. Stephanie South's biography of José. *2012: Biography of a Time Traveler, The Journey of José Argüelles*, 2012.) *A Day in the Sun*, consisting of separate poems, or cantos of a single long poem, naturally deals with and expresses a great sense of loss, of the transitoriness of existence, always couched in the themes and topics central to Ivan's work:

> how the poet organizes for his
> own garden for his own feckless
> dive below the soil for his for-
> saken by god illumination by
> the root of his hair pulled by
> the Muse through the glass
> into the distinctions of light
> and the periphery limitless
> night swans ululating a mass
> eleison! each is one of us a
> "the" without syntax...

Jack Foley, in his blurb on the book's cover, neatly encapsulates the nature of this book: "José Argüelles redefined the western calendar and pointed the way to a universal harmony, a "convergence." In Ivan's work, the universe is expanding and contracting *at once*, and speech, far from clarifying, constantly returns us to the fact of Enigma. The world is wild, exciting, in constant motion, but also horrifying, painful, an endless blow to our Narcissism. Both visions can nourish and sustain, but *A Day in the Sun* beautifully offers us the elegiac, shadow side."

Fiat Lux, 2014, was written in about three months in early 2014. It is a long poem divided into cantos which use a variety of forms and voices, and can be read as a kind of account or imagining of the creation of the world, as the title suggests. There is a melancholy in the tone throughout, which Sharon Doubiago, in her comments at the end of the book, ascribes to a "...moving, recognizable sorrow for a twin brother dead." The idea of a poem or a mind containing/perceiving/invoking the totality of the universe is present here, as in so many of Argüelles' works, but here it is more likely to be couched in terms that suggest that such totality is imprisoning, closed, and not expansive and liberating. From the poem's opening:

> the end which is also the beginning
>   the insectary of the mind
> yclept γνώμών
> carried over the shoulder backwards
>   into the river of time
> ransacking the jewels of heaven
> no longer interested in the mere range of languages

Olchar E. Lindsann refers to this as well in his comments on the book: "These prophetic anxieties are a babel of stories, of voices, of worlds, they are the fragments of languages, scattered like shattered beer bottles or amphorae along the highway. They unfold with a tragic tread in long incantatory lines, heroic episodes wherein sentences are dashed upon the rocks of punctuation, slain, sacrificed to Poseidon; or else, bristling with a *metis* both grammatical and psychological, continue on, journeying through strange worlds, Byzantium, Las Vegas, the pages of a book."

The melancholy tone is clear in this fragment from canto III, "Leçons de Ténèbres":

> not the single nor the plural
> but the uncountable near the nexus
> of sunset and vine watching the slow
> motion of empty cabs drive by in
> funereal procession whose mighty death
> whose massive stone with just a nick in it
> is being conveyed to the lawn of eternal distance

It is also present in almost every topic the book touches on, for example this passage about language, or language as one aspect of the chaotic mess of consciousness, from canto XX, "The Miasma":

> has forever flown the ancient mess a forlorn
> adjective subject to blank periods of excess
> the thickened plot the cloud smitten ovarian
> flight in what subjunctive mood stress howls
> wildly like hair in arrears mirrored in pools

Yet the very fact that this work exists, that it tries to place the self and its consciousness in a vast universal context of all time, cultures, places, is an affirmation that there is a *value* to what we are or to what we try to know and apprehend.

Duo Poemata, 2015, contains two long poems. With their references to classical studies and archaeology, they are more explicitly and exclusively focused on ancient worlds and cultures than most of Argüelles' books, and do not include many direct references to the contemporary world. The first poem, *Ilion*, is subtitled *A Transcription,* and is in fact an example of his concept of all poetry being the same poetry or story retold. In this case it's Homer's *Iliad* ("Ilion" is an archaic term for Illium, or Troy). *Altertumswissenschaft*, the other poem, works some of the same Homeric territory, although the stories are framed in a somewhat broader context of history and archaeology of the ancient world.

Although this book has a more specific focus than many of Argüelles', it still uses all the range of stylistic and formal devices in the author's quiver, and is infused with his unique driving diction, trying to say it all, at once.

In his cover blurb, Jack Foley says: "At the beginning of "Ilion – A Transcription" Ivan Argüelles writes, "just so one world goes away / and another comes into being." Like the best fiction/fantasy, these poems operate at the intersection points of "worlds" - which is to say at the intersection points of mental actions which have about as much in common as Lautréamont's umbrella and sewing machine. But the "marvelous" of these poems ventures further than even Surrealism."

What it ventures into is a vision and invocation of the world and history as something complete and always present. The Homeric world, as well as all times and places, are still with us, and much of Argüelles' obsession has been to make them visible in such a way that they can be perceived as part of the present.

COLLABORATIONS

Ivan Argüelles has collaborated with a few other poets over the years, such as Jake Berry, Jack Foley, Peter Ganick, and myself. One of the first to be published was a chapbook, *Purisima Sex Addict II*, a long poem done with Jake Berry, 1997. There is no part I; calling the work part II was a deliberate subterfuge to confuse bibliographers, but it also suggests that the poem has no beginning, and perhaps no end, an idea very much in keeping with both poets' ideas about poetry.

The poem is a seamless collaboration and truly reads like the work of a third poet, who perhaps betrays having read both Argüelles and Berry. The poem is centered on erotic longings and fantasies:

> she came at me with that little girl smile and said,
> "Do you wanna lick the bowl?"
> the floor hit me square in the face
>> WHAM
>> back to the ENIGMA
>> back to that Euphrates waltz
> the stars guttural song in the backbrain
> .....
>> but shouted loud in hindi
>>> by that thin and naked dancing girl
>>> strutting in the ruins of Mohenjo-Daro
>> hand on hip
>>> mojo cigarette in her mouth
>> her special dialect is dynamite
>> her kiss is the fuse of life

Saint James, 1998, by Argüelles and Jack Foley, is a thick chapbook of an approximately two-month email exchange between the two poets, consisting mostly of back and forth improvisational poems, (is not all poetry, especially in its origins, improvisational?), each responding to the previous one, like a "battle" between 19th-century Gaucho poets. It also includes a poem by Baudelaire translated by Foley with four pages of commentary on the poem and on how it might relate to Argüelles' work, and some discussions on matters of poetry and other poets. One of these discussions is about "imaginary girlfriends", a topic relevant to Argüelles' work: *"Have you ever had one?* I have 'had' all of them."

Dead Requiem: New Poetry from California, Ivan Argüelles, Jack Foley, 1998. This includes two separate long poems; "Requiem", by Foley, and "Dead", by Argüelles; plus "E-Mail", a four-page collaboration by the two. Both poems share a somewhat conversational diction and ask a lot of questions. Argüelles: "who is that stiff?", "what did the doctor say?", "how many voices are there?", "what came of it?", "was there ever anything idyllic?". Foley: "can you tell the difference between my family and a loony bin?", "who are you, mother?", "What is holy/about a book?", "what emerges now?". Both poems, and the collaboration, explore and question issues related to what "poetry" is in the world today, in the midst of our particular culture, contemporary history, and, especially in Argüelles' piece, in the context of the broad range of ancient worlds he so often refers to and relives in his work.

Neeli Cherkovsky says in his introduction that the two are "...drawn to measure themselves against the utter darkness and to ask all that they can from 'That Song'". He's suggesting that the two are inhabiting, recreating, and repeating an ancient and still vibrant world of poetry; an ur-poetry that is fundamental to what we are as human beings. Although the book consists of separate texts by each poet, it is in fact a collaboration, with both poets addressing some of the same questions, each in their own way, but with some similarities of approach and style.

cosmic karmic raga, 2000: this poem, by "Vyasa and Bahina Bai", is a 46-page collaboration by Argüelles and Peter Ganick. Ganick published it through his press, and added a series title, "Indian Literature Series, 1" to further enhance the deception of its authorship. According to an email from Argüelles, "Vyasa and Bahina Bai: Vyasa was a mythical figure who supposedly composed all the big ancient Sanskrit books like the Puranas, and Bahina Bai was a medieval female Marathi saint poet". The poem, in six cantos, appears to have been written back and forth with each poet adding several new lines at each exchange. One voice, perhaps Ganick's, is more "philosophical":

> where to be a necessity of previous lifetime context-
> ualizing the end of a millenium, having been here
> more than which one's Self issues from the mouth
> of Brahman inviolate in its memory of thisness...

The lines immediately following these, perhaps by Argüelles, are more "poetic":

> a garden of shapes we walk through in this lifetime,
> shapes from real life, the life of illusory beings being
> somewhere else, the elsewhere of those beings
> launching dekarmacized territorialisms once or twice,
> meditated upon in its fullness, the sporadic music

Both poets have had a lifelong interest in Indian mythological, religious, and literary cultures, and this work is a celebration of that fascination.

Chac Prostibulario, 2001, by Argüelles and me (John M. Bennett) is considered by many to be one of both poets' most ambitious collaborations – although, being one of the perpetrators, it is immodest for me to say so. But whatever the case, during the first half of 2001, Argüelles and myself began an email exchange of lines of poetry, not with any specific intention, but just out of an enthusiasm for what the other was writing. The result was a quick evolution into a full-length book in which the poets exchanged seven-line stanzas, each responding to the previous stanza. *Poetas gauchescos*, as it were. The first stanza was written by both, each adding lines:

gunner hits tragedy in low slam hoff//max snarks especiality yr
bee low the bore dere a rose yr mexibasca sauce r so smoo
che's oldie ham's o faster dribble sno defensive chews yr
card//board ou tt ake 'n japones yr divvied
sp end angel yr angle hair yr mockassassin boot: uh (charring
root a lamp sticky p ills yr nick le g lints be
neath ah table, shiny with yr breath

...with the rest of the book consisting of alternating stanzas:

necesitas parabrotas como nubes de arena! me siento como nadador
de rimas perdidas un dialect in circular ruins, a textual e menda shun
jaqueca de ritmos átonos the tin a' greek stuff on the shore just rusting
with achilles n his cute li'l shadow play, dwarf n duende at super bowl,
puke to blue jeezus all morning long, helen and her banshees cancún
alley
an' you braggart anent soggy pantaleros two pistols to the wind y niebla
de mierda en merida, chiapas chopsticks surfing like choppers in the Nam

blam thing yr cho ppers gritty en la alcachofa (surfy through, la rutina
jerkular a leaking greek en macedonia antontado pis
tolado in the alley lodazal like cubes of rain! ("cRusting
chanchre bowl a writ more chapado and a quilo giggling luffs
against my wall my boiling enteritis dia lecto why I studied
entumecido esa mapa de la mierda chiapas albania en la mountain
mojada heavy thudding behind the trees falling crows shutup

My guess is that the first stanza above is Argüelles'; the second, mine, based on certain vocabulary choices. [Argüelles: rimas, duende, blue jeezus, helen – Bennett: alcachofa, lodazal, enteritis, mojada] But I confess I'm not entirely sure, especially considering that each poet uses words from the previous stanza by the other poet. It is worth noting that this work was created in the period when Argüelles was writing *Ulterior*

Visions, and Bennett was writing *rOlling COMBers*, shortly after his *la M al. Chac Prostibulario* contains stylistic elements from all those books. As can be seen from the stanzas above, *Chac Prostibulario* is characterized by multi-linguistic punning and word-play, and a joyful enthusiastic tone, all rules of standard poetics thrown to the wind. In his blurb on the back cover, Anselm Hollo said of the book, "...ist ein ootwageous cuncocktioun ov linguadge in unb estado ov tootal disschewelmento y abandonmento, un bytte loik der grayte John Lennon's immurtal 'A Spaniard in the Works,' et aussi un bytte loik le grand Saynt James Joyce's woiks, but a lot mo' apokaliptik!..."

Décima Mucho, 2001, also by Bennett and Argüelles, was written, I believe, later that same year. It's a chapbook of 19 pages. A décima is an old and still-used form in Spanish-language poetry, consisting of 10 short lines with varying rhyme-patterns and line lengths, often octosyllables, and often is a form in which the poet improvises, which is very much the case here. It is often used as a form for popular song lyrics, but is also used as a poetic form on its own. At the time, Bennett was writing a lot of these, mostly in English. He sent many of them to Argüelles, who responded with hacks or glosses or other reactions to them, with décimas of his own. These call and response décimas are "experimental" versions of the improvised back-and-forth décimas which have a long history.

Bennett, for example, sent Argüelles this:

Le gal

Saw forth an regal schlong
supper attitude attire, your
shave clump listed, frothy
eyes game a sump. looser
pants you "stayed", sta n
ding in a hole. ah home
minder, less chump than
pissed! age a while then
"dance". your fire clutter,
long pail and coursing law...

Argüelles then responded thus:

Le gall

shaw s fourth from the left
il legally that 's marxian for
doubt, whistler s dea daunt's
tea cozy with plasma plum jam in
spewers from either cheek as gas
Oh lined his alley frothing
lincoln cubes til the log built
high around her brick house lilt
s a byte to the right fall ter
a long the bul warks ram pike

IN CONCLUSION

Ivan Argüelles is clearly one of the most unique and authentic poets
working in English today, and I dare say one of the most authentic in any
language. As we have seen, his uniquely identifiable voice runs
throughout his work, but each of his individual books and poems has its
own unique timbre, point of view, its own movement, tone, thematic
centers. Each work is unique. The nature of his engagement over the
past 40 years or so has been far more than a desire to write "poetry";
rather, poetry is the air he breathes to embody a complex psychic need,
the air he needs to *be* in the life form and time he occupies. When you
consider Ivan Argüelles' work, you are not looking at a literary career,
but at something basic about human consciousness and unconsciousness;
indeed, you are looking at something basic about the being of living
things in general. His work is one of our greatest treasures.

BIOGRAPHICAL SOURCES
Stephanie South, *2012, Biography of a Time Traveler: The Journey of José
Argüelles*, New Page Books, 2009. The early chapters have a lot
of information about Ivan's younger days.
Ivan Argüelles, Wikipedia, [nd].
Ivan Argüelles, in *Contemporary Authors Autobiography Series, Vol. 24*,
Gale, 1996, pp. 1-30. Also see *Contemporary Authors Online*.

BOOKS BY IVAN ARGÜELLES

Instamatic Reconditioning, Damascus Road Press, 1978
The Invention of Spain, Downtown Poets Co-Op, 1978
Captive of the Vision of Paradise, Hartmus Press, 1982
Tattooed Heart of the Drunken Sailor, Ghost Pony Press,1983
Manicomio, Silverfish Review, 1984
What Are They Doing to My Animal?, Ghost Dance Press, 1984
Nailed to the Coffin of Life, Ruddy Duck Press, 1986
The Structure of Hell, Grendhal Poetry Review, 1986
Pieces of the Bone Text Still There, NRG Press, 1987
Baudelaire's Brain, Sub Rosa Press, 1988
Looking for Mary Lou: Illegal Syntax, Rock Steady Press, 1989
"That" Goddess, Pantograph Press, 1992
Hapax Legomenon, Pantograph Press, 1993
Tragedy of Momus (in the anthology *Terminal Velocities*),
                              Ocean View Books, 1993
Enigma & Variations, Pantograph Press, 1995
Purisima Sex Addict II (with Jake Berry), Luna Bisonte Prods, 1997
Dead/Requiem (with Jack Foley), Pantograph Press, 1998
Saint James (with Jack Foley), Pantograph Press, 1998
Madonna, a Poem, Runaway Spoon Press, 1998
Daya Karo, Luna Bisonte Prods, 1999
City of Angels, Potes & Poets Press, 1999
Madonna Septet, Potes & Poets Press, 2000
Cosmic Karma Raga (with Peter Ganick), [by Vyasa & Bahina Bai],
                              Potes & Poets Press, 2000
Greatest Hits, Pudding House Publications, 2000
Chac Prostibulario (with John M. Bennett), Pavement Saw Press, 2001
Décima Mucho (with John M. Bennett), Luna Bisonte Prods, 2001.
Tri Loka, Potes & Poets Press, 2001
Orientalia, Luna Bisonte Prods, 2003
Inferno, Beatitude Press, 2005.
Secret Poem, Chalk Editions, 2009. [e-book]
Comedy , Divine , The, Blue Lion Books, 2009
What Are Probably My Memoirs, Chalk Editions, 2010 [e-book]
The Death of Stalin: Selected Early Poems, Beatitude Press, 2010
Ulterior Vision(s), Luna Bisonte Prods, 2011
A Day in the Sun, Luna Bisonte Prods, 2012
The Second Book, White Sky Books, 2012
Ars Poetica, Poetry Hotel Press, 2013
FIAT LUX, Luna Bisonte Prods, 2014
Duo Poemata, Luna Bisonte Prods, 2015

ORPHIC CANTOS

ORPHIC CANTOS

*la mia vita era tutta "un'ansia del segreto
delle stelle, tutta un chinarsi sull'abisso"*
Dino Campana, Canti orfici

1.

how does language work
by subterfuge and shadow
by echo play of the vast Unknown
or is it because we are on death row
playing with substitutes for the word *mother*
employing enormous syllables of sand at day's end
far from noon's catastrophic light
it *is* because we are on death row
leveling the air's small brown hills
with consonants of oblivion and decay
some distance from the paragraphs of flame
established at either terminus of the horizon
to indicate a passage of time and space
through the narrow defiles of sublime ether
struggling to remember whose was the echo
that ricocheted like a small music
between the afternoon's frail leaves
when collapsed in a heat of fierce dissonance
the body sought the stone's cool refuge
beneath the blasted convent at road's end
were ears enough to deceive the sleeper's dream
does language work passing and repassing
a sacred thread through the arcane eye
immobile in the myth's fantastic atmosphere
heavy with a redness of impenetrable mystery
by subterfuge shadow and echo play
the divine intent to understand the inchoate
memory at the root of each child's name
is it because we are on death row?
and no longer comprehend among the grasses
that grow between the fingers' shadows
how long it is to the very next day
how little we have traversed all these years

leaning over into the abyss
to see in eternity's opaque mirror
what semblances we are to the recent dead

2.

smacks of syntagmatic
back snap sugar
loafed into reels
of leaking windows
hump leaved
and delivered greener
than memory's echo
shakes a bit
above smoking hospice
dying is simply
other than gasoline
in the tight rod
leading from synapse
to duty's folded
side swipe

the sea with faces of a hundred thousand suns
the woman with eyes the color of salt
the black wind that never goes backwards
the protean egress through funnels of ink

to decipher the text of marble runes
haunted ever by the infernal echo
repeating the same words over and over
names proliferating among the waves
hands rope-burnt air shaking like mist
eyes against the splintered mast
grain spoiled must running over
sour streaks in the evening clouds
how is the way back any different
than the way to the underworld?
is there anything inherently adjustable
                        about zero?

would shadows in the form of words

would incandescence in the midst of sleep
would the great roman profile at full noon
would the mayoral horse in the plaza
would the great mountain at day fall
would anything at all in the migraine
how do we persist week to week
shifting the order of syllables on the page
expecting a different outcome each time
and by the next month to discover
that red has always been underneath
and that the king of Hades imminent
with his upturned scepter and echo
making both trees and waves to quake
how do we come out of this margin
into the full display of language?

stones to cry weeping grasses
hermetic context of shaded vales
small deer come to die for heartbreak
rustling in the eaves a longing
what a distance from echo to echo
living on the edge of the blade
earth turns over its sleeper
dusting the early frame of time

textless   if my face is pale

3.
white caryatids white rocks white deserts
of the sea of night   somnambulants!
headless white statues pure
in their tenuous aridity
perforated immobility of stars
in their secret passage to eternity
shadows of mirrors releasing thousands
of mirrors of shadows   somnambulants!
which is the soul and which is the body
of the soul errant in the vast cupidity of night
to suddenly arrive at the colossal cities
mythiform truculent jubilant radiant with dust

myriads of noons in the steeple of space
around which clamor elephants and tortoises
for a moment it is the stillness of a photograph
water seems to resonate in imperial distances
enormous whiteness of the false sky
painted in the laburnum flapping wildly
only a stochastic process can bring Eurydice
to memory vine-waisted swarming with bees
in the dense cupola of her black hair
                              somnambulants!
and in the next moment anxiety
jewel box in the heart of night's blanched corpse
echolalia and serpentine of black onyx
opaline frustrations of the Mysteries
how vast the multifarious designations of language
suborned by the shoulders of the Himalayas
reduced to the vagrant powders of the ruddy planet
Rudra's own necklace of human skulls
making night gleam with the million coral teeth
which can never come back to haunt
stones weeping tears of blood
grasses lying down in sorrow for what has passed
in the small white fraction of infinity
as if a man sustained by the ankles
could ever capsize the numerical and stygian boat
which ferries his chaotic and divine recollections
to the teeming port of the afterlife   somnambulants!
thither do all beings tend summoned
by illicit headaches nasturtiums and cathedrals
gleaming like glacial blocks over a Mediterranean
turned upside down in the Tunisian sky

what is it you want of me, Lala?
peripheries of red and black peppers steaming
lungfish and sidewalks of boiling Cartesian thought
integrals in a hallucinatory topography
endless mile of glass rippling horizontally
intent on hearing the orphic lyre
tuned to the eighth string for the perfect note
to aspire to the Thirteen House
burrowing through Gaia's blank thigh

and never never obtain to Eurydice's envelope

somnambulants!

4.

evening falls down from the alpha crest
no one in sight just whispers opaque and
rivers running underground somnolent zetas
head to humus and listen how brown it sounds
dun and vertiginous at the same time like
the rumor of a very distant catastrophe
Tuscany silver hills of dusky memory
realm of the goddess Ceres deep yellow
the brim of her eyes captures the crepuscular
swing of the swallows diving at the campanile
itself a recollection of smoke in its rigid plumes
Ceres bare knees feet like rustling grass
her hair suddenly a phantom of church domes
burnished gold at sunset one shoulder free
the other bound by a silk cord about to disintegrate
hers is the news that paradise is in flames
purple heaths wrapped up in an icy fire
remote and fast the horizon freezes the mind
in its pre-Socratic origins and everywhere
the mysterious sound of water being borne
by the disseminating Tyrrhenian winds
Ceres her upturned nose the straight line
of her unapproachable lips the long swirl
of deep mauve cloth scarcely hiding the contours
of breasts and hips fleet in line and off she goes
swifter than musing deer into some thicket
the darkening air fills with the chirring of crickets
or the fine tuning of bee swarms returning
from the noon heat of yellowish pollen storms
clouds gather in seductive oriental formations
soon night ominous with her purple pallor
will set in on the deserted alphabets
language in ruins dewfall of rustic vowels
phonetic decay in the archaic ivy
strewn the dead leaves of the even deader Oak

below which rotting consonant clusters maze
the mulch with indistinct vocables hazy recall
of a colossal oratory and poetics of heroes
now namelessly scattered face down in the dense
far from the intricate Asia of the constellations
whose mute roaring announces nothing
but the murky spell of the afterlife

what is Memory but a mesh of dwindling echoes
etched in a pointillistic and evanescent ink
across an incomplete mountain range
someone dreams of from time to time
before dismounting from his chariot of smoke
to lie down beside a broken set of signs
head first in the twilight
murmuring murmuring *"Eurydice"*

5.

I am flooded with light
to speak as an Oracle to sing!
in what fierce inch of sleep have I ever been
if not the extension of the unfinished Poem
the threshing floor of language the haunting
of words never completed for ecstasy's wild thrill
the irrevocable few seconds of being with the One
and then for looking back to be at a remove from time
banished from the cloister of the Dedicated Heart
swirl the galaxies of infinite flame
in the mind's impoverished cell
and then to have to remember repeatedly
the error of the sun in its burnished glaze
how does Echo fail to really recall not memory
but the thing that memory represented
the pale shade of a visage as if blooming whiter yet
in a ceremony of flowers poisonous to touch
beneath the moon in its reddened phase
how does the shadow fail to be reunited
with the body of its soul that mistaken imprint
hovering in a twilight air brown with fainting
and to hear constantly those cries of distance

longing in its most remote ochre recess
where grasses no longer increase their destiny
where a water as if lifted by an invisible hand
pours itself into the thought of language
thirsty for the dream of expression
famished for the harsh rocks and crags of Thessaly
where torn apart by againbite the brain
relishes its raving forlorn madness
where everything is uniquely destroyed
for its beauty and sovereign impenetrability
where I am nothing if not the Oracle
the babble of divine utterance
the speechless invocation to Light

unhunh I am the rudimentary the implausible
the dissonant speech act of incomprehension
the pharmaceutical device that unhinges perception
not poetry nor the broken chord of the unstrung lyre
not *meaning* in its syntax of human resemblances
whatever resides in me is incomplete a ruin
relics of the all but forgotten alphabet
the gods devised to communicate the irrational
antithesis of the visible lyric wreckage of the eye
demolished archaeology of the ear
not poetry nor the pretty banalities it engenders
but the misbegotten formulae of the daily catastrophe
that brings noon down to its burning ghost
cancelling the supplications to the deity
with a fierce all-withering simoon
sweeping out of a post-meridian conflict of deserts
beyond the values of sound and harmony
the few inches of sleep buried in sand's multiple orgasm
it is a nothing of oracular blankness
ultimate red shift through spaces intricate with negativity
howling craziness probing through rock and air
song of unfathomable depths
for what I cannot have back

I am flooded with light
to speak as an Oracle to sing!

6.

"His fader was comen of King Pluto
And his moder of King Juno …
Orfeo most of ony thing
Lovede the gle of harping"
Sir Orfeo

Legend in her flimsy white frock plucking
months of flowers for her nosegay
what do I care! be they jasmine be they rose
"close the doors, you uninitiated!"
be they Maenads raging at my throat
envy like wildfire devouring sacred wood
and evening hush of smoke and moving thread
suchness of nothing in the petrified sound
to move backwards the rivers to the crest
numbering to zed the waters of down below
make of king Hades his realm the darker yet
queen Persephone her voice return to mourn
colors deep the dank brown stained yellows
burnt sienna hashed carmine dense mauve
maroon violet indigo fading into vast helium
until red eats them all in chthonic ranting
and umber and distant teal emerge fog-drenched
but whose voice wan of pale diphthongs weeping
against a sleeper's din of remembered deaths
'tis that I hear oh dreadful in this undressed bed
promises in ochre depths wormwood patterns
traced in somber greens hues of livid disarray
a universe without color a labyrinth of blanks
blanched skies of inconstant constellations
wheeling invisibly above fortune's stormy sea
massive clouds of purple oaths break their waters
dire plunging human errors like shattered masts
seethe under into the grayish colloidal mass
music I ken sweet strain a raga from the Ganges
its labyrinthine theme weaving in and out of nerve
naked ghosts sunburnt from death's other world
seem to call drowning out that sleeping voice
wishes are fractures on the tongue's toiled skin
who dies the quotidian phase in disrepair

who indeed rounds the idiot thought of hope
I sense hands plunging upwards through surf
bulbous eyes of the unseeing reach for air
as if tufts of it could be gleaned and harvested
and a next day surely be on its way by dawn
cataracts instead dash their furious liquids
into the brace of fen and mangled rock
how much humanity yearns for the authentic
for a song unrestrained to burst from the lyre's vein
not so much to assure but to confirm mortality
and not unending deathlessness AOI
my harp my quoits my wandering sandals
my shifting alphabets my mists of total distance
my mountains my pure unfinished hills the dun
my path unshaped my singing in the night my
beasts tawny eyed fauve gentle crested or plumed
rapacious raven black peacock iridescence my
brambled woods briar strewn impassible hostile
desolate haunted impossible of egress blackness
leaf that bleeds speaking branch of broken vowels
my language my dialect spun around its eye my
pidgin bawk talking hesitant stu- stu- stuttering
spewing where beauty finds its soft
my loss then my finally utter total lorn my abject
my unstressed syllable my shh
   "close the doors, you uninitiated!"

7.

mmm I could have invented the alphabet
had I not been so obsessed with You
it could have been a whole different world
landscapes inner directed cloud wonders
bursting white orients of flower and sound
is it that I register nothing at all now
the senses ripped out and sent traveling
because of my darkling obsession for You
how the harp sounds like a silly tinkling bell
gone the deep forces of its perfect notes
held so high no god could withstand hearing
imploring beast and rock alike to lend tears

instead I bleed blank powders dreaming hells
vivid no more the garden's opalescent dawn
in shades of gray and paler still the rainbow
behind whose shivering imminence my mountain
like a small dun colored mule collapses breathless
all because I cannot shake this obsession for You
they took you away those blind hunters of a noon
and switched you for a fuse or shade of blue
is it that dread fixes the apparent world with awe
and sinking trenches vivify the waning light
no, no, they placed you on a trembling leaf
and sent you sailing down the under Stream
my ivy twined wife of an hour's time You
whenever I turn to look and brooding trees
shape the winding air like a lunar blast
and whitest of all things memory the obsession
pallors of cobalt and cuprous dank basements
floorless and wild with competing shadow-plays
colossal myths reply their tangled mourning threads
ancient in this havoc of caves and false destiny
a misery among miseries counting endless fingers
as I crawl among the universe of evening grasses
how can I never find the one that matches
spuriously bleeding from an invisible cut
itching to touch *skin* once more the song
how was I fooled by a simple photograph
in believing that fading dusky *thing* was You
my obsession my tremulous opaque vertiginous
my something of a distance my sleeping thumb
my unpronounceable longing my whiskey
my discolored yellow saffron ruby baited one
my city of perfect quadrants dug deep in a well
my hallucination my abdication my fornication
where will you sleep tonight?
mmm I could have been the alphabet
the roaming siege of letters scribbled in air
sandstone amorphous dwindling script
yellowish bracken misread ungiven vowels
the coiled reference to the unending snake
which is You my obsession and destruction
sempiternal graveyard of my feelings

they lifted you from that wandering noon
those eyeless hunters and quarried you deep
beneath the silt and mulch of time
they left you where I do not know buried
beneath seasons of ravaged oak leaves
and who am I but a bearer of unknown letters
signal of noise in the arcane galactic silence
scribbler in the sand evoking monuments of ether
on some wasteland to the east of the water
who goes circling and circling the inch
where myth has hidden Your voice
my obsession my ninni-nanna my omicron
mmm   mmm

8.

we passed through the land called Unreal Omegas
we passed through the land called Unreal Omegas
we passed through the land called Unreal Omegas
far from the edges where things blur & declassify
far from the worlds of meaning and matter
when time was young having just been born
the *last* in the series of births of time
seated on the throne of the dead the girl-
whose-name-cannot-be-said *Persephone*
speaking the hill dialect of those without death
rustling and humming in the language of trees
we passed through the land called Unreal Omegas
fictions of sand announcements of wind ear shafts
that flood with the body of the serpentine sea
immense red of the distance of the thought of
eternity just two inches below the war scar
hispid blasts that raise the waters to infinity
where the great but unknown souls float
among them *the* woman generated by a turbine
in a lost *bolgia* of Dante whiplashed stoned
we are never the same again we can never be
as we thought weightless birds golden winged
levitating through the ethereal scripts before time
when a letter bore the height of seraphim
blazing ingots of purity and the sublime

we are not *that* neither can we aspire to such
etching with parrot plumes repetitions of the Name
the unpronounceable the unspeakable the the the
imminence of the Unformed deity shadow
without memory stairs that go all the way down
a cigarette smoking by itself when no one is looking
a green fright wig burning in the shop window
a snake instead of a wife lying beside the bed
millions of tongues going on at once about sleep
 we passed through the land called Unreal Omegas
this is the mercurial Aeon of Thoth the megalith!
the greatly expanded blank histories of the Wheel!
but nowhere trace of my little bride the Child
woe for the taskmasters of Hades who grind the quern!
my sweet consort bathed in a divine saliva
whose hips undulating bore red and blue lotuses
through the greater Mysteries outside the Portico
how many times can she have been so near
a shape without form a longing for the unrepeatable
union with the alchemical metals of the Invisible
am I spent in melodic scales of Farther Asia
to sing lament and threnody the baleful ode
what is to recall but that wisp of a thing the *Child*
errant with her hair of voluminous temples
with her peplos tight around her vine-waist
attended by the bee swarms of great Delight
only to go lost in the folds of some eerie myth
darling sweet endlessly wistful her almost voice
a craving for swans in flight who with their wings
spell out constantly changing advertisements
that sky is four fold and forever disappearing
that human error is a glyph carved in ether
that
we passed through the land called Unreal Omegas

9.

the uniform of the text
the braid that wraps around the long unwinding column
who are those people whispering at the end of the hall
BOOM there's a man upstairs!

a thing that makes human sounds darkening
the boots of the text make no sense
each time it starts moving *they* get excited
to learn a new language to shape the lips
removing the tongue to articulate
the behind the vowels a messy scene
murdered the word every time
the lingerie of the text flimsy
pink staccato embroidery around the uvular
they do without the definite *and* indefinite article
sometimes it feels just tropical a miasma
and regard their temple architecture as supreme
built in sequences of heat and verdigris
until culminating with a peak of vibrant ivy
the skin of the text layered in thin sheets of sweat
as a result of constant sexual play
pairs of consonants the ones called retroflex
employed during discharge of ecstasy
they make these small click-click sounds
when they can no longer endure the illusion
the spectacular thing about *skin* is its text
not the texture of its song not the film version
but just who are *they* whispering at the end of the hall
it's infinite it's just killing me
these bilabial sonants the speech of the deathless ones
memory of their hooded figures
like circumflex accents tottering on the rim
collecting leftover rain in the gutters
where they perch thirsty deities to avenge
some poor mortal his broken wife
then they roll their eyes back and howl
the moon is a remove from catastrophe
greek variables in the drama of syntax
"Orpheus!" they call *"Orpheus!"*
the purple buskins of the text
inveterate byzantine symbols ornate and useless
tumultuously shining in the nowhere
narcolepsy of the fifth tone pure music
this is failure of Athenian statecraft
an entire history of phonetic decay
shrouded in a text of indecipherable hieroglyphs

man is a two-timing worm an unspeakable
the immeasurable sinkhole of depravity
and wants his wife back does he?
and those shady figures whispering at the end of the hall
BOOM there's a man upstairs!

                    10.
tell me about the woman in the myth her whiteness
her abduction by the eyeless hunters her wooing
in the wood her antecedents in the clouds the stuff
she put in her hair the coloring around her eyes
the way she pouted her big painted lips the saffron
occlusion in her mind the legends about her feet
her voice captured by the phonograph the light around
her when she woke the absence of skin in her song
the meaning of the vowels in her name the breadth
of her face coming to be the iridescence above her head
the archaeology of her hearing the promise of deathlessness
given to her the lies and deceit which felled her the random
foot work of her passage through the labyrinth the massive
storm gathered around her presence the seas she evoked
when dreaming the moon spells of her speech acts
the things she saw that nobody else could see the skies
and the distance of space that flooded her vision the one
and the nothing in her breath the presence of a small rain
as she dressed herself the falling away of time because
she stopped to *look* the single hand capable of circling her waist
the unending serpent of her desire the glistening chrome
of sweat that covered her breasts the car drawn by humped
bulls that conveyed her to the palace the underground
manor where her pallor was increased the terror of the
sudden night descending on her pale bare shoulders
the indecent softness of her mouth her fainting spells the heat
that took her from the knees up by surprise the emerald
pendant that reached to her navel the braid of gold leaf
encircling her hips the red and blue lotuses that sprang
from her steps the delicate ivory anklets with bells she wore
during the Mysteries her ruddy excitement at the approach
of her husband the longing like a ceaseless smoking dream
how she came to be a shade in the multitude of shades

how she came to be a shade in the multitude of shades
she's a photograph of light
she's an advertisement for a cosmetics firm
she's an accident in the syntax of the archaic
she's a syllable in the unpronounceable name
she's what never comes back in the dark
she's the glossy magazine cover of a lifetime
she's the last letter in any alphabet
she's the reason why poetry
she's the footnote at the bottom of a page of water
she's the ever elusive wisp of hair on the brow
she's the unknown partner in the round dance
she's the moon's impenetrable backside
she's why I cannot sleep beside the stone
and make moan the Thracian rocks and crags
with my lyre's unstrung note
a song an almost sounded word a draft of air
the greening of breath on the leaf a swoon
what age is this what sands slipping through the glass
where in the world all this unmown grass
a finger gone lost in the weeds
a

11.

seems like just yesterday
   I ran into death
      death was a mirror
which I walked right into and through
taken by my image death said to me
don't I know you from somewhere?
don't we all know someone from somewhere
Tuscan ridge flint hard sky
burnished edges of nowhere
right into the mirror and through it
death was my twin the reflection in the glass
walked right through him
into the other world the one behind
the Tuscan ridges below the flint hard sky
ghosts of rock and stone looking for
the entrance to Hades somewhere in the dun

landscape of fog soft hills and weeping Madonnas
narcissus yellower than the crocus
dwelling in the pupil of the eye
whom do you see if not me?
bathed in the alcoholic light of an Umbrian evening
from on high the piercing call of the swallows
navigating in a vast melancholy
over the spirit cupolas and domes of Gubbio
have been here before sometime before *time*
dressed in shifts of ochre and haze
though I cast no shadow I was of those who breathe
and restless search nightly for a bed
as a sort of consolation
in the cold unplastered rectangle of conscience
narcissus yellower than the crocus
dwelling in the pupil of the eye
whom do you see if not me?
to recall what it was in the pharmacy
was it the crystal ball or the mortar and pestle
inert in the opaque space that exists
between this life and the next one
and whose voice booming descended
from the attic announcing the various fates
yours mine and that of the *other*
the one in the mirror

seems like just yesterday
her mouth lush as the pomegranate
her kiss the seed of death
you craved more the bittersweet red
dark ruddy wake of her passage
through the *selva oscura*
her silver-sandaled feet barely touching earth
as she ran lithely through the brambled maze
what dank cave took her in
paler than white her pallor a sign
in the night of the imagination
lush as the pomegranate her parted lips
what poetry is this yellower than the crocus
what dense ochre season in the fens
dun colored hills fog drenched

Madonnas weeping behind rent veils
when there is no way to turn
but into the cracked mirror
don't I know you from somewhere?
the cavern in the pupil of the eye
and the shrill cry of the swallows
chasing ghosts of stone and rock
the pharmacy which is the entrance to Hades
perpetual the evening trapped in brown glass
round and round the lightning shattered tree
charred remains of the effigy of love
dripping from the recent lacustrine rain
this poetry is only madness a blank
in the time without space
moving into the beyond of the mirror
like the moon's ineffable backside blanched
reflecting nothing
       a river between two earths
the upper one where the gods play at dice all day
and the lower one where ripe with death's seed
each of us struggles to remember
the light how it dazzled
in the morning's dewy silence
a mystery the shadow
that came to devour it

narcissus yellower than the crocus
dwelling in the pupil of the eye
whom do you see if not me?

12.

the years went by in a single summer
all lives ended in a single day
trumpeting elephants on a blade of grass
sun in its splendid and constant error
night the unbidden with its image of death
white faced unmoving through the sacred vowels
a language of prescience and foreboding
sounding distantly in the ear's arcane halls
who is summoned to the infernal court

and who is warned to do nothing at all
spells cast over the shadows of men
sleepwalking like children on the stairs
doomed to wake and remember nothing
of that day but for the bruiting of elephants
and the monotonous buzz of insects in the weeds
who was the woman all bangles and gold
who leaned over perspiring with musk
her eyes kohl-rimmed her mouth a red secret
what did she want grass stained breathless
in the single afternoon of our lives?

I see you there crawling on the wall
don't think you can get away so easy
this is the labyrinth the underground
the court of the king of hell Pluto
this beautiful music that enthralls you
oboes recorders viola da gambas harpsichords
chaconnes and passacaglias and grounds
is an illusory fabric woven in your ear
the orchestration of bees stunned by heat
coming into the dark of their work
when colors fading run into endlessness
a disappearing white paste on night's rim
crawl as fast as you can on the stucco wall
your shadow will not stay by you
nor will the sticky sweetness of memory
abide in the ransacked cave of your mind
a hive of detritus and broken furniture
dusty avenues through which you climbed
once thinking to persist in the light
all that was the desultory perception
of a desperate soul a mortal enticed
by false promises by some divinity
the goddess in her girlhood gauze pink
the rumor of a distant love a solace
a poetry that you kept writing in letters
borrowed from the oracle at Delphi
a poetry that has nothing to do with literature
rattled sequences of hymns and odes
elegies and threnodies to the multiple

and varying faces of death encountered
in the instantaneous mirror of the moment
that single afternoon carousing on lawns
waiting for the gorgeous advent of the stars

13.
the impeccable mauve shape of her hair the Muse
I invoke tripartite Selena Nymph Hecate godsome
silvery sheen of leaf turning in the auburn light
fastening the locks in place the braid twined ivy
'round her lissome waist supple the gracious leap
shaking ever so slightly and pray her bare shoulders
pale and white to bear these inspirations tongued
in threefold intonation violet indigo azure hued
the blue of the crescent moon in her matted jungle
pelt fuse of oriental and the spotted panther skin
unh chugga chugga chugga the violent sun's chant
drilled in libya's sandstone words iconographed
one-eyed mythiforms revolving in heliotropic orbs
to spin and keep weaving invisible airy histories
unending cycles intensely red for shifts of otherness
her many armed longing the desire to die just once
I sing the maze this perplex liquid sound her vowels
a voice the dactylic evoked sonants from beyond
lush distances ripened for the adolescent thrill
a song many-layered the atmosphere duly rends
quires of thought whitening in a pyramid of light
do this time undergo and from subterranean rills
bring back darkness to evolve the polyvalent thread
a tale to color porches of memoried evenings ago
longing the yes and reaching green into the vast
the triple voided space hers the luxurious 'gyptian
starry threshing floor whence set forth armies dusky
chargers into the oncoming frothy tide a man to drown
did ever then recall his sense a world revolve in verse
quickening dead flesh plunged into the massy deep
being thought waters of how many dense the chorus
salt and against the skin the music explore tracing
verdant luster at times the colossal women on balconies
blanched and sighing the heroes long gone to battle

this epic unfold the eye to train its sight on remoteness
the vale where such as we were once shadows grave now
their minds to mind imply a simplex darker still the one
how then Oh Muse discord content and fugitive rounds
display the ochre masses cloud rolling hills extending
into twilights the unending lawns moors the brooding
cannot children learn the rote of mountains incomplete
to lore and 'magine once more the earth yielding greaved
warriors clod clinging clangor strife fraternal threnody
air blackened with missiles whistling a finish to worldly
woes how complex and intricate this night becomes
ores of rich polish mirages of palaces labyrinthine old
sorrow the many pleated who wears your hair tomorrow
how is such this the tale oh tell me many times the Muse
multiple in raiment transparent the immense pallor Oh
and to the city underneath descend and ply the raveled
streets burdened with hexameters from the unwritten ode
me knowest Thou? the plaint lachrymose unspent it goes
further and deeper into the galactic mass the big unknown
in which of the universal inches unwinding is her face
ever to be seen again the grammar of recollection gone
her small cries the sad and wistful against the window pane
the little rains that slowly flood the ear's brief archaeology
then deaf to be true and lightless wander a ghost of mind
ah much the traveled and nameless the countless lands
a slip of her skirt a glint of her ankle a clue of nevermore
be mine then when if again this round its smoke returns

14.

the singing in me O mothers!
even if I wear the blue crescent
in my matted locks haunted my eyes
against the dazzle of day's false promise
light azure over tiny Etruscan cities
been here before in a buried epoch
twilit ochre distances hills of remote
unreachable as soul yearning baffles
in me this singing this dolorous
were I to return in what form
the animal most kin to me leopard

or a god-inspired bird chanting
mock reveries to Dawn's cold lamp
would I ever get back what I most
the lost yearning aimless wander
such a thing that was a living
a flight of cloud melody ringing
ivy clad her skin a shining intense
as over rock and stone clamber
body weary numbering years by grass
a fiction rounding vale and dell
to summon green I think a massy
heaven turned upside down
and shepherds in courtiers' rags
hymning the ever lost a love afar
did never the nerve hurt so near
the heart's cruel nave of shadows
so grasp I then this lyre and tune
an air that surpasses mountain death
a universe of running notes a scale
approaching red in heat and style
to some cliff rend the outer shell
a man's this dump of empty thoughts
a cistern of bottomless sense a
the and moreover O mothers!
a madness weaving through stores
of ancient poetry and words unkempt
do wild waves wash away the shore
and sand spirits sighing darkly
what is more than sorrow this
shaking in the woeful clime
a legend painted in frosty rhyme
a visage sundered a pallor pained
this shattered season a leaf bears
veins of incorporeal silence spilling
and planets rage immemorial
their epic of cannot have her back
again and more I go into the trace
blackening weeds and russet sump
does Pluto's echoing voice demand
does the aisle of plundered sales gifts
does wrapping her skin in around

the brief chanson of Juno spurned
white armed her eyes ablaze
live charcoals ruby jets of ire
will keep from me the thing desired
Eurydice by name her cloth defied
stepping prim on treacherous gravel
sliding then first again invisible
no hand implore my beseeching
tremble vowels of lengthened time
or master syllables I cannot spare
her back again no more the lorn
absent days race their clock
to some still point to endlessness

15.

what a night! the operas of Monteverdi and Gluck
the plan was to go to Paso Robles the next morning
if only we could see the god just once before
say he's a boy or a shout! diaphanous presence
of the wholly invisible manifested as music
or the pure light of high summer vibrating
that is Dionysus who will release the cars
roaming south on highway 101 like animals
blindly making their way to the Pinnacles
reading the librettos in candelight confused
roles of or between man and girl the descant
odor of roast pork and resin night settling in
but the arias just gorgeous on the painted stage
costumed shadows wandering among violins
a skeleton at best the memory of the Pleiades
at the café table scribbling verse on napkins
when you get there give us a call at the castle
be sure to take your berlitz and a baedekker
guide blue aux enfers the playbill acid corroded
making a map of the poor directions *sotto voce*
with only a flashlight we tried to read the text
irritated by the chirring and whirring of insects
infatuated with the feeble flare the will to die
something like the dance of the blessed spirits
too much alcohol and chain smoking bleary eyed

who could perceive the deity was there beside us
trembling with inspiration and incoherence
take most of the following day heading down
the coast watching for seals and sea-nymphs
marine haze and inviolable presence a mystery
or deep discussion about the dharma and zen
suburban anecdotes about the college philosopher
who starved himself to death to prove a point
the point was there the ineffable soprano voice
darkness clothing the soaring notes of her grief
an excess of red dyed into a spurious sash wound
around her ivy-like waist the winsome lissome
reminiscences of the Tyrrhenian sea shore below
Cambria almost see her the Etruscan girl shy
in her pigtails and frail freckled shoulders seated
there on a rock jutting out of the spuming waters
call that a divinity! it's when you can't remember
anything about the "spell" and days have passed
eating mussels and crab cakes in a Santa Barbara dive
salt in abundance thick slabs of butter on crusty rolls
white wine chilled to the death frills of green spray
music that comes at you like thunder not remember
was it last night at the opera or was it at Vesuvio
across from City Lights where was it we connected?

it's the shock of recognition that takes you out of the self
puts you in a place you've never been calling out to a heat
to a nameless wind in an orchard of grey-leaved olive trees
if there is a place to put the skin to undo the mind of its
troubling absence if there is a rock in the meadow or a
jewel or even the trumpeting of an unseen elephant but
night has its way a boulevard of neon confetti a flash and
glitter you know it must be a god manifesting to tell you
nothing about yourself except that you have become other
the awful loss of duality the shining from deep within
exacerbating surfaces that are only the appearances
of things Φαινουμενα *a celestial revolution in a blank eye*
what is at last sleeping inside you opaque marble statue
waiting blindly for the brief syntax of light to reappear

16.

I notice that she's been biting her lips
a sort of classicism in the fringe of hair on her brow
or totally naked beneath the peplos held at the shoulder
by a single brooch she moves unsteadily toward
the pierian fountain a jug on the left hip
wherever there is a Nymph death is close by
whenever you hear that rustling something invisible
a trouble in the format of light falling
uneasily from the window of heaven
something is going to go wrong today
biting her lips a loss of serenity a kind of craziness
in the black pupils of her eyes staring into a void
as if predicting a fortune a storm a vortex
as she moves lazily toward the well outside the walls
when she pronounces the word *water* a hush
a cathedral of silence encases her a terrific
pandemonium of unseen things hurtling in the air
you can feel absences about to occur a mental
process that requires all the significance of red
to determine that this is the moment this is
as she steps one foot unsure of the other
along the dusty donkey path toward the watering hole
a dun colored ridge in the distance seen by her eye
a memory perhaps of Zeus when he was a child
having the thoughts of an infant divinity
setting into motion whole other worlds of thunder
and rocks and projectiles of pure light into the ether
she is having this reminiscence swaying her body
blindly as she paces aimlessly toward some still point
in the mass of heat gathering around the afternoon
biting her lips what can the trouble in mind be
there was a time when all the elements were one
until Discord and Envy or so they say
today as on no other in the vast serenity of sky-
drenched earth does that proposition seem more distant
the force of the Archaic holds everything in place
beings like statues in their marble perfection appear
to breathlessly await the instructions for moving forth
even as she hesitates momentarily by the House of Time
to consider the Unseen and tosses her big hair back
does a wild roan colored satyr lie in ambush around the corner?
the compact intense density of the meridian hour

buzzes with the foreboding of an insect catastrophe
dust in yellowish whorls clouds of purple pollen
lift and become stationary in the staid beams of light
a remote voice calls out for some fragment of thought
she stirs moving again beyond the distance of a song
this is the atmosphere of eternity when the godhead
assumes the memory of stone and trees petrify
it is what the Nymph brings on shifting as if dazed
through the noonday city of Dis toward the well
jug trembling on her left hip face a flood of perspiration
as she draws near to what the Mystery is
that thin demarcation between gods and mortals
the invisible violence that stuns and turns the brain
against itself in a zenith of shadowless inspiration
months turn into minutes minutes become infinite
all appearances take on the speed of light
she is here and she is *not* here
insistent drone of the unforeseen hidden in grasses
that spread yawning into the abyss
in her right eye a neolithic apiary turns
and in her left eye the semblances of writing
spread like an incarnadine ink
yet she keeps walking slow motion toward the rim
of the well where a diaphanous presence awaits
seated on the very precipice humming like a hive
it is poetry the translation of the unbidden
immobile in the swarm of heated ideas
the persistence of longing and echo
if she touches the sacred precinct there
and she will when the Hour loses its breath
then will ECSTASY proceed from the void
ineffable madness of Omega piled on Omega
wherever there is a Nymph death is close by

17.

intense dream of Claire Birnbaum again ageless like Helen
suspicious eyes hair still done up empress style dark chestnut
unwilling at first to kiss then yielding ever so sweetly
was this like Helen also a simulacrum an ashen vagary
of sleep when words featherlike drift one into the other
and nothing is understood but the intent to communicate

from the beyond and just how many Claire Birnbaums
in Florida alone Fort Lauderdale Coral Gables Plantation
night comes swiftly on the storm tossed sea and already
the peak of Pegasus fades into inky mists and from Olympus
the gods watch with amaze as the lone ship plows watery fields
depths of mystery Orpheus his lyre tunes and sends the bark
fleet on its way towards Lemnos comes swiftly darker still
the empty Fort Lauderdale airport the humid boulevards
that thread bleak asphalt into the everglades high cheekbones
like those of the moon shining between peekaboo clouds
and what distant mountain casts from so far its silence
over these driven waves where with one false move to drown
a shadow that even at noon what consternation in her eyes
emerald cast and even after more than 50 years her skin
that of a seventeen year old nor fear for the harpies swoop
taking morsels from their very lips Selene by any other name
her oblique sheen over the treacherous main purple swift
as the cormorants diving the prow spearlike driving foam
dividing the watery course with fierce white lunges a voice
lost in the snapping of the masts a simulacrum like Helen
words lost of sense in the surging invisible tide drift a man
is a dump of thoughts incomplete as a mountain seen in dreams
with tear dimmed eyes watched the homeland detritus and mulch
slowly fade away while Orpheus hymned to Artemis to steer
them clear of the craggy rocks and shoals from mount Pelios
marveled the nymphs at Athena's wondrous deed the heroes
whether in the murk my little wife more resembled Elizabeth Taylor
kohl rimmed eyes and lids heavy with turquoise paste Cleopatra
or Natalie Wood strip dancing on a bare stage as Gypsy what
was she whispering to me so many eons passed jealous gods
took her away passed the headlands of Meliboia where evil
winds constantly blow and dolphins leaping accompanied her
seeming like so many sheep in a man's trance to have at the thing
invisible shafts flower-tipped that enter the heart and moaning
sheets drenched with brine driving down the hollow freeways
night with its multiple and confusing intersections signs pointing
all directions but the correct one flood the soul with such sorrowful
lyric to Lemnos where the thoughtless women the year before had
exterminated all the men she looked at me stupefied meeting
shadowy indistinct figures this way drawing back into the recesses of
Pluto speechless and groaning fear has nested within them and Aph-
rodite sowed anger thereupon having been dishonored and spurned
making incursions into Thrace how could we ever have known each

other and so briefly unreconciled each into what darkening alleyway
lost a life
lasts less than a summer
descended through the fearful gate down to the stream of Acheron
which is oblivion among the many dead there faceless
she

18.

"I am a man possessed!" to have at this epic to ever understand
what is classicism marble truncated statues crying to have back
the perfection "to re create the past" talking in hexameters and
obscure images before painting occurred or the puzzle at the gate
handed to everyone a portion of the text an idyllic light glorious
landscape of letters and word fragments as evening burnished
in gold tinted twilight a time of heroes and enigmatic gods whose
appearance in muffled dreams or speech acts of a sphinx a woman's
voice elaborate and seductive behind curtains of chalky sweet pow-
ders tracing in the endless sand emblemata and oracular responses
ample darknesses sutured to human skin rounding the bend a wa-
tery repose between barking rocks or the siren song of midnoon
when did it happen otherwise in the heated dust of the agora or
strife in the circus maximus a crowd of thousands thumbs down op-
posing the advent of a new deity shrouded in the gorgeous
linens of Isis mourning the bits and pieces of Osiris and rush
the furious middle sea beneath the implacable sun rhetorically
disposed to the glassy mystery of the aqueous surface dilating
round the world map *"man possessed"* tossed into *medias res*
him Muse the sing many wiled and versed in shadows who from
literal shores to the alban temple mounted first his climb white
among lotuses red and blue born the omphalos splayed cretan signs
women the head-dresses like oriental and wrapped in ivy fringe
them chant in russet grasses the eye's meadow spread a beyond
language greens and blues the charioteers who likely greek resound
circling furiously the obelisk to avoid the light storm who swarms
like chorus of bees in their hair revolving empresses colossally robed
wound in bangles and rings and anklets a secret destiny written
on the invisible brow and wend our way through narrow defiles
to consult the Sibyl in her wary glass cage like unto a cicada
lone in an endless Sicilian estate when suddenly BANG!
we're in a movie theater blackness surrounds and the screen
ignites with a lavishly choreographed rendition of everything
since the Fall of Rome in a faux german Expressionism that

shows seated on a tripod in the back of a smoky cave the great
Orpheus himself after whom the movie theater is named
his castrato soprano voice exalting in one Handel aria after
another we fall asleep we die unto the text we follow a thread
back into the labyrinth we despair in despond we forget how
to speak we become as mice racing aimlessly we chew our tongues
off we become red eyed excited wanting to masturbate making
tiny little chirring noises we don't recall where it happened we
whoever whatever we have become studying latin in the ninth grade
we run to the blackboard to examine the hanging colored map
we looked at the place names in Etruria we know where it is
we ask to be pardoned we are dizzy fall down hit the floor taste
blood imagine we are falling from a trireme into the middle sea
we are drowned then amazed at the multiplicity of worlds

waking sulfurous fumes a wave of nausea nudged by a deity
what small wings she had your little wife but lacked presence of mind
she went under in a trice all shadows and bloom an august afternoon
in the glade leopards watched nothing moved by the spectacle
helpless all but knocked out by the drug you watched in a haze
first she vomited by the holy lintel then wavered and stumbling
entered the office of the damned her pale oval face ghostly
fumes of pitch and bitumen enveloped the whole bringing tears
to your eyes losing by the minute any recall of the latin lesson
the way the oars slanted into the glassy waters of the middle sea
where did she go lost to sight so suddenly divorced in a mirror
the medicine cabinet was empty she'd taken every trace of herself
colored powders magic unguents sexual toys antistrabismic pills
you followed taking the precarious winding path vomiting too
as you approached the sacred portal knowing full well you'd be
mistaken for your twin dead these three years yet proceeded
mistletoe in hand reciting in a trance the mantra of retribution
hunh hunh hunh invisible beings surrounded you ejaculating
the voice of a muezzin fainting straight away practiced dying
in your ear as never before the world of sand became greater
than anything as you slid though level after level of darkness
until devoid of human emotion you surrendered your random self
fully initiated at last in the mysteries of Oblivion

19.

what he said:

come be mine for a night nothing
more I desire but your lips priceless red
the slip of a waist you are
ring of ivy besom and depth of love
don't hesitate be mine forever
what she said:
un hunh you gotta wait for the dawn
my lips not priceless red my
slip of a waist ivy twined
not for you just yet
my ochre's gone mad and darkly
I engrave my mind to forestall
what he said:
I sing this orphic chant I revel
in your unending light
your moonbeam spell your yellow
hair frizz your everything about you
my drugstore queen   come on
I know a nice motel just outside
the Vale of Tempe   all shadows
and plush red and lavender seams
like heaven   who's to know?
what she said:
you're mad *ragazzo* with your
tra la la singing all day long
who's to know? why look at them
satyrs and centaurs leopards and
even the rocks that cry hearing you
they all know what's up
and me in my flim flam underthings
you just ogling me like the *ragazzo*
that you are all dun and brown
flinging eye shots my way
all the live long day
chorus:
you're gonna lose that girl
what he said:
it's your peekaboo skin
it's your skylark voice
it's the bees in your hair
it's the burnt sienna you call mouth

it's why I have no shadow
following you instead
it's the grapevine of your waist
it's the burnt afternoon of your thighs
it's the siesta of your kiss
it's what I imagine paradise is
stuck in the fork of your road
it's the end of time in your eyes
it's the sandstorm of your mind
it's looking for love in a drugstore
you're in every phial and pill-box
it's the sandalwood incense of your skin
it's everything and nothing because of you
it's the logic of your breath
it's only you *Eury!*

what she said:

big talk bad boy I ain't budging
I'm just an oak nymph playing coy
Apollo's my dad and he's all light
I dance when I may and devil may care
run through the meadows
of a dazzling day
but marry you so quickly
un hunh lover boy
chase me chase me if you can
through daffodil and hollyhock
sing your heart out *ragazzo*
strip me bare when you can

what he said:

be my little wife if only for tonight
I promise you nothing but nutmeg and joy
your breath is short and I am in the leaf
from the far country I come
where night lives in the stalks
and the lizard stakes its claim on rocks
be my little wife if only for an hour
this life is as brief as smoke
vanishing in the empty sky

chorus: *you're gonna lose that girl*

what she said:

OK just for an hour if that

I'll cozy up to you bend my ypsilon
to your crazy will hyphenate my thought
bury what I can of my bee-drenched hair
undo my lace unzip my skin
spill rose water and unguents all over me
hold your lyre at the eighth note
perfection of music in my ear
let me know it's the end of the world
upside down in a bath of myrrh
cut me off from my many kin
bar them from the wedding rites
make me whiter than pale in moonlight
lotuses blue and red be my crown
fragrance of opium suffuse my mound
ragazzo I know whence you come
the uplands where night dwells in grass
and serpents in weeds abound

what he said:
I have chased you as I could
and stripped you of your very skin
held you for the eternity of a minute
and lost you to a mirror's dream
chorus: *you're gonna lose that girl*

20.

suffocating in the light, a , life comes around , or
else remains empty , afternoons of blank nowhere ,
but , for the music caving in , on its , self , lesions ,
disembarkations when no one's , looking , infernal
units of thought , to get through a , day , recalling
what was sweet , what , was , the enormous glass

the effort to move , inch by terrific inch , in and
through the day , counting the hours within , the
Hour , how could she , why did she , where is she ,
? , can a movie theater , be so , can the avenue , can
anything ever be recovered , watching the ceiling ,
for a , sign , a mere symbol, a glyph in red , fading

instead into a , twilight , suffused ochres and tawny ,

summer colors , a dwindling of intensity , months turn
into minutes , cannot get out of this , vortex , writing
and re writing the , epic , a tale of betrayal , by light ,
by anemones and deities , lurking in the , (l)eaves , why
this version of breath , and not the other , the red one ,

the , enormous planets suspended , invisible , a lamp
above my head , a small flame licking , apex and advent ,
can headwinds be so adverse , can tollbooths , can the
minute hand wrenched from , its fate , walls of unseen ,
the apogee of , and the nadir of sensation , because , why
the little tart , cleaned out the medicine cabinet , fled , a

to live , the rest of one's life , re creating , the substantives
of memory , to live , if you can call it , that , a storm
of paper lies , lawyers' fees , indications of vitality on
the moon , to look into the eye just once and see there ,
what , ? , a landscape organized by , color , starting back
wards from zed to , blank , too much aspirin , dissolving

the fakes , who are the inauthentic , and her small skin , the
porphyry brooch , the byzantine calculation , to flee , dross
and levantine , period , an assemblage of air too dense , too ,
can't hear for all , the , beside me the leopard , immobile ,
waiting for Mozart to start up , again , the books he wrote ,
the master negative , gyre after gyre of , all in a minor key ,

this is tragic , this is a fossil , this is an , invertebrate , this is
, if we only knew , a shadow play , an irreversible text , a sorrow
writ on the back of a palm , leaf, incursions of black ants, clouds
of gas , Dante , minute deities trickling , conscious of doing every
thing one last , time , this is water , a section of sky , basins of
ruddy ink , big high boulevards , racing in the , tropics , heat

islands of , fortune , bickering about the , a divorce , a schism ,
in the body , eruptions on the skin , worrisome evidence , that
, is mortality , insolence , she didn't say she , wasn't coming
back, she just didn't , say , running out of time , just , envelopes
of hair , mysteriously inserted , whispers , suffocation , how much
existence can a , take , ? , termagants , basilisks , sandy wastes ,

dreaming , arena emptied of consciousness , only wafting saffron
powders , millennia , she was expert at dining out , distinctions ,
arhats carved from teakwood , and , mulch , humus , planetary
detritus , bees swarming around the idyll , that afternoon in may ,

this is really tragic , dionysian interpretations of , civilization , more
heat , turned up the volume , singing the inner *"me"* , rhapsodes

blind apprehension , tuning the one-stringed instrument , took
everything out of , behind the mirror , sexual toys , hair brushes ,
velvet underthing , stray hairs , brunette , hmmm , living document
called breath , attached to her memory a set of , anthills , separation
angst , one of those roman empress updos , big tortoise shell comb ,
half sized moons pasted to , just inside the cavity , the mind , that is ,

fragments so precise , too painful to recall , small piece of skin , at
best the heights of , caprice , and inside that drawer , still another one ,
chinese puzzle , red velvet plush , just sitting there , transmogrified ,
inside the almost empty , movie house , buzz , vomit , comic books ,
extinct characters talking in captions , white levitating , supernal
as are the gods , the gods , no going back , what was the song , again

O lady of the wild hair , trying to piece together , vedanta , subsequent
editions , even further back , darkness around the edges , suffocated
by light , barely make out who is , talking , appended to her voice ,
ligatures , vowel combinations , melodies so sublime , around and ,
roses lotuses dogwood eglantine , purity of thought , righteousness of ,
measures of flame , strict , how to pronounce correctly , OM , transitory

dying is , from one state to the , next time around , see you in the mirror ,
argent shades , barely visible figures , wearing someone else's clothes , the ,
section about , yes , the soul , *animula vagula blandula* , heteroclitic , eerie
version , of , way she shifted from one aisle to the , other , half way to ,
paradise , is a park , when the phone was invented , when drifting from ,
sphere to sphere , ever more distant , longing , yearning , sighing , far

the , is a , articulation of the ineffable , phonetic decay , aphasia , rushing
ether through the , ear , tones , deafness , can't hear you , everything sifted
through , return to dust , loss of form , shapeless as air in the night , echo ,
hiss , zzzz , hush , shhh , lingering in a funnel , sliding , long dark transom ,
the , depths , bottomless , when hands are no , more , when , as you were ,
speechless , looking back , at me , why , sleep , sleep , huff , thunk , shhh

21.

monkey's home! look in the mystical mirror
out chasing ghosts all night long what a face

and die again the lonely death motherless

through naked wood and darkness haunted

or within desolation's labyrinthine moor

cloaked in the dust of archaic myth wording
spells to mask what is felt every passing minute

lampwick soot congested paraffin colored hell
unreadable the blank woof of the unspeakable

ink tainted face stains a night without sound

and yet to recall home threads its red beads
round the white throated bride of memory

sweetly descend into ivory hills of eventide
the resounding sea in the ear's small shell

syllables of dun colored slopes a distance

what a monument of dust and blear the eyed
thing coming over the ridge a lantern to espy

make out what they say failing that to sleep
motherless monkey his soul to breach a saint

a high note held to perfection while decay

junction of proximities for the sake of love

isn't the dusk here in the overgrown grass
and the cool of oncoming planets so rushing
to kindle that old flame over again the big one
some noise in the head's archaeology crashing
beams help a choking twilight can't see so well

it's to be sad a memory dismember me by a

where bottomless as unlit ocean floor other
seeks its self formless as powders floating
around the statue's unbidden shape ah cries
for its monument back the vast incomplete
like the mountain in the forgotten painting

when we were trudging upcountry in search

in their ascent to a broken paradise parked
by the deserted lodge in Arden Wood betimes

sounding out the vedic syllables uninstructed

are seeing something between furious winds
branches taut breaking leaves in a swirl
bee swarms stunned trying to escape winter

like the day you called to say you weren't
returning a rerun of last year's bad movie

twisted into verse by the experimentalist
who happens to be you in this dark diorama

shafts of incoming light through the mind's

distances of incommensurate longing as if
to drown without anchor to the fathomless

"to live in a country without philosophy"

22.
other fragments include the passage to
the song you knew so well frozen in the back seat
while the car plunged directly into the maelstrom
driven by some relatively obscure deity from the east
discoursing on the seven branches of learning
what was that?   ornaments of sand
adorning the perfect Pythagorean body
music spherical endlessly revolving in a sky
the size of a mint leaf
travesty of juxtapositions the twenty eight days
when men and gods walked together
in the country called *Eleutheria* the flower blessed
what distances! what increased yearnings!

turned to look and the sacred ones were gone
leaving in their place cities of arcane dust

a violence in the noosphere an instantaneous shining
equivocation of silent lunar catastrophes
how else can this noon be translated
but by fireflies and the nonchalant appearance of nymphs
soon it is later than the Hour
evenings of burnished Tuscan statues
when the third and fourth floors of inns light up
a violent rush of winds blinding night
these hills were not here before
this transcends flame this transcends water
here was the egress to the confluences of hades
this small portal protected by the *numen*
tongues parch eyes burn memory dries up
to cross the lintel intoning numbed vowels of a mantra
to lose everything

eye fixed on the phenomenon
the immobile nothing of the beyond
shakes my hand my other does
we let ourselves go into the irreparable
wants his wife back goes on and on at the bar
the music strikes up its seventh note and holds it there
we can go back to where it started
we can go back to the twenty ninth day
when the gods were no longer with us
we can count all around us the rows of "them"
as they first manifested in the poem
we can gather the fragments and try to piece them
it's all an enigma ink strokes on an empty paper
shifts from the red planet to the aggravation
of living here between wars and monsoons
besieged by swarms of insects bearing human faces
going under is a struggle

an enormous plan projects itself
a map of the ideal city of the *nous* exteriorized
blazing white cubes elevated above the surface
and women who come out of the palace doors
their hegemonies of hair piled up like pagodas
puzzled glances in their radiant violet eyes
have seen my *Eurydice* I ask
they go on by as if invisible into the Museum
where they will look at *the thing* under glass

traffic lights blink red on and off
tirelessly throughout the night
unredeemed I retire to my rock
where sleepless the leopard sits
animal beauty spirit host

each fragment less intelligible
islands like unto adrift in the sea of Being
none to the other easily visible
sleeping restlessly with the sense of loss
to have *that thing* back even if
for a minute in a mirror
impalpable tantalizingly "there"
morphosyntactic aspects of a language
we have never really grasped
the immense incomprehensible
of consciousness at odds with itself
me you is the other

23.
the girls weren't they something
each and everyone no matter what they were
wearing doing thinking an absolute puzzle
Legend in short skirts or Echo wearing a nose ring
Myth in her phantomatic organdy chiffon dress
the Muse herself in skin of pale white see through
summoning with a single finger the mistakes
of history to draw blood from the lessons
queens princesses courtesans and nymphs
accidents waiting to happen at the crossroads
going in and out of half constructed temples
lying in wait in the shadow of the sacred oak
bent over river banks to exhaust the waters
with their good look reflections
silver mirror reverberations in their languid pose
faces instead of masks masks instead of faces
eyes shining within the thought of beauty
butterflies of light! throne-goddesses of ivy!
is it any wonder that in the very end
they were the trembling oncoming darkness
the unspeakable thrill of an unknown orient
deadly night-shades descending over the visible

those girls hiding from the moment of truth
behind painted screens of the galaxies
slowly emerging pallid wispy partially dressed
in grass the instant of their mouths O
ruddy dissolving into a dewy crescent
more than half the sky was theirs
earth their mother shivered as their feet skimmed
dancing like fireflies over the shaking firmament
which of the so many all so similar and elusive
was mine? which pouting in a boudoir of cosmetics
and pink lingerie was destined to be mine?
"what you love you can never possess"
thus the sibyl in her green glass opacity
one fade afternoon in the bright be-all of existence
air gathered itself into a soft violet knot
time ceased moving on its fiery wheel
but the girls they kept *being* persistent
as a swarm of bees circling Mount Hybla

here among the dead in this weather of wreathes
of withered garlands of crumbling fanes where
the immobile is the image of perfection the girls
playing hide and seek between the cracked marble
columns of abandoned temples flee darting like mayflies
over the sluggish Styx faces a blur of smeared lipstick
and rouge eye-highlight liner black streaks over
their ghost pale cheeks sticking their lolling red tongues
out provoking the manes *rising inert from beds of*
coal dust and ashes it is in the dialect of ancient love
play and mourning that they intone their childish verses
resounding faintly in the enormous garden of Echo
where weeds bracken briars and thorns abound
catching on their non-existent skirts scratching their
long skinny legs running bare over ossuary mounds
who is it they are chasing or from whom are they
fleeing in fugitive bands like angels who have lost
their identities fluttering broken wings in an archaic air
how intricate is the lack of light the loss of form
the memory of shadow which of them so seductive
in their distance of forgotten music and yellowing
incomplete mountain slopes gathering where they
can flowers narcissi and asphodel swooning colors
mauve haze and purple tinted blooms twice dead

with recollections of the upper earth of the summers
when girls reigned adorned with a mimicry of light
lying in great fields of heat arms open waiting for
someone like me which of them is the one

24.

black thread through deep green side winding
darker sea crests in the ear's faint tautology
rock drills sleeping crystal formations roseate
like dawn's fingers groping thin sheets of ink
violent surging from underneath procrustean bed
lamp tallow signatures faintly smoking vowels
uninhabited waters swirling eddying fathomless
around dreaming distant existences coming to be

light! for the briefest of minutes streaking the all
spreading canopy-like a blue fan whitening into
abeyance fractions of things sent centrifugally out
unconscious as space is disrobing itself of matter
to remember as shadows do the instant of recognition
before plunging pell mell into the fiery mass of ether
what did I do wrong? mind blends its thought wildly
groping with its tiny hands of rain for the edge of time

thunder drumming depths in the veins pounding
heart senses oncoming the darker strength night
a music rising from stone a weeping in the grasses
for some untold loss some fragment of illusory passion
unrealized section by troubled section of the unimaginable
you deposited on some sandy spit wasted and marginal
where can I locate you without compass in this storm
how can I direct this tangled unwinding of memory

a man's just a fraction of a thing nerve skin and salt
bone thrust into ivy recollections waking on the other side
a millimeter from the forge of the greater matter reddening
opposites that accrue in a hazy light like fireflies buzzing
toward some unspecified loss is it to rage then forfeiting
the human emotion to a herculean diameter out of control
agonized and ignorant of the bigger why of the quantities
the gods mete out in their myths of caves and fornications

bolts then of lightning threatening purplish cloud masses

the empyrean wreak dissolving fundament and ether alike
precipitous and dangerous the cliffs of heaven the visible
things that swarm in the perilous scope of your amazing eye
does a cascade of immense orchestras pour into your ear
sleeping as you do on the outside of thought's universe
fiery axles plunging chariots quartets of horses aflame
everything in your palms reduced like sand to the infinite

when it has finished bathing in sorrow when grief's wing
glassy and shattered has ceased beating against the frame
will you stir again then agitated consciousness of delusion
asking to have back that shadow you surrendered on the lawn
when the eyeless ones enticed you with promises of paradise
just words a forest of syllables parallel systems of expression
confusion as to which *"you"* is intended in the honorific
or am I to blame mythologizing *"you"* in preterit darknesses

blood-red amaryllis sapphire intellect ruby-throated hummingbird
memory a distillation of colored mirages blowing like powders
in the air's forced entry known to the Ionians as the *soul*
was it shadow-stalking when I pursued you into the Vale
whence none return the howling of winds and unseen beasts
nocturnal abysses geographies of the unending accompanied
by swarms of migratory bees mad to find your ultra hair do
with what diction address the entities who govern the ineffable?

I am a poem I am a havoc I am a wreck in human skin
the thing is the beyond of the unspeakable a refrain in madness
surrounding the occult physics of what it is to be a girl do you hear
the business going on in the stone do you ken the waves washing
over board and the drowning of the one man within the two
what a symbol is in the waxing moon and when the wine spills
darkening the face of the Master and the stairs multiply by three
going up and divide by five going down what is the next chapter

let us count the number of times it takes to write just one single word
using a vedic system of astronomy and the dawns come rushing all
fifteen of them through the cloud-burst and Indra king of the gods
holds the trump card dashing his car all about the simulacrum of heaven
it is this orient I hail from and these animals tamed by my lyre
that bring the sands of sleep into the contentious kingdom of *amore*
it is nothing but a topography of broken hearts and bleeding arrows
convulsion of rock formations and lava beds conspiracy of firebirds

everywhere it says a *love supreme* but just as quickly the curtains

come down in a blaze of raffia and spit while embraced the phantoms
who have exchanged names and personae a dozen time lie breathless
beneath fortune's panting wheel a small plume of bluish smoke scribbles
promises in the arcane script of the coffin makers who worship Osiris
in all his bits and pieces and the storms come springing the doors open
and floods of intense heat amplify the sense of total and utter loss
the premium of passion in any language littering a flush of dead blooms

Primavera! your naked stunning leaves me outside and vertiginous
whelmed by anxieties of never knowing why do you answer to no one
walking the senseless surf that borders the very unconscious of sky
I am borne by lettered pygmies to a baldachin and laid down to dream
I am in Hades with father Pluto the world of stone and labyrinthine
masonry the hemisphere this side of the Lethe looking for you
cosmic daffodil among lepers of inconstant shade and those whose
skin is a song of interplanetary stress vagrants of futile oblivion

do I choke on my own green syllables plankton and miasma of dread
because to never have back what I owned is destiny which is aphasia and
alike the infernal system of remembrance words mumbled to tree trunks
incomplete incisions that initial the twined ivy of lovers doomed to
afternoons in the crocus that grows solitary among Olympian marbles
ruins of the Ruin circling endlessly a gyre of unfinished beginnings
smoking and not smoking the designations for *mother* and *captivity*
in the language of One who has lived for loss and that alone in time

25.

not much time left for anything but
the hymns secretive recondite mysterious
a deity never to be discovered hidden in the ivy
a voice echoed through the bright red trumpet vine
a brother gone into underworld mists imploring
there *must* be a god of transitions of sweet wafting
for the souls departed that want also to return
somewhere in the white turbine of the invisible
where singing the fifty daughters of the sea
make of the marine air a palpable transparency
skin itself the Song of mirages and delusion
hymns that require no music for they are *the* music
syllabifications of the blank echo of evening
remembrances culminating in archaic streets
backwaters where the sun's magnificent spoils fester

undone by Dionysus who draws in the purple shades
over the mystic garden where Dawn and Night sit
in trance formation longing for the green
that transforms for the archaic of yearning
hymns to the very sun that devours them
as they devour him in turn taking that entity
into their soft pomegranate mouths
talking holy nonsense babble to the world outside
is it because we are twisted unable to see straight
for all the indivisible that lays before us?
is it to great Pan we turn this hymn?
the roaring in the sky is his signature
but great Pan is dead all the shepherds know it
their lament creases the atmosphere with a red shift
that renders Selene the moon unconscious in her orbit
what is left of all the books we planned to read
let alone write in the language of transformative vision
all alone on the banks of the stream that purls
eddying slowly past the Library
day dreaming a life away the small pauses
when for a minute and awake we *"see"*
and lapsing into coma again pen these hymns
the illegible ineffable visions of the Other
        who else is there?
or am I talking to somebody new to a divinity
intrinsically melded into the lush verdure
outcropping wildly around the capital of the Delta
and I call upon Demeter and Hecate and Persephone
and light sparks all around the cubit
that contains Psyche her small breasts tightened
by a silk ribbon and her hair in golden ringlets
do then these Ladies lead me from the hustle
of the daily routine into ecstasy
closer to death and dying than to quickened breath
lightning bolts of the ether and storms
that take place in the little siesta after orgasm
chung chung chung I hear reverberating
in the ear's immense distance a motor
which must be the call of Unreason
and I hymn out of mind other deities
Hera of the powerful white arms

and Artemis formidable for her deadly aim
and lord of the afterworld father Pluto
to whom I make mute appeal
to have back my Eurydice *"the wide justice"*
repeatedly I perform the piece called the Mysteries
and a hush reverential and puzzling falls
from stone to rock and cliff
and back again sighs blandish the sulfurous air
baroque arpeggios chaconnes and passacaglias
like fine fiery rain call the spirits to dance
round and round in the absence of shadows
their incorporeal selves become suffused
with the intense devotion of an unknown love
hymns! I race through the printed words
that dazzle and diminish before my eyes
singing numbly the force of the Lip
as it meets chastely the cold caryatid
whose beauty is an eternal recollection
of loss in the fast dissolving white night of time

26.
"Send your madness, O Pan,
to the ends of the earth"
lessons of the primordial the wistful the never ending
....
............................like a second cadaver ....
the river so swollen it took the bridge with it
where did the city go the magnificent city of the Sun
pyramids and market places from all corners ....
....
once you reach the junction where the flags unfurl
and .... ask if there is any other way
white balustrades jutting out from the dark
you can hear voices quarreling inside women maybe
high reedy singing .... plates smashing walls ....
do you remember how it was? Mnemosyne was there
in her dark green velvet wrap-around ....
there was a ventriloquist and several dozen gods
faceless ill-humored ....tusks
....................to see them ....

great islands appeared in the vast water of space
and the murk between the glittering panoply of lights
.... a fierce joy .... troubling
first there is the illusion you were born and living there
talking to thieves and priests alike a riot of words
then there is the delusion that among the many girls
sporting in their primavera colors and tatterdemalion
one was meant for you her broad white oval face
here fish-like eyes red and flashing against the pallor
that set her off ....
.... how many times on bended knee pleaded
askance looking tossed her raven locks side to side
taunting teasing cajoling wearing that drug store look
too refined for ....
afternoons in drowsy sultry splendor sheets wringing with
sweat yellow orange spackled dense the air suffocating
her bare legs erect above you anklets of coral ....
....
did you really think such luxury could last given the misery
of this planet ....sent you raving moon-mad
destroying repeatedly your many-stringed instrument
dashing your brains against Thracian rock formations
.... how little and yet how infinite ..... grass
weaving pliant memory with its small hands ....
....
driving a buick 88 up and down the country lanes shouting
at every tree her name as if ....*borderline*
gonna lose my mind couldn't get that song out of the radio
.... hours of dust going up and down hill and dale
crashing .... city of the Sun
endeavor to remember why it was ....
first time was the last time or no time at all circling whirling
buzzzzzz ....swarms searching her hair piece
how many lunations in a bathysphere ....
how long it takes to reach the number one in an inverted pyramid
what is the matter .... cannot herald her coming (again)
suited out with complex hair the kind they wear in the underworld
her vast and white face a blank of centuries ....
moving through infinities of sand her subtle slow motion body
to have it at the ends of time to...

.... Mnemosyne was there
ZZZZZZZZZZZZZZZZZZZZZZZZZZZZZZZZZZZ
I am at the origins of things : insect kingdoms : heat
over and over writing her name with spit
on a single eucalyptus leaf that is
dwelling within me is
the ineffable

27.
otherwise the excruciating period of waiting the
insufferable wasn't it   the door opened
the gravity the sheer darkness that accompanied
announcing nowhere to be seen though the shadow
remained stuck to the wall the moving likeness
a profile in gesso white pallid remote the her saying
what a vivid recollection like a dream in water
you can never tell here among these defective mortals
assaying small replicas in gold or praying to idols
exquisitely sculpted and painted iridescent dravidian
the tell tale logos flagging in the artificial sky
what was meant to be it all comes to that
and what can never be what is the use breathing
here and here among this lush verdure walking
as it were counting moonlit hours that shine down
on a landscape of desolate and mournful rocks
sitting in the ruins of a once great quarry
or was it a city or an aggravation of contents
listening to the underground river the black thick
sluggish stream it is the enticing like a drug to hear
a music as sudden as it is unlikely in the drowned ear
an article of notes ascending sublimely into the ether
un hunh and still unable to recapitulate exactly what
bright red things in the heavens warnings and
mutilations of gods who have spent too many hours
in the seaside motel with "girls" and the sighs
the multiple of the immense seas just outside
the boundaries of thought the unspeakable reflections
within the breast's rent attic ghostly skeletal
aspirations to have at the likelihood it is really "her"
question marks of a wronged syntax a lover's grief

unpronounceable syllables carved in an air of marble
inconstancies and subjugations and betrayals
all the human delusions called "tragedy" the inimitable
sparks flying and rage or despond beware the her
it is not literature it is repulsion the antipodes
the upside down masts of wrecked ships
in an extra galactic sargasso signaling futilely
to the wayfaring souls who have lost their way
naiads fruit flies caustic whims what is it the eye
can't see in this miasma and din this mad rushing
to what ends to what unearthly goals unperceived
I am what her could be an ampersand without direction
the intervals between lives and the symbols
they stand for the percussive threnody on the shore
wasted the once glorious fleet the mind's own trap
listing tilting drowning southwards to a tropic
flooded with replicas of "her" the lovely the winsome
the young how old was she when we first met
speech acts defying balance and then to fall
shudder posing in the refuse and byways of Atlantis
O mothers! the distance demanded for recovery
glottal impositions stops and hiatuses
hyssop jasmine fragrances untranslatable
memory wrung out to dry on a rope of sand
the insane it is occupying so many zones at once
the simultaneous elevation of all the bodies
she is through pages and pages of liquid aphasia
into the epic half-starts all about
and yes it is a cognitive thing this amazing
loss of everything in the sudden flush of inks
what was visible now but a punctuation mark
in the far off of nowhere *ay ay ay*

hush of silence murmurs whispering
in ear's recondite pink seashell a nothing
nowhere divided by zero poetry
essences streaming invisibly through the hole
at the other end of the wicker work cosmos
a chaos lipless ungrammared darkening
richly violent in its porous soundlessness
leaving in its wake a symphony of alephs

diminishing lamps that once decorated
the bride dim recollection of skirts
a wind filling the pleats an unwinding
fade ever fade the small

28.

"wielder of speech,
  the dreaded and respected weapon"

foremost in the realm of the deceased
interpreter of the complex conductor of the long gone
behold your aerial deceits deriding mortals
even in your ruined fanes where it means
to be hermetic keeping the great Secret
and you Others I also praise
the horse-god the earth-shaker Nereus too
of the depths and whose steeds rush
through windless Hades by dire Acheron
where there has been a shift in consciousness
where a life has been altered by the Muses' gift
and You who keep to your darkest selves the Queens
nubile nymphs vine-waisted girls caught unawares
to share your unending palaces half a year or more
whose sudden return into the dazzle of day
blinds even as wheat and grape ripen in the glare
how often do we fall unconscious in your lauds
ceremonies and banquets where the dead propped
by slaves in white skin struggle to listen
to deeds attributed to them in bardic rounds
in verses of crafted rhythms in tales and variations
of histories recited by trance-blind seers
and sacrificial fires blaze into the distant night
sending islands off into the remote west
and talk of thunder and sky big with clouds
massing in martial formations above old Anatolia
where in powerful mid-air the series of thoughts stir
bringing confusing dreams and portents inky
what can never be rightly understood
though the heavens are observed minutely with awe
as the sun drives his chargers bright as melting butter

through the errors of the revolving hours
……………………………………………………..
what can never be rightly understood
obsessed by what was seen *once* and only once
to have it back to enlarge it to amplify it
so it occupies the whole southern hemisphere
where the galaxies appear brightest most remote
to name it *feminine* unapproachable exhausting
with enormous hair and face hauntingly blank
blanched powdered the color of albumen
blood-red lips and eyes fish-shaped flashing
rimmed with smears of black kohl hypnotic
translucent sheen of skin spread like a sky pattern
across the furious winding sheets of sleep
………………………………………………………
learning to speak what does one really learn
imitating shelves of sound boxes of vocables
syllables that linked correctly make a prayer
like a little prayer hermetic redundancies obsessions
repeating endlessly the names of gods the god the many gods
the goddesses the only Goddess the demi-ones
the transposed heads of heroes cut short in their span
vowels without discretion zooming southerly
mythiform secrets kept in cretan caves
Kypris the holy one shaking her love-mound
in the pearly resonance of dawn-echoing dew
and the conches the sea-shaped instruments pealing
is it the end of time is the cycle of years finished
has sky finally been reduced to its infernal inch
cutting along an equator of senseless heat
have we at last nothing to say after so many lessons
copying the speech therapist whose hooded figure
moves in and out of fading daguerreotypes
as afternoon draws to its tiresome conclusion
we hear doors shut voices stifled muffled cries
one after another of us disappears
………………………………………………………
what can never be rightly understood
meridian when together the bedazzled and I
gathered crocus and hyacinth to make nosegays
garlands easily withered promises not kept

perspiration like dew on her upper lip
the wisp of a memory the thing bending
like a thin reed in the dragonfly's shadow
by the small water running darkly
back into the underworld

29.

the catalogue of heroes of those dinted spurned
cast aside on the dreary grey-surf pounded coast
as the battered ships set sail back again to home
names lipless and unsounded in the increasing night
suchness of deeds once deemed glorious now lost
unuttered bodies hacked to pieces brains strewn
why go on agonizing that this has happened that
so many dear ones friends relatives rest in oblivion
brother lend me your shadow for you need it no more
let me in your place descend to the unlit halls
where eternity is just a unit of measure

remember the pleasure it was making verse
the delight like child's play memorizing stanzas
that praised death and its ethereal kingdom
now it is come to this serious office confronting
death's living reality the fierce knot in the air
which unwinding takes us in its burning noose
when did we first realize we were dead though living
was it on the supreme and instantaneous lawn
when summer the infinite one of heat and glory
when Delphic Apollo smiled down on the leaves
we looked & saw each other as dead already
young our years were verdant and keen singing
both visible and invisible to the swirling cosmos
such is the transitory blade of grass that at once
its end is come no sooner has it drunk the sun
so you fighting with your shadow in the verdure
one minute a halo of brimming light above and
the next you are imagining a voice is within you
seeping out into the soundless dark and gone
to ashes windswept cornices of unseen rock

glass bees painted on the world's ceiling
trellis of twining ivy caught between whistling winds
a hemisphere the size of ink and the poem deep
embedded in the chaotic measures of its flow

is it because suddenly conscious of light's gift
and aware of the vast ether and multiple worlds
the possibilities of breath and color that we come
to quarrel over lesser distinctions and invidious
the gods see this as their chance and make heroes
of those who are altered by insight and smite them
ah this is the course we have taken this the stony path
shunning the painted and splendid mansions on the hill
for the contentious and complex mobilities of thought
entangled and illumined at the same time by a possibility
that perhaps we are not our *selves* after all but
something dimensionally other
so you in your brainy sinuous way come to this door
avoiding as best you can Artemis' eager shafts
earth comes rushing at us a swarm of leaf and insect
heat and its varieties of red illustrate for a second only
the infinite instant of love wrapped in fragrances
of musk and vine headstrong delivering us forever
from the light
careful one step to the left and into the Acheron
you plunge   mighty Soul!

30.
the last time I wrote that poem
the alphabet was arranged differently
the sounds were more archaic the pronunciation
verged on the rapidly incomprehensible
taking full advantage of red
and all its various and often violent tones
and for whom it was meant and for why
her wavering dimpled crescent faced
her assumptions about where the piano goes
in a room full of nostalgia and
the last time I read that poem
wiping from my glasses the ichor of the gods

and pointing to an audience of the invisible
angels and demons alike in suspense
candelabra and tiny lunar satellites
shook above the decreasing world map
and signatures of the bards dissolved in sand
the last time I destroyed that poem
to an auditorium of the unseen
elephants of the sun crashed the paper
moon nymphs with enormous black hair
danced on stilts like peahens before the rain
libraries of arcana emptied their contents
rivers lost their deltas clouds and clouds!
there was no reason to have written that poem
whatever went before or came afterwards
in waves of inky miasma what did it matter
words out of joint syllables ululations
imperfectly sounded vowels and diphthongs
consonant clusters clicks hisses buzzing
exhausted swarms of river ants crawling
upwards toward a vedic symbol for Dawn
all the vast anterior of language
nothing finally whatever informed that poem
junctions where sleep and echo concur
where ivy twines around the goddess's waist
leaving a faint imprint like a kiss
intersections of marble and gas
a universe going backwards towards its infancy
smaller and lesser galaxies like cuneiforms of flame
imploding soundlessly in the devastated ear
and the next time I write that poem
if there is another time for such indecencies
what it has to say and how it can be sung
whether there is a lyric vibration
that adheres to the infinite skin of her
for whom it will be dedicated
full of blank and mad devotion ampersands
and ligatures of wild and desperate communication
yes the next time I write that poem
when in my leopard skin of rhetoric
I reappear as the novel Orpheus
the rock frenzied stoned and totally deviant one

lyre in one hand and paragraph of serpents in the other
and I will sing mantic and dispossessed of mind
the thousand attributes of my Bride
the girl nymph nubile thing of the crazy grasses
how many times will she manifest all utterly
the suchness of white pallor and distinction
among blue gilly flowers and dragonflies
whose transparent wings cast images
of wavering indigo nothingness on a water
of non-existence the absolute end all
of love shifting diminishing evanescent mirage
and as many and more times will she be lost
innocent of hades immersed in a sulfuric
and dazzling music of otherness forever gone
the massive of longing and melancholy
preterit of what could never be
my Eurydice like a cubist painting
ascending repeatedly the stairway
that never goes all the way
then this is *that* poem
which should never have been written
this is *that* poem
which I cannot remember writing

31.

is the mind spherical coming around
to eat itself for againbite
is thought nothing but a wax impression
vainly trying to maintain memory
against the heat and light of passing time
what is a purer substance than transient dew
which clothes the Nymphs like a white raiment
dancing in circles around the goat-god
in hills and rocks of far off Legend
can I come back to myself without mind
do the Hamadryads accompany not me
but my shadow ever walking the crescent
unperceived entering cave and grotto
where something or someone dances frenzied
do the Maenads await outside hiding

eager to snatch and tear madly at me
what is the excuse for myth to play such games
how many times have I exercised this art
plying these verses through invisible ivy
training words to become more than their meaning
because I too remain the outsider
the uninvited the stranger the one Without
whose domain is ever the wild and unkempt
the far from the main the solitary discourse
who sees in a single leaf the pattern of galaxies
and loss and the terrible spirit of yearning
today is the only day in time
everywhere else is outside the sacred precinct
there will be no yesterday only greening
there was no tomorrow only barren
each instant contains a seed of infinity
each infinity explodes in a yellow pollen haze
it is constantly noon on the planet of Sicily
clusters of magical beings hover around the water
they all *know* what has happened in the mountain
they are filled with amaze at the sacrosanct
the voyages underground every July
the fertility rites the circle dance the offering
to the goddess who is the One and the Many
by night in my trappings of haunted beast
tuning my instrument to some lunar theodicy
to enchant the unseeable what do I experience
but the unknowable the secret in the margins
breath coming through the dense verdure
that swarms to strangle the light
I am capsized I am on the verge of non-being
there is within me a dactylic music
a humming and drumming of intense chords
wired up to the eighth note and no higher
the second this happens and it is every second
I suffer a vertigo that sends me to eternity
dazzling suffused of multiple concurring constellations
it is never to wake and speak again
as a mere mortal it is never to wake again at all
dreaming the inky seas of the mind's bottom
where language suffers a syntactic accident

memory echo and the ability to *see* peripherally
without expressing a single syllable combine
to make inchoate the chaos of originality
I am that also and Thou in my midst
uttering out of profuse eons of memorization
the whole of the Book of Eurydice with its parallel
inches and reconsidered conflagrations
always coming around to the mind's declinable fortress
the so many small eyes rotating in an idyll
by the bosky mere where the outsider in his hide
tends to the wanderings and vagaries of thought
tiny impulses to shake from the shade
some ruin a relic of beauty a polished stone
a refashioned bone a lock of hair
places where stepping out of her skin
Persephone might have conducted the lost one
back to the light

32.
so many irrecoverable things just floating
in the diaphanous to whom address such losses
without naming them keeping them invisible
out of time and place distorted fragmented
unutterable a snatch of music a half tone
a register higher than recalled a reedy sound
taken away in the may breeze a cloud section
once enormous now tufts of friable cotton
rushing backwards into the unseeing eye
to sleep again under the leaf to stir in grasses
looking for the cut finger for the footprint
for the egress that leads darkly unwinding
back down to the small unlit doll's house
to whom address these losses in twilight
when heaven's purple hinges come loose
and the vast rippling awning of thunder

blind lanterns! deaf and empty hills!
return to me the disappeared of memory
does light itself no more contain the factory
whence flame and sensuous matter arise?

smoking irises! imponderable hiatuses!
I have lost my voice imploring you O shadows!
disjunctive syllables softly falling from the pearl
into seas incarnadine that swirl dreaming
around spent rock and crystal impassiveness
have at the missing body with knives of fog
sunder from the fading pallor of once green
bright the sunken text of unbidden secrets
lore of sandy infinities! maze of hazel tresses!
unyoke me from the massy stellar plains
so plunge again I might into unformed waters
bleaker still the drifting page the unkenned
what was written there with foaming consonants
unpronounceable languages erased by salt
emphatic reds!

it isn't that I have no more initials to sign
no more love letters to pen and send by dove
no more exegetical comments on the mysteries
to narrate *sotto voce* to the Naiads at the well
it's that my persona is no longer indelible
but soluble dissolved in an aggravated weather
that my masks once gilded ornaments of stage
have been torn off to litter the evening lawn
world is a crazy storm of indentations and sighs
rains that pass through glass into the crucible
byzantine baldachins saturated with humidity
personifications of trees and hail and lichen
spectra at the door demanding free entrance
stone and hillside pine for their quarry and
inevitable night

the speckled cloud the grasses of many hues
the spotted kine evaporating like smoke
come evening and the enigmas in the air
bluish transience of everything in the quiet
submerged the mind the lunar veils spread
so little left to die for a nothing dressed in white
to whom address these shapeless yearnings
how far does it go before simply turning blank
Atropos Lakhesis Klotho ! fates who all knowing

pitilessly watch cold earth revolve in its ellipse
governed by entities of imperfect intent and aim
it is nothing to you that my hands grasp shades
insubstantial spheres of trembling ether
which were once the body of summer--woman
airy inexorable heat between silk sheets and
like water rushing underneath impalpable

was I meant for some greater music
or have I been dead all these eons?
spent in the leaf growing in the mirror
borne away by the eurasian coffinboat
into some heaven of marsh and russet grasses
where the mind cut off from its rock
eerily loses itself in a grammar of transience
volleys of distance and perpendicularity
where archaic thoughts ricochet
remembering a thing of immense beauty
shimmering in a meadow of eternal primavera
unapproachable but in passing dreams
the ineffable

33.

this is day of eternal shape
this is day of non-stop yearning
this is day of the maze and the honeysuckle
this is day of the darkest hive
this is day of buzzing swarms
of insect communication to the stars
of grasses thriving in dappled clouds
this is day of the non retrievable sky
this is day of living quicker than ever
this is day of utter despair
this is day of massive blank
this is day of fleet Artemis
intent on smiting Actaeon
this is day of immense water
this is day of celebrating Zeus
whose mind is ever on the House
or this is day for climbing Hera

whose powerful white arms quiver
this is day of the labyrinthine coil
this is day of the endless Hour
this is day of haunted summer
of baleful leaf and herb
this is day of hummingbird and light
of wings and ants and heat
this is day of nothing less than zero
this is day of utter despair
this is day of Hermes and his deathless sandals
this is day of the unfathomable
this is day of erased cuneiform
this is day of sacrificed black ram
of the of the of the
why can't this be day of mourning
of sorrow in the fifth degree
of black honey threnody
this is day of Persephone's little doll house
this is day of father Pluto's dominant rage
this is day of Ishtar and Isis
day of Delta and Omicron
this is day of no honor
of and of and of the all encompassing
day after tomorrow
for why do we walk on our knees
shedding tears of blood and purulence
this is day of the smoking altar
of choking incense and dead mayflies
this is day of holy pornography
of the absolute end all of human sex
this is day of utter despair
this is day out of time
no day at all the last day ever
this is day of animus *and* anima
of obfuscations of the pinnacle
of day of the day of the other day
when nothingness comes to riot
and whatever went lost the day before
whatever most sorrowfully went to play
in Persephone's tiny little doll house
that day is come around

in caves and fearsome grottos dank
in silos and abandoned fanes
in dried riverbeds and blasted hills
of thorn and decay of loss
this is the day of *that* day
bilge and heaps of detritus
human rot excrement on the walks
day of massive city detonations
of urban nightmares ruddy
this is day of Chronos' death
this is day of Saturn's emasculation
this is day of mythological orgasm
of shooting stars and artifices de feu
this is day of I don't know why
of sovereign madness
this is it today of endless death
the thrice praised Lady of the Crossroads
Nymph Bride and Hag
this is day of restless bone
this is ultimate and groundless
this is
this is I don't know how or why
she is walking other earth
a planet ahead of me strapped
to speeding metal vehicle
a god task to complete a
finishing the conscious life
this is day of frank incense and storax
demolishing the sonata form
burning up the linguistic interior
phasing out the dactylic hexameter
this is truly day of many unknown gods
deities who govern shopping hijacking
wayfaring plundering rape and booty
minute gods the size of midges or termites
gods with hyaline wings and snouts
gods who are rank with ire and envy
day of misfortune and despond
goddesses Melinoe and Leukothea especially
who preside over the Invisible and Unheard
this is day of bilious rancor and regret

day of remembering the shape of Troy
as it burned and smoldered
and totally day of unrecognition
this is day of sweating over last night's mistakes
having won and then lost
true love and the forever vow
everything is in hues of deep to darker
grasses lay down for terrific winds
seas surge up from the center
out of control tsunamis
volcanic tremors break Gaia's spine
herdsmen barely familiar with the calendar
wonder whether Monday is perpetual
this is day of utter despair
this is day of strabismic vision & galactic confusion
this is really day of the Twins!
Castor and Pollux brothers of fated Helen
this is day of fatal moon swap
when sky dissolves like an aspirin in water
this is day when I go crazy
with the knowledge that nothing is repeatable
this is day holy to Mnemosyne
goddess who keeps oblivion at bay
at her feet I worship imploring
this is day of final sleep
of unrecalled dreams of breathlessness
this is day of eternal shape

34.

what can the poem matter any more
is it magic incantation mystery secret
not to be divulged or chanted aloud
criticized for its cryptic incoherence
for its melodious sublime unending
      untranslatable
meaningful only to initiates of rites
unspeakable and ineffable unholy
it is about nothing or the whole cosmos
it is chaotic deliberately misspelled
inarticulate a linguistic catastrophe

phonetically unsound obscene indiscrete
what it praises and hymns to the skies
      enigmas
shadowy vehicles driving through mind
echoing echoes of the long gone one
afternoons inebriated on solitude and
the poem half finished or just begun
a palimpsest wine stained illegible
inchoate verses meant to chime in air
smoking when the second line begins
and brassy refulgences obliterating
the better part of the text already
a partiality in a backwards script
to be read in an Etruscan mirror
summoning darkly the after gone one
laboring to read the initials marginally
placed the iota subscript frequent
references to omega rather than zeta
lacunae throughout making unintelligible
the entire piece were it not for chance
mistakes of orthography and arrows
pointing to the heart of the matter
somewhere after the praeludium
where cloud masses form volumes
of rolled pergamum or papyrus
doodling crocodile heads and cactuses
nilotic lilies azure fading indigo violet
intention to make red speak for itself
undressing the scribe's alter ego
the indwelling woman who *is* the poet
but the poem the poem itself where
how when is it did it come to be a
fragrance of thoughts like jasmine
dissolving in blank verse sideways
or in reverse etyma and spoiled conjuncts
spilling off the erased pages in profusion
of abstract colors like pollen or mist
swarms of buzzing references to arcadia
to the archaic to the arcane to the ancients
yellowish fade of the mid section where
a faint signature indicates a dying

to the world a hesitation to move on
but never an ending only the hemisphere
of missing contexts sinking below
the water-mark a sort of language
expressing doubts and right thinking
the poem a poem many poems in one
thumbing through the incomplete index
to the first lines on sheets of paper
that lack pagination this has to be chaos
an obligation to test the reader's ability
if not his patience to get through "it"
this unedited lyrical abracadabra a forgery
or a calque on previously misguided efforts
an adolescent pining to imitate Kallimachos
diction as flawed as it is faulty peppered
with savant allusions to a prior world
one of fauns satyrs cunning stupid gods
drooling after the poet's love of choice
enduring violent tempests shipwrecks
pathological encounters with the *Other*
a wandering home through rocky nights
drunken essays with a left handed pen
scribbling for hours the same word
imagining the unimaginable in *French*!
anti-vision of the visible in parenthesis
discoloration and hiatus of the unspeakable
dot dot dot in envelopes of pliable ink
until word weary the phraseology pales
leaving abrupt chasms of metaphor
cliffhanging above dormers of drowsy
splendid imputations of the ineffable
et cetera and more et cetera reddening
in the hermetic dishabille of false endings
repeatable quires of blanched nothingness
saying everything possible soundlessly
vowels etched in *selva oscura* burnt sienna
ochre dun twilit hills of enormous distance
inexplicable lapses of syntax and punctuation
spanish accents circumflex acute and grave
castanets in the ear haunted whisperings
hunh hunh hunh Homeric diphthongs

on the tip of the tongue then aphasia
in twelve orders migraine and tumult
of vowels nonsense and hobson jobson
culminating in *medias res* epic blow
latinate discourse of opposite lyrics
orphic misinterpreted misunderstood
rife with typos misspellings white-outs
never meant to be read aright if at all
a shadow script verging on oblivion
all about the girl he lost in Hades
tuned the lyre made music the poem
a song a singing despair filled verses
half finished barely begun never again
handwritten spiral bound notebooks tossed
into the garage to be forgotten the poem
unearthed in after times a yesterday
of inimitable nostalgia in meadows green
beside the purling stream of crystal waters
reflecting in its swift passage her face
bent to read in the dark racing liquid
her poem

35.

this is what I read in the Pleiades one night
dear so-and-so
what is ungiven is not yours to ask for
troubling green is the borrowed summer
some few leaves and blades of grass forever
and sky's a wrinkle in a folding carpet
spacious and infinite as sand
what is left unseen you cannot touch
whom you want to possess you cannot have
give no more thought to undying love
trees abound in the grove of time
by evening bare and sere they waver
mourn as you do it cannot come back
photos and keepsakes memento mori
Orpheus the waves of the sea are uncountable
as are the vagrant islands of the heavens
pray however much to goddesses Hera and Artemis

they will not return what was not yours to keep
pray to Persephone the whole night
hers is the sovereignty of the unlit house
she will not relent nor will dawn's lamp
illustrate for you a glorious day
fogbound your mind continues to circle
reciting incantations and mantras
dark syllables pregnant with secret meaning
words that cannot be deciphered
languages no one can transliterate properly
yours is the world of the Book
the realm of fragile consequence of pages
subject to the corruption of time and nature
insect hoards wait to prey on your consonants
menacing waters a single flaming spark
the enervating passage of sand
through the hourglass all conspire to destroy
that Book fiber by fiber and what it spells
the unimaginable province of a single name
Eurydice of broad justice her meaning
nor can consultation of the astral bodies
kenning the hermetic lore of the planets
fixed and moving bring her shadow back
to the material projections of space
fragrant is the morning jasmine
and like the dew that vanishes too soon
love's reminiscence is just as transient
colors that to the eye once bright
like red in its power with an eye blink
return to shade and pale transformation
Orpheus why cling to what has no form
to what no hand can contain
ether vapors airy nothingness
sphinx and chimera of the imagination
voices of forgotten lawns playing in twilight
to dust to less than dust migrate
into the ear's impalpable oblivion
saying her name and saying it over again
do nothing to substantiate her body
now nothing more than an empty hive
ignored by the bee swarms of Hybla

your Book is not memory but it's faintest echo
the all but unheard in the court of Chronos
the grand night of words is a passing mirage
light years come and go through
eternity's see-through inches
yet you boundless dreamer on your rock
perish thumbing your Book's unseen pages
no wonder nightly dumbfounded you sit
nowhere to go nothing to count
stunned in the minute verbiage of fireflies
whose halos imitate star-light
in vain trying read this disappearing text
thus the message of the Pleiades
and I liable to theft loss and perjury
in my small earth-maze stoned
abandoned by petty house-hold gods
listen intently for the clue in the grass
waiting just waiting for the shadowy vehicle
that brings on the cold endless rain

36.
"Lull thou asleep, to wake no more, the
pair who on each other look"
Rgveda. 1, XXIX

an end to language an end to things
to express the ineffable in the content of shadows
and shadow-beings who in pairs linger longing
for light and the chance to take shape once more
here this is your red kimono and garland of blue lotuses
here these are the sandals and anklets which you wore
dancing before the ice age
was it the blush high liner the rimmel the black kohl
that set your face off from the rest the night of the tsunami
was Legend set in place narrating with slight variation
the way we met beside the glass that obsesses with flame
was it to touch just once the mythology of your skin
and to make a song of it
and to ask of ourselves what was good and just
in our dealings and what was it the god demanded

from us that in the end language was of no account
that things as they are named lost all contour
was it yellow your face paled vanishing in blank
was the rosy hue the lemon tinted pallor of your cheeks
that no sooner lit disappeared in twilight
what was the cause the light withdrew its waning moon
which deity was so offended that speech ceased to circulate
hands became letters groping in the dark to spell
and you with that large paper fan shifting like a bird
through time's inevitable transom flew
for we have drunk from the cup of ignorance and error
finding faulty the way through the world's bower
darker still night us parts and shadows weaving
our paired souls far from one another in weeds stumble
bracken foul stains the once bright green
our springtime's gone our shining dawn's a loss
maleficent poets twine our fates in ivy's fatal curl
no more Mnemosyne recalls each our names so fair
underside the incorporeal mate plunges
looking in vain for its mutual half the bloom
and thunderous echoes the distance ply
but none your famous sound returns

which is the inch above the vowel that colors red
which the stitching in the flesh that anchors love's recoil
I cannot remember to name the thing nor why
every is the time that yearns to think aloud our vows
what's a smile a whisper above belonging
where's to go round and round the vine-like waist
how dizzy the pliant summer day its sun slant
can't you once call back through the thicket dark
or has oblivion your lips contained in waxen chill
a tongue was once the prattle in hexametric verse
styles that change yet sing immutability's renown
render no less the shape you took within the classic ode
sweet linger the syllables pronounced mysteriously
when to the ear your disembodied voice poured its omegas
all the universe refracted in that original echoing
shimmered for its moment before imminent decay
space and the grammar of its redundant reticence
expanded the realm of silence beyond fire's recall

the lyre I lifted into the airy height
the lyric I intoned being divinely inspired
mere vocables of senseless ranting
no language to them known no translation to heaven
just the inch rising above your brow that colors red
just the catafalque where they lay memory of you
unbodied ungiven the all unformed

there's this section called *ahuramazda*
and another section carved from Egyptian basalt
covered with hieroglyphs of sacred mutilation
the sphinx that ate Persepolis
the chimera whose entrails a galaxy devour
why am I tossed outside the field of language
why is this achievement reckoned antidimensional
I fly with the avatars into the tumult of desire
naming and not naming each statue they call history
after the one and the one and the one
still another section a single piece of sky
aerial lifts that run up and down the scales
making of the spheres the great Noise of time
I wrote that part wherein it says *"Sink no more*
my Fate, Thee I call when waters have no shore"
many other such nights pass in a second's blink
beds upturn mattresses tossed and burnt
the sidewalks collect with vagrants named Orpheus
each more damned than the last
a begging cup with a world inside and two left hands
tuning a single-stringed instrument to play
when evening falls and the god's ruddy kine
are sent into the faultless hills to sleep
here am I but where oh where oh shadow
can your restless spirit be?

37.

satellite planets hovering on the rim of thought
white powder in which the dead recognize other souls
this the anti-earth of Persephone the thin lunar crevice
known as salvation for those that succeed in hanging on
a daimon resides in my head pushing sideways into inferno

legacy of ancient poetry untranslatable traces and dreams
of the other life where the elysian fields extend behind the moon
cold cataracts pour into gassy space the relics of the epic
I am if nothing else the stifling afternoon of Sicilian myth
fragments of rock and vegetation dried air volcanic ash
from which arise spectra shuddering from the noon blasts
pleading to have back some shred of shadow a small darkness
a daimon increases his infinite size within my aching brain
there are things my thumbs cannot know to touch that burn
without sensation of flame that contain forbidden metastases
echoes of the first death for those who undergo the second one
when I reemerged from the oracular furnace feet first
my body was radiant this the daimon's irredeemable gift
who filled my mind with the voices of a thousandfold gods
in the lair of heat which is the chrysalis of the omniverse
how can a man ever return who has *seen* and be greeted
by household members as the same when he is polluted
infected by the miasma of being *other* the outsider?

a petty fable jumping from the chariot to earth
the unwholesome goddess inheres to her mortal prey
breath endowing and seizes his limbs in the love act
contractures and stigmata characterize the corporeal domain
perceptions hair-thin of anterior lives vanish in the light
a man this once wandering between stone and rock
mind consumed by the daimon a fierce rippling
fire and ether demand their utter spheres alone
and him leave lost wingless pilgrim without memory
to traverse aimlessly the half familiar terrain
was this his summer once was this the lawn
from which he surveyed by night the starry masses?
do I want out of my head? can I get anything back?
cannot tell the difference between a god and a mortal
the one hides behind a marble statue pretending
to be the statue the other resides inside the marble urn
pretending nothing but the dizzy universe of ash
the daimon inside my head determines the distance
between the two and never tells the truth
entangled in the chronological vertigo of myth

Aphrodite daughter of thought how many are you?

and equally infinite is the number of Cupids
surrounded by their annoying green-winged house flies
swirling inside my poor skull destroying all decorum
so smitten am I ever to escape this amorous infection
or am I destined to revolve between the seven heavens
and the consecutive but numberless floors of Hades?

mythiform worlds crazy ash white disorder the body
simulacrum of the series of deaths rotating in space
just inches from the small aperture inside my mind
where the daimon pushes and pulls and threatens loudly
summer's out the end is here trees all die too green's gone
smashing invisible and immense objects against the air
I am withering vibrating wavering in the middle of sleep
dreaming what is happening here is also happening
on planet Love where all the girls wear Eurydice faces
pale paler than the moon's last thought dissolving
like a mint on the roof of the god's intricate mouth
and which god that is and what name he can possibly have
and just why we are inside him recklessly driving
large polished metal cars through the invention of white
right into the remaining hemisphere of the cranium
the despair of a vowel one too many and the end of time

38.

stochastic process of the sky
        love is not eternal
loss is the spectacular thing out "there"
        enervating gyrations of stars returning
from the dead
            what is it we're trying to recover
where is it we think we're going
        what's up there so fascinating
and down here in our wattle huts and sticks
        sleeping even when awake
dreaming even while most alert
        who is it we think we are
puny entities endowed with breath
        yet being stifled the *other* stifle too
to know what cannot be kenned

the fire within still burns
air all around stirs its ungrounded sound
do we dance to this untuned lyre
is what happens to the wind at night
the same as the long unwritten poem
what is the nexus between two hearts
that have never met
what restrains the *one* from surpassing
the never counted
I am baffled by this illumination
by this source of nerve and battery
whatever we do we are but liquid pouring
irreversible and indivisible
invisible do the gods ever want to imitate men
what is the conversation here
what are the sounds of the words
that make sacred this marriage
or is this the sacrifice the stone cast
the knife elevated the altar smoking
what is the distant sea if not
reflection of the heavens
come lie down it says everywhere
and the small grass listens for thunder
aggravated rock splits in half
earth assumes its under side
steaming and relentlessly dark
where wander the doubles of all
some rent in various parts
others still whole in hieroglyphs
that none can read unless as the ineffable
how came we to enter this bole
to assay the furious nether being
to embrace and to separate
bleeding from the unmitigated kiss
the tooth's imprint on the lip
like the leaf fixed in its afternoon
indelible for the memory of it
echoes no more but waves of the unheard
that enter dissolving in the divine
error of the soul
celestial vagabonds wandering lamps

whom do we seek in the starry vast
    you I remember on the lawn
a flurry of fireflies your mind
    candles lit just once your eyes
all that was ever thought
    however labyrinthine
you expressed in your constant gaze
    mirror of the empty otherness
prism capturing all shades of red
    glass and pyramid of song
your skin that goes on and on
    sand the infinite residue of time
that passes through the lunar hue
    yet nothing of you comes back
nothing remains of that wedding day
    but a finite perspiration a damp
beneath the arms a swooning cloth
    tissue paper fade that pales by light
an afternoon without pages
    blank an astronomical number
masks at last that cast no shade

       39.
if the gestures of the gods are indecipherable
those of men and their languages even more so
sleepwalking through the labyrinth of life
signaling to one another with fingers crooked
assailing the brain with lusts and desires
provoked by promises of paradise on earth
encounters in the dark with talking shadows
whose faintly heard words echo in the underbrush
some distant intaglio of light some glimpse
however brief and passing of the Beautiful
in her shimmering raiment of lunar silk
that was it! the mind cries describing an arc
falling though the interstices of a thought
too intricate to maintain too incoherent
to be interpreted rightly by the lamp of day
left confused errant rambling on dusty paths
the mind and what it beholds wanders lost

a transient in the unnumbered hotel of Dis

the reason to write a poem is not to communicate
the reason to write a poem is to be incoherent
are indecipherable the of the gods a gesture
of men those their languages more even so
crooked fingers sleepwalking labyrinth signal
a life dark shadows faintly talking paradise
of promises provoked an earth underbrush
echo glimpse of intaglio some distance brief
however lunar the Beautiful passing light
the reason to write a poem is not to explicate
the reason is to contradict writing a poem
which has no reason to be written other
than to maintain incoherent the dusty paths
is a mind lesser because it misunderstands
yet applies errant the rambling lost of Dis
shimmering the unnumbered transient falling
silk hotel beholds rightly too intricate arc
is a poem to be irrational enigmatic by day
and if a gesture indecipherable however gods
the sooner imitate mortals in speech acts
not a poem to have reason nor to be coherent
for over half a century sitting here windowless
in hades with this like memory her a pallid planet
circling the distance of sleep with mute syllables
make no sense write no poem speak no act a
god ineffably bloodless envious of the dying

when I left her by the porch eventide moon just up
dust clouds heralded night through a small transom
delicately placed and her hair thick with smoking
residue wasn't she about as wan the pretty a thing
don't look back a warning signaled through rock
her hazel eyes a thing inside them curling wispy green
echo no doubt in transit to another world softly dark
what was moaning in the grass her footprints dew
stained if another just like her a shadowy essence
through the trees wearing a costume of human skin
too confusing being here and not here at the same
she whispered into the leaf shaped ear and crying

in a way no one could hear her green tears a lake
subtly lifted into the gauzy atmosphere fireflies
eerie red shifts remoteness languid columns spiraling
from her hair the thickness smoking a goddess could
have been her left by the steps painted white like
absence of clouds everything disappearing

40.

"misero amante"! there you go wandering
in the brush encountering the occasional shepherd
the oaten reed the untuned lyre the scattered
notes of an unheard music under baking skies
relentless azure of endless noon searing the brain
what's left to think you've made a mess of it
the divine plan the descent into sulfurous realms
chapped lips hands scarred and eyes steaming
hearing voices night and day plying invisible looms
summoning errant planets from their ellipses
talking to imaginary statues for god's sake Man!
wearing shirts inside out spending hours on a single
cigarette in a bar named after a volcano seething
and if evening comes which it never does doomed
to patrol rock and warren in endless midday heat
flagon of warm red wine gone bad in one hand
rosary of amber beads worn thin in the other
pray tell which goddess of the countless will hear
your raucous defiant voice will lend an ear
to your leafy plaint your ivy scoured indictment
"scrivete occhi dolenti!" what was once tender green
now sere patches of twilight's distant Umbrian hills
where gods disguised as honey-thieves maraud nightly
how can it come back the instant of divine undergoing
swerved from a diffident hour into the timeless end
when all that happens has ever happened happens
no more again swathed in touchless flames your mind
the swoon the fainting away into pales of rose and vine
an inch of thunder resplendent in the unconscious ear
whoever told you there was but one lintel to cross
that the room behind the Room was the secret abode
that for every god there is *another* god unwinding fate

look at you bathed in a dark liquor talking at no one
while swarms of holy bees hover above your head
everything is but a fragment of some unknown whole
omicron and zeta of a fictive ontology of light
lives go weaving in and out like threads in a thimble
red twists into blank white passes through amaryllis
an eye a grieving eye writes its unfathomable memory
in hues of lunar ash and rivers pour underground
bearing away in a mad rush the eloquent shadow
the one that accompanied *her* through infinities of sand
while you in some sublime striving thought to touch
her unending body passing through the harbor of night
what was it but water of waters depths of liquid
madness really the splendid pool of her unformed mind
"misero amante"! the next time you write this poem
when you are shaking as with ague on a frozen lawn
and reaching for some island of recall your eyes
filled with smoke from the inextinguishable cigarette
the next time you run at the mouth with words
searching for something that will define a sound
a ringing in the brassy air that clarifies not the loss
but the absence of it the potential and the impossible
which stigmatize you as a mortal in a winding sheet
as you go clamoring after the sourceless music of ink
impenetrable thought amplified in a dream mosaic
comprised of vowel after vowel of soundless drum
the next time you read this effort scribbled in ether
you will come to know you will come to know at last
what you were never meant to understand
"scrivete occhi dolenti!"

                        41.
filigree and firmament, *mother*
grass weaving clouds longing, *nymph*
starlight fireflies singed wings dying, *mother*
hush panting silken sheets smother, *nymph*
so it goes the eternal round the song immemorial
leafage shady bowers ring of stone and graveside
deep whitening presence *what is a woman?*
when was the first time stepping out of the dark

rustling in the grasses of memory the
what was it the leaves almost transparent
in the unreal light of an unremembered dawn
something dripping in the eaves a sensation
coming out of sleep's embroidered dream
of a previous life when was it heard stepping
across small gravel still wet from dewfall
across an enormous room with paper lanterns
orange and yellow and burnt sienna her
in a floor length dress with floral pattern
signaling with her eyebrows arched
eyes patiently burning with the hills of distance
dust involving whole worlds of inky enigma
could this mean what flickering in the dense
moving slowly in what seemed an ocean depth
lives and lives apart the simultaneous evenings
when the talk in low whispers was all about
and outside the screens the language of insects
planets revolving in wide trajectories of longing
echoes of barking or vehicles shifting gears
headlights tracing long tree-shaded avenues
into the absolute nowhere of abandonment
or was it an illustrated page of a magazine
what is a woman? proceeding like a galaxy
of cosmetics a guilefully painted artifice
hair luxuriously sculpted into thick cathedrals
dyed and ruffled by an unexpected tempest
in these eyes wholly otherworldly tsunami of lust
turquoises of Egyptian splendor and cinnamon
to drown in them to lose the man within
to have never been as before an individual
in the maze of bright red lip-gloss and fashion
now a seed a blackening embryo of desire
exchanging identities and sexual discharge
in a wanton and willful unknowing
which is the who in a parade of flashy skirts
maenad bacchant or wailing banshee
ravishing and eating the god who created her
or is it I the man inside the apparition in white
ungiven forlorn who first without wishing to
saw and seeing loved uncontrollably what a woman is

coming in and out of earthly consciousness orphic
nostalgia for the pure origins the undifferentiated
between seed and acorn between bee and honey
remembering so many unnumbered summers
voyaging to and from the oracle her blood red mouth
pomegranate spitting to ravel and unravel
many answers to the single question *what is a woman?*
locust swarms devouring the ripened field
linen sheet wrapped around the sacrifice
smoking nostrils blazing attitude locks unkempt
white arms powerfully rippling feminine as the sky
whose multiple mansion the clouds become terrible
darkening and ravenous for light before pouring
out of a single vein immense black rains
her the once little thing inside the hollows of a doll
sitting there inarticulate speechless dumb
all blond curls and rouge daubed cheeks
the pink of her the small yes I want to kiss her
sweetums the illegible passion in her stare
inch by inch skin extends its song into the leaf
opaque incomprehensible   life!

morning glory hollyhock dogwood blooming
                    invitation to the dance
who that mysterious thing is wrapped in white
mirage moving through night's fixed minute
insane to know her deathlessness
becoming and not becoming in the swoon
enormous enigma
                    unformed
that gives shape to all passing matter
perfume of the stars! essence of light!
          S H A D O W !

              42.
          this is confused
I thought I told you not to come back
you withstood the first interpretation
imploring with vacant syllables and hissing
a response from the Pythian oracle

when Hades abducted Koré
by the yawning doorway you stood frail
beseeching with your flowering hands
some invisible deity lurking in the weeds
to have back your ring finger
bloodless moments passed between then
and the swift eternity of the bee swarms
that descended from Mount Hybla
to inter your shadow near the rock grove
afternoons without you going blind
searching in the spaces vacated by snakes
yellowish bracken earth nothing grows
when Hades abducted Koré
we used to go to that Greek restaurant
in Paphlagonia and you'd recite snatches
from the *Book of Going Under* sunlit
confusion between lives agonizing
that this has happened before intertwining
ivy and smothered leaf and heat so dense
your breath came in furious red halts
to have that ring finger back from the weeds
an unseen god playing his gambit
the way the light slanted on the olive branches
was Athena herself present?
or that other goddess strong limbed of the hunt
squinting her eyes into the brush aiming
to kill something before sunset
did you dart from the menacing shadow
into the false lamplight a terrible mistake
when Hades abducted Koré
the argent anklet slipped from your foot
glittering there for a brief and infinite second
something grabbed you from behind
hot breath of the panther reeking of liquor
when I turned so much confusion
torn grass dust swirls flying air condensed
into a profoundly dense ball of flame
like a demonstration of Ionian physics
I heard your voice whispering a lament
it was bedtime in the Hesperides
the mountains were drawing their purple shadows

lengthening along the rippling unknown sea
ridges of deep mauve shivered hoarsely
the evening planets rising watery and malevolent
took their places in the mortal constellation
when Hades abducted Koré
the illustrations in the book slowly disappeared
page after page turned emptily
fragrance of many dead flowers lingered
cold verses all but forgotten sifted by the winds
reminiscences of when we gathered
whole afternoons like aromatic bouquets
in our embrace falling weightlessly into the well
where sloe-eyed deer stunned waited
licking salt blocks as we passed shadow-like
to the fundament making no sound
dreaming confused voices alerting shifts
in the thousand grasses dampening below
where the impalpable body makes no impress
unheard demands puzzling the dormant ear
can make no more out than that
a confusion of
when Hades abducted Koré
singing

43.
yellow everything air clouds distances
how could the music sustain this color
this unbearable memory of the other world
you used to appear on the avenue wearing
your summer skin sauntering beautiful hips
down the hill parasol of white lace twirling
sun decking glints of reddish bronze your hair
what you saw at that moment coming forth
like serpent shadows gracing the grassy knoll
something tainted your full lipped smile
an evening suddenly blotting out noon tide
reached out for me with your thin white arms
listening intently to the heat hidden cicadas
their persistent monophonic chant secretly
embedding in the ear code words for death

that was a july of splendid luxuries fully green
wrapped around the lissome nymph you were
echo of the Echo your broad face radiant
with a thin perspiration like dew freckles
high cheek bones indicating your asian birth
(did Bacchus bring you in his vine covered car?)
 together we were bound for the hot corn fields
paying no heed to the medics' dire hints
that from love's embrace proceed catastrophes
instead below bright air's superb architectonics
in each other sought enigmatic intaglios
tokens unworded promises troth and faith
in how many languages did I sound your name
translating each one with a new glassy syllable
never before heard in the world of myth
each time different more lush more intrinsic
to the ivy that grew rampant in your stare
divine and ecstatic as are the planets of midday
what childhood did we espy in the burdened leaf
assailed by hordes of red and black ants
warring against a consciousness that informed us
truth is we were both already dead lying
there on that open field scouring the heavens
scrutinizing the labyrinthine azure for a clue
to the source of the mysteries a single letter
from the unformed alphabet of clouds and birds
stately you sat on the stone *that does not laugh*
ivory comb in your hand your hair bound
in crimson fillets already distant apart from me
though still shimmering in your proximity
to the sacred precinct of the invisible beings
who govern each waking thought and desire
you lay upon the rough ground your profile
in secret summoning Aphrodite the shining
who accompanies the wounded of Eros
only to abandon them come twilight on shores
haunted by heroes defined by their imperfection
already a mirage a faint apparition a specter
blank wordless drifting inches above earth
you struggled to articulate a sentence a phrase
but only succeeded in spitting pomegranate seeds

everything about you becoming dusky particles
shifts of color that blurring indistinctly merge
into night's enormous assemblage of dreams
such was the brief the instantaneous afternoon
we spent together somewhere on the floating islands
shadow embracing shadow in the fiery trajectory
our minds left behind in an empty room
while from a balcony in the heavens the gods
leaned over to watch the flamboyant puppet show
soon becoming bored or annoyed with even that
to return to their mirrors of elusive identity

44.

which is the ago of when this was taking place
why the where of it with or without persons
masked as shadows invidious of the invisible
what is the whether it happened or not here
or whenever in this or the other world exclusive
of or including not this but that mythiframe story
in verse of how it was that when it first occurred
was no later than the second time it was recalled
which is to say rhapsodes to the contrary in a cave
in a mountain by a rock near the spring next to
a tree over a grassy knoll under the midday sun
when the body casts no shadow and memory
alternates with oblivion round and about fragments
of the ruin peopled by headless statues whose intent
is to summon the gods at this period still nameless
informed with furious silences and aborted speech acts
to create in this multiform but unshaped world in chaos
fusion of the divine and demonic who in their chariots
whatever it is that draws to smoke returns lovely
as distance itself the instance of coming to be seeing
in the all amazeful air lit up by planets of longing
suchness of the possible like moons of dissolving aspirin
and when this does happen if it does in a dream trance
who are the characters of the masque dancing feet
lifted millimeters above the surface and a tremendous
water rushing underneath and the dark and the abyss
when that was the ago in question the when of time

handful by handful registered in alphabets of sand
porous rock through which filters the was of light
once the filled of the omniverse thrilling a single note
on a string yet to be affixed to the portion of music
is it that I am sleeping this sequence of what words
why is never the issue encircled by potentials of color
more likely red than not in its infinite shades and variants
spread like a tapestry beneath the evolving figures
rhythmic and fluted elongated into the estuaries of space
galaxies no less plunging through the nascent eye
what it senses of burning the very ago of its memory
is it brains we are talking through funnels of ego
nattering insects swarming making way through
foot tall grasses immensely green childhoods minute
on the lip of the notion of the feminine wet and luscious
fruit given to eat when the if stutters is it asking
for more to realize a shape the totality of the whole
personified as the eventuality of any given human
which is a petty subterfuge a search for the escape route
which is the real when of ago the fist in the mouth
dust to choke skies all over the painted masterpiece
with its crenellations of pure ether ready to burn forever
when that is eternity in the instant of unknowing
wake to that and suffer the lamp and the fluttering
of wings worth a while to be there or wherever it
can be whenever it could be landslides and ricocheting
echoes myth of the girl by the well waiting for the hour
incandescence and radiance starlight and absolutely
nowhere else if it is not here right in the now of ago
lapses of thought gibbering in the ape of memory
white becomes whiter loss is more alone than when
and if solitude is a rock and sculpted events speak
a whisper then and naval battles and arrogance what
are they what is anything beside what is missed
what drowns switching off the light turning a page
blankside of recollections remoteness and lonely the ago
the whenever I can't remember of the thing it was
abiding in the me of sleeping in the small in the very little
it was being *that* whoever it was it the the the this
this crazy feeling only happens once every millennium
I am up and about I am strolling through an ago of sulfur

I am the magazine of illustrated everything jumping
from rock to rock alter ego and unconsciousness of what
whenever that was whoever I was why and because
at the same time singing in this mad and circular ruin
of a portion of music the beautiful and never of again

45.

and invited me to come aboard
   ay! to sing to them
some of whom I recognized but the others
   remained unknown to me
dark the density of grape pulp
   in squadrons twenty thick
and their hands fastened to the rough oars
   on the helmsman's shoulder a bird of omen
their names sounded in my ears with a cadence
   Μοψος Ευρυδαμας Ακτωρ...
in the tumult of rushing waves threatening
   to splinter the mast and bring it down
tenebrous hours of black salt and sweat
   not to see more than a hand's length
palms sutured to hewn pine
   remembering in the blustery gusts
a girl with honey colored eyes hair like sand
   somewhere in the bleak Thracian outback
listening with ear intent on the tuning
   plucking abstractedly at the strings
to which deity dedicate this number
   Demeter and Persephone the dual entity
being mindful of the unlit house
   which is the end of a man's career
and scouring the atrabilious night sky
   fierce and moonless roaring
with invisible demons and the fear
   the world seen from afar
a petty place riddled with half ruined cities
   crumbling towers perched on rocky summits
temples fallen into disgrace and weed
   inhabited by mangy goats desecrated
how could any god thus honor us

to sing then to lift the heavy heart
and the mad torrents of water darkening
lips cracked with brine and bilge
sounds of men grumbling or retching
sturdy canvas ripped in half like paper
a man's lot this riot of sodden chaotic uproar
cuprous stains on the mind's sheet
to read the writing there the scrawled plea
to raise the voice in lyric pitch
employing dense dactylic hexameters
to convey the rich dread setting forth
linking to this or that oracle a reason
bidden by some twisted interpretation
to accomplish what!
is the space of a lifetime
no more than this tortured inch
a hero's nothing but a fractured bone
a storm-tossed being derided by god
and woman alike on some sandy spit
to die as if by some noble sport
plagued by debt fraud and extortion
apparition of the lissome mountain girl
chanting her lilting hindustani speech
bent over to say something improbable
gloom gathering its faded gold
into the texture of an incomprehensible verse
do not hold great store in these tales
rock and crystal shattered by a single bolt
yellow streaking glass across
solitary fragments of a hymn
nor is there a light above to guide
in her supple girdle Aphrodite bare limbed
to none true fickle to all
rising from the dawn-colored foam
and on the far left an osprey
the great grey eyes of Hera
takes wing into the nocturnal torment
sails unfurled by contrary winds
spume and fury horizonless puzzle
to what end this ill sparred voyage
to make music in the musty hold

blindly sleeping the wasted bodies
 undreaming held in other worldly thrall
fate wracked doom spent disorder
 remote from the sunlit slope where
by the well a child-woman lingers
 honey colored eyes hair like sand
mouth suffused with wild thyme
 her song this is striking thunder
crazy and endlessly revolving
 like the Muse who has eaten of me
what good there is to play

 madness and illumination

46.

if it is not in the system it will not hold
stars flake their light chipping away for eons
the hand and what is its shape and why does it
lying there between lakes of blue acid the soul
bestirs recalling numerous former careers
lives spent in leaf mold working like a caterpillar
or suddenly sprung full blown in brassy armor
flinging spears and quoits at the invisible
been a century since anybody lived in this room
determined to study language and its fallacies
if it cannot be found and there is no way to it
and the museums fill with artifacts of polished bone
ledgers of cuneiform and hieroglyph where is writ
the preponderant myth of heaven is its Tree
and fish that fly and scaly things that crawl behind
who will a god create to care for all these things
that have no answer only a mystery it is to be
and being go under in the flood and dream a life
that never was among the indigo lilies of the Nile
can so much sand in the warp have its context
which revealed fills the night with stellar maze
been a century since anybody lived in this room
sitting in the saloon musing on fly specked matters
avaunt! have had sex with so many cannot count
whose faces shade into one another pale phobic

luster of office holding on summits their legs
wet amphibian who they must have been sleek
coming forth and behold! heroes one after another
dead for the light that rapes their gleaming armor
and can I tell you something else about the past
archaic ant mounds citadels built of sliding shale
and dancing nymphs round the Dodonian oak
each is one each is many perishing in the grass
beneath the hilt and force of some daimon red
that has dragged from darkness a human form
radiant in perspective and animated for a moment
only before returning to the damp map whence
and what's more the fickle things once used
sought retribution by way of kingdoms of pumice
marble passageways to the underground baskets
piled high with multigrains yellowing heaps rotting
will any prevail among the mass of undetermined
and what holds in the center flying from the wheel
a pin stuck deep in the eye and all it sees great sun
fleeing westward in a chariot of molten glass AOI
been a century since anybody lived in this room
memorial erected to the once and only god Zeus
who remembers to lay at the stone this gutted hasp
a splinter from the section of sky he once ruled
and cannot explain to the wayfarers the why of
this shady dell and hard by the cool spring tended
by the child-woman fearful of someone's ejaculation
for sport cleaning her peplos and stains ineradicable
does air hold a finer thing than this shimmering
this mirage of the mortal city ten ells deep in mud
and the traffic in and through its polygonal structures
a ruin by nightfall mortar and dust and burnt beams
the stench of its denizens quartered by the invisible
fie! when a citizen had but to step up to the podium
have his say about destiny in his hands fuming entrails
coloring the air with small writs of habeas corpus
the perhaps of the because in every lingering doubt
aren't they just like women those figurines gossiping
in the mural and one more thing! say you just arrived
and your purse has been cut unawares the livid you
are blaming the citizenry in crowds rushing to see

the latest circus event trapeze and burning ropes
girls sawed in half by automatons in human guise
sawdust the color of late Umbrian evenings sighs
longing for the beautiful it was on the other side
of the mountain before the great battle and hush!
been a century since anybody lived in this room
we pass trembling from *bolgia* to *bolgia* stepping
careful not to trespass the unlit domain of Pluto
though we are verily in his suburbs summoned for
judgment some of us headless others without trunk
bleeding in the leaf where a voice decries the humiliation
blank envelopes passed around with extra hair inside
to be employed when the masks are distributed
me that's Orpheus in the middle of the great arc
and the animals who by name come to lick my feet
why is it a recital is demanded white shadows flicker
in the deep pit on the left sulfuric waters a nausea
infects even the dead who are commanded to stand
an immense Noise rips through the vestibule cold
bearing with it the numerous names of a nymph
a single one whose repeated entries into the stone
have been minutely recorded in the reading of the text
her that's Eurydice I mean gassed one summer noon
for inflecting her verb into a multiplicity of lamps
change does not come easy there is a culmination
of debts and the shriven souls riddle the porous rock
you can still hear their cries above ground in the month
when swarms of fireflies come to crown Mnemosyne
and what's more! ah the pagan rites all but forgotten
I give to each of you silent ones a chaplet some hellebore
the opportunity to sing in daylight one last time
been a century since anybody lived in this room
when nothing more holds matter flies to distant space
each quadrant floods with ungiven luminosity
small beings the guardians of sleep buzz persistently
it is afternoon of the great Reawakening, Dreamers!
each hold a blade of grass each look for a finger lost
soon even the resonance of Echo will fall silent
looking upon each other none will recognize the One

47.

who maintain that life coincides with breath
and that only in those few fleeting moments
is commerce with the gods possible
the machine that goes on and on and on
nausea at the pit of the stomach reconsider this
that on the day of birth that on receiving the light
one is already an inhabitant of the underworld
earth is of no weight fire and water from which
all things spring are of the passing moment
a statue who bemoans the hewn marble left behind
is of better consequence than all the days of breath
thus my brother Shadow holding forth
mid these grasses moved by a restless summer wind
a tree I grant you a reverend rock 'pon which I sit
regarding with monumental silence the summit
of Olympus one with the immemorial skies
have more than we the finer share of existence
quarrel we do and now and then a fight ensues
from dust comes oblivion that wraps us around
its dreary mantel and sweeping takes us hence
to the cremation yard to the ossuary to the hole
where figures in solitude and misery like unto us
knock about senselessly pining a grievous loss
though not recollecting what name attach to it
I too like that once of a splendid springtime morn
felt experiencing the great delusion of immortality
and sang I did the beautiful the finery and ornament
of all that surrounded me mountain meadow brook and
to what avail for smitten by a love I deemed endless
and divinely spent in that emotion considered everything
within my sphere of knowing cloud weft sky swing
azure the very limits of the brain swarming outwards
with a music a rush of harmonies like unto the planets
who in daytime dance their stately sarabande anon
but what weather what tempest foul no sooner struck
and tumbled I did from the cliff of ego into the depths
where Chaos with delight mingles Gaia and Night
and all the howling titanic entities indifferently
is there worse retribution for breath than this wound
I call this woe *Eurydice* I name this calamity *Eurydice*

for what else is a man but faults and dishonor of love
improprieties of mind jungle nerve shibboleth
to turn back to revolve to stumble to falter to blame
to undo the carcass of passion and sew it up again
filled with the stews of lust hoodoo vertigo and pain
if it stop breathing simply to evolve into something else
if there are stairs that *do* go all the way and heights
brighter than that which we can *only* imagine
acribiliter sanctimonium loqui! stupendous words
or merely verbiage garbage in the waking ear
sounding stops in meter countdown prosody
fictions ultimately by which we respire inhaling
heaven's imported fragrances lemon balm rosewood
ere we transpire dropping weightless through the floor
clasping airy bodies of absolutely no substance
I will write her name then on the celestial tree
carving syllable by syllable the nonsense of amor
regrets deceits flaws imperfect vision self deception
and to remember only half the face or that the name
belongs to another face entirely in the masque of death
that life is merely this brief sequence of breaths
and that the gods by some sort of chicanery exist
only for that brief sequence being otherwise gone
flown through some eerie transept into the other world
taking with them simulacra of mortals painted perfumed
dancing like wooden puppets in the Ramayana play
where brass gongs resound and bells and conch shells
echo into the unending darkness all around
will take you with me if only as the nerve-end
that thrills ever so slightly whenever the small rain
or when waking beside me your impress on the sheets
yellowish damp and a coil of hair burnt sienna in color
nothing mattered as before and breath taken in and out
piecemeal days tattered and slipped through the cracks
holding a nothing tight against the heartbeat until
finally all is a blurred series of fading hues phantomatic
mirages clumps of grass torn from a disappeared lawn

then at the end of the walkway startled we encountered
facing us magnificently serene majestic poised *the stag*
certainly more self assured and sublime a creature

than we the composure of his features the depths in his eyes
this was indeed a spiritual epiphany a form of grace
a moment when breath suspended rendered us gods
assuming for an instant the totem body of that animal
who disregarding the sudden apparition of our human forms
mysteriously sauntered away from us into the night

> *"death cannot get a hold of him, death becomes his body,*
> *and he becomes one with these divinities"*
> Bṛhad-āraṇyaka-Upaniṣad

48.

from this little dust from this vague shadow
what chaos plunge with what intrinsic name
declare the self a void a thing rife with riddles
anonymous actors in a continual film loop
the two we thought we were being sequenced
between blades of grass and tormented desire
watching light go through its multiple phases
before becoming the ever fade of a puzzling
moon-shaped evening somewhere beyond
the unit of thought a man is wearing shoulders
mounting the glass through which to peer
into his own past evocative smoky enigma
faintly etched with carbon amidst the galaxies
dizzying gyres within and without consciousness
now and then to recognize in an old photo
the remnants of a sun-splashed afternoon
in the vast ruin of the amphitheater of time
slight figures gesticulating in a play of words
long lost even to the prying archaeologist
who discovers absences instead of clues to sound
phonetic decay arrested morphological development
half formed letters buried in an archaic sand
copies of symbolic animals snub-nosed blind
petrified in the immobile black sun of the pharaohs

isn't it sublime stuck on the parapet like this
all space our gazing hole a tremble in the mirror
hold me like you did again and never let me go

I'm so cold tonight so old and misery no comfort
but your fade of a shoulder you're losing weight
me again in your split bearing arms so medieval
so you can't just bear it like you did dust covered
gliding from planet to planet in the mizzen stream
a foaming you was and built like a jerry cracker
height of darkness and the big tower rigged up
with wires going from Greece to the ancient lore
wasn't it a time buried me chin deep in the sand
counting from infinity backwards for me to cry
but I was your lizzie fling your oneiric alphabiddle
dream swooning between songs of abacus and wedge
no sleep too deep no smoke too thick I used to dry
some little mountain I used to be some darkness
steep wouldn't it be your used to be a strawberry
cream a muffin of love two slices of ether pie a
whatever else I did I kept to you a secret yellow
anemone a crocus slipped into your major fist
some feathery sleeping nods I'd like to remember
inside earth's trembling envelope green turpentine
ochre rumored slings about town sarsaparilla and
a modicum too I used to rasp in your berry field
oh what's a summer to the mind's recoil a heat
smothered in red as far as the beam can reach an eye
seeing was a bitter ward and so every often you'd bilge
the dip of lees swarming with micronauts too thin
to feel too wide to grip a faint I did a dance without
feet sliding from your midden grasp and swoon did
I a thought like Aphrodite surf swum up to the moat
how many of me did you think I could be so short
the span of breath and multiply in the grassy fane
suchness of an august midday spooning all verdant
vine-slip of a waist tongue all a loll in the perspire
loom of language I thought you was making up
letters all the time formed half formed upside down
meant to read aright a scribbledy hobbledy book
you'd face to the mirror and shout what a glass of
a time you was making out chimes and lyres to put
a wild beasty to trance between his furry muffs ah
you'd echo so soft a sweet-ended poemetto mmm
me what about me all broad of justice in my brow

mistaken for one of them the eyeless hunters nabbed
shook me out of my wits sent me under plow white
witted the gift to a Mistress Blank good wife to him
father Pluto to deem me a sward of the endless state
there down under crabbed and weed spun pine I
mourning ever the shadow I cast across your fate
what day was that what ancient almost never of a
and here round about this tiny jewel we spin not
registered to mate again each the other opposite
the whole on this invisible pier flung to starry seas
swift is nothing more nor scent of screw-pine nor
touch against the velvet felt some skin a distance
because you looked I f-f-f-f-ade away mostly pale
a shhh hush ungiven lips to kiss most vasty space
and sounds no more to word what I cannot say

increasingly silence is the better music the sublime
a higher tone a note unsounded beyond the pitch
nor earthly ear to rhyme or crown the invisible melody
why ken these souls a past and matter to them a fixity
of sense when breath its halo spun from light is gone
it's all echo framed in primrose nothings of a pale
a finish final to the touch of things a swarming
dizzy imperfect thoughts caught in time's latticework
why ken these souls a past and matter to them a fixity

                    49.
who's to say why the flame goes up and
mountains buried in sleep and the world
is it we are ancient already dreamed spent
a lamp flickering in the Aegean dark wind
a seed yellow archaic waiting to bloom
opium poppies drowsy with oriental heat
or buzz of ancient bee swarms from Hybla
to lose a finger in the childhood of grass
who's to say why we don't clearly remember
by small streams silver rills trickling brooks
a life passes in a matter of seconds it's over
look up! flying alphabets of winged things
spell out for us the inscrutable the ineffable

looking back again the trees have gone away
in their place ruins of once lustrous palaces
mansions where gods played hide and seek
with Nymphs whose skin was absence to touch
white nothingness of pleasure and destruction
ashes sown into the dark fundament of mind
never sure whether the known was real or not
or whether what comes come back is the same
as what was left behind vertiginous moon-like
only the vague sensation of sand upon waking
apostrophes of cognition flickering red dots
that flood the eye then empty it of seeing
what's to decide when to forget what color
flowers possessed why the dust storms came
what road was taken to go around Paradise
in order to enter Hades what words Demeter
employed cajoling you to explore the beneath
it's all a story within a story traced in linen
the bare outline like the blueprint of the sky
all but legible or the origins of clouds in speech
recalling the first letters crooked insignificant
scratched into leaf or bark and the sound
stretching as far back as infinity summoning
the incoherent mass of deities to take shape
to give to things names and contours to flood
the empyrean with an even greater history
now totally gone into oblivion sense and all
just here and there the yellow crocus peering
through a vine or the ardent morning glory
climbing the invisible trellis that goes nowhere
heavens of somnolent water or deserts of air
can't you at least tell me why you didn't call?

50.

isn't the least of it the slender remembrance
the day of the Lotus-Eaters or years with Calypso
friend, you've ruminated long enough
forget the cattle of the sun and who herd them
Eleatic discourse to the contrary what have we to show
but myth and plague and extermination

every cycle or so the world blows itself up
thugs shooting flying machines out of the sky
or ego-blinded nations enslaving others in the desert
only to be consumed by an orient of self hate
what good to consult the riddle-bearing sphinx
or to sit solitary on a beach cliff musing forever
about the city we once envisioned high on its emerald
perfect in all its rectangles and pyramids
were it not for the invasion of red ants
the incursion of termites midges and house flies
the swamp we made of our lives erring at every turn
what did you come home to, friend
but a tribe of traitors swilling your estate away
pandering after your white wife given to the loom
making of the night an intricate black puzzle
more exiguous than a syllable of sand
what's to be done?   volleys of flame
jettisoned furiously against an invisible enemy
slogans reiterated vociferously in a hill dialect
as if to bring heaven on the side of the enraged
the *this* and the *that* at war with the always other
mind itself the enemy wild juxtaposition
of opposing targets elephant and tortoise
swung into midair and suspended there for eons
while slings spears and arrows make thick the hour
when was light ever so rare so deeply incarnadine?
and in each room a gibbering ape a likeness to man
masturbating and roaring a self willed triumph
nor are there reasons to hope for peace
across the dizzying and shifting dunes missiles fly
evidence buried beneath the gnat's castle
slender epistles written in lymph on sheets of air
making demands on the unseen for release
yet the body that heavy sack of greed and lust
tarries bearing its own shadow to untimely doom
vast territories of the Unmapped laid to waste
as generations of the homeland's finest perish
in a single puff of smoke   AOI!
friend, what did you find there on the deserted beach
but an agglomeration of dead warriors in buckled greaves
quarreling over a single dice misthrown

and the snarling snot green sea rushing at the fleet
dashing it to splinters glutting with salty brine
the drunken home-sick navvies in their cold longing
never more cried the anguished mariner going down
in purling eddies of blood pus and sea-foam
how can this be the dream of reason the razor's edge
who can cast a net to the fathomless deep
and expect to ransom a life just once   , friend
is it to score a thousand and call it victory
when all around shattered altars fume with disregard
and from the skies pusillanimous deities pour sulfur
and the hundred cities of the peninsula disappear!

a body is no more than the syllables it takes to speak
and speaking chase and rue the malignant sprite
friend, lashed to the mast and heard the Sirens sing
how did the furious wind bite and sting your cheek
and yet wept for the beauty of what you heard
is my song no less nor my grief to mourn such beauty
caves of wintery silence tombs of endless stone
nothing is writ upon them if not the chisel's echo
the writing thing to recall wars and love's bitter
intent into the depths of memory then subsides
in pulverized vowels no hand can reconstruct
but waver sinking in inky melancholy the end
from which no glory returns to sound its note
no unsung hero spine snapped by hostility
regain the shimmering light   , friend
unless but there is no *unless* nothing but
stellar distances glacial interstices ashes
dispersed throughout the colonies of thought
unbidden words made up of alien sounds
mind's constant clash with unconsciousness
the unspoken farewell the tear not shed
the   [zzzzz]   , friend

   "And I exhort the unlearned, by reding to learne
to bee more skilfull, and to purge that swinelike grossenesse,
that maketh the swete majerome not to smell to their delight"

51.

"And in my minde I measure pace by pace
To seke the place where I my self had lost"
Henry Howard, Earl of Surrey

in those days she wore a bouffant hair style
what the poets call *faux empire* deep red chestnut
in *those days* says it all not content to simply recall
but to attempt to reconstruct that body of syllables
pronouncing the heat of summer or the grammar
of unreason mounting sounds in the mind's water
is it she there standing in the middle of the floor
elbow deep in humidity piece by piece of clothing
falling dreamily to the rug itself a sea of inconstancy
swirling with fading colors in one invisible wave
around her ankles slender pendants moon-carved
why go on why mention elastic girdle & lip gloss
or the Prolegomena to Greek Religion when outside
burn fifty automobiles sacrifices to smoking Moloch
how many centuries has this been going on in *those days*
treading unknown letters the symphony of her disguise
one mask behind the other in a display of pure ποίησις
red becomes more than red a terrific almost audible hue
shifting in the mirage of the wasted august afternoon
more Nymph than bride treacherous in her secrecy
beside her an invisible future just waiting to implode
suggestions of suicide and music Liebestod mystery
empty movie theaters haunted by phonetic structures
windows that open out on the abyss of the Holocaust
or the eerie rumors fading on blasted radio sets
reporting the aftermath of Nagasaki in castrato voices
behind clouds packed with undiscovered scores of Vivaldi
how could we go to the movies knowing what we did?
she left me in *medias res* a walking zombie reciting
what I could of the initiation hymn of the Orphics
counting the avenues remaining before the Rock
it was the other way around I simply lost her one hour
when I let her go to the medicine cabinet by herself
everything was instantaneous a geometry of parallel lives
fifty years of negotiating with father Pluto to no end
up and down on the crazy Luna Park circuit to nowhere

electricity jammed into an envelope for the hair-dresser
weeks and months spent writing and rewriting the same ode
reading it to the house of mirrors every Thursday at noon
smoking that famous and endless cigarette with tattoos
speaking only Italian to the unseen doctors in attendance
swallowing green turpentine and turning inaudible
on and on and on what else is there to say to confess to
never mind the insomnia that lasted a decade switching
to planet Jupiter for relief and I am still rotating lunacy
as a diversion between chapters of the unwritten Quixote
I am this fix this junk in the arm this hallucinating hyperbole
inventing as I go the paraphrase of an event yet to occur
exhausted by never being able to return exactly home
a horizon limited by its inability to employ language
to define to contour to eliminate finally its *raison d'être*
to go back to her hair-do back to the way she combed it
in dense oriental waves like spasms of black water
what the poets also chillingly call *reductio ad absurdum*
in those days all the fashion a rage to mirror the self
in miles of plate-glass show window never sure whether
to expose Narcissus for the repetition of his persona
or just to let the whole thing blow away shattering
forever the mind's multiple self-deceits
her hair in big empress terraces shaped into place
lacquered and thick as a swarm of bees in ecstasy
her hair a pagoda of license and deathless corruption
perfumed sprayed lit up like Aphrodite's navel jewel
sashed and tied and bowed with a hundred bright ribbons
coming through the door with it tall and faintly shaking
its undulant masses big with enigmatic suggestion
walk away with it she did right into the other world
the one behind the mirror she used to fake her mouth
into an immense Omega of echoes and
will I never again touch that superb
it's all dit dot dit dot dit touching the hemisphere
where desire darkens into a midnight absence
her just a motion in sand a
body of syllables
in *those days*

52.

wended we our way to the Nekropolis
our guide Hermes
      the wing-footed shone no light
        a long dark thoroughfare
lined on either side by series of eyeless statues
      history monotonous and forgotten
when we came to an immense stone portal
did Hermes then fix a small lamp above
      and by their absence the stars
what is it we had come to this place for
      a rustle of paper flowers *the*
could read in the brief illumination a name
      carved in the arch high up there
a niche where owls nested hooting
      their blank yellow eyes sacred
to Athena who keeps a car and steeds hidden
      this dark metal projectile
and this thing so slender it fits into a slit
      this is called the *soul*
to which of us does it belong
      and to Hera quick in wrath
and these fire pits burning night and day
has Hermes flown away leaving us bewildered
      if one tears a leaf
resounds a tearful voice in language unknown
      step by unsure step downwards
gravel and loose rock grassy tufts
      what is the word to employ *"open"?*
muffled sounds strangled utterances
      pray to Artemis pray to her brother
Apollo pray to whomever what good is it
      this vast and bleak heath
that stretches far into the future beset with
      ruined obelisks fallen gates rotted steps
and beyond this small petrified bloom
      yawning masks of those lost in flame
hundreds of years before or after
      was this restaurant always here?
and this conjunction of stars painted askance
      and this retrograde alphabet shading

off into brief inaudible prayers
    shattered hands less than nimble fingers
vowels of distress sent off like shot
mother of mercy the distance a life was
    this dry sluice this bank of eyes
this was once Tiresias or was it
    speak no more be aghast for the afterthought
down that corridor where women's wails
    echo a pattern like sulfuric rain
these are called margarita
these are called death's heads
    these are called button willow
    by the grace of *Ahuramazda*
if we can conjoin these disparate phases
    linking the animal to its totem
subordinating the relative clause to its
    the main verb just hangs there in mist
waiting to be used correctly in epic style
these are called jumping jack flash
    these are called forget-me-nots
    these pallid vine like growths
I cannot remember what to call them
    if not You   the *abysmal*
septic tanks busted in a circle
    image of Mary Lou in corroding rust
a section of light carefully discarded
    behind the flapping tarmac
approach not the flickering Delphic emblem
    Dionysus son of Zeus torn to bits
Maenads in white face blood-thirsty
    tarantulas and human-faced jackals
zeroing in on the tent housing the
Hermes,   shaking the branches
    mistletoe and rue   the abject
the ones over there are called wolf bane
    next to them are the asphodel
    between them are the asterisks
just how many of *me* are there?
    and to Demeter always bereaved
offer this small bouquet of anemones
    and to her circular daughter Persephone

beware the ambulatory bush
      and to her   daughter Persephone
and if she be burnt for a witch
and if she be put to the stake for a witch
          we have come after the harvests
then will the rains of autumn pour
and earth's ghosts drink with glee
          consult with Tiresias again
moreover clouds will consume language whole
          in particular nouns of sand
dissolving in adjectives of despair
the left hand know not the right
          margins of heaven pushed back
sky reduced and placed neatly inside envelopes
          addressed to Atropos *the world born dead*
did Hermes not foresee it
          this is that and that is this and art Thou?
of broad justice her brow and a
          fan made of human skin ventilating
the small aperture near the dry-well
          this is not north of anywhere
this is Hyperborea   this is Manicomio
          and this little thing here
this is the escape valve
this is the hissing of time
          this girl here without a body
what is she then?
                    Κόρη,
touches that which is in motion
          existence of so many different forms
a word difficult to pronounce
          as are we the, dead

      53.
what is the size of thought?
is it dense as brick?
is it incommensurate as ink?
is it because or do we have to start all over
once time's done its round
all ashes gone and hard to get a handle

floats and metamorphoses it does
a thought interpolated and inside still
another thought dimensionless without
depth width or substance circulating
and recirculating *ah* to get over it
to have a career seamless at the joints
miles apart from the center which is everywhere
seeking distance in the very proximity of it
sleeping deaf in the hard earth
blind to the fabulous variety of afternoons
in the quilting and patching factory
if you would be mine could I lend you an ear
to drain a thought by to have a meadow
big as the hue that taints a scope
no larger than an hour no finer than a week
ancient as an ant heap gorgeous more so
than the cloud that fits in the left hemisphere
of your wandering brain gathering
the sheep who forage on the legend of red
dreaming that is a thought as formless
as vertigo or the paint that bedecks sky at the top
just when eventide brims her skirts
in a ploy of triptychs whitening toward the surf
impalpable that runs skimming the lake
that dark emerald water where you lost your face
thinking it was the other side of the world
thinking you could catch it if you could only jump
but don't! I shouted watching your shadow
take leave of you immersing its self
in a myth of oak leaves and hamadryads
but a thought? can it be measured
any more than death the bottomless?
where is it we come out in the second hour
why is it you are never there
by the door at the window next to the well
drawing from the unfathomable an unshaped thing
a simulacrum of a thought
a sheet laid out to dry on summer grass
you in your pink and finery evaporating
like the dew which as an imitation thought
beauty! if I could only write down

this one thought I am having about you
ever since the air with its inevitable hands
rushed and swept you into some dark dormer
far behind the mountain which is where
they say thought is buried
waiting for its resurrection
is a thought a ruse a trick a reflection
of something that can never be defined or outlined
something that must remain what it is
an enigma *the* enigma
so it was one day *the* day we went to play
lozenges and skittles and the Nymphs
weren't they at their best all jeweled up
for the round dance thoughtless reckless even
become naked and swarming with passion
all the gods named and unnamed
as if for a wedding in attendance
with all manner of flowers and garlands
and skull yes dangling around their necks
it was the thought of it happening
the thought that cannot be measured of it
bright immense endless Ay!
it can never be again
this is that and that is nothing
what was happening inside out on a day
that was no day at all the *unthought* day
a day the size of ink
denser than brick
minutes spaced out into eternity
like the dress you wore made up of the months
all sewn backwards to confuse the years
but disappear you did a thought all consuming
of mind itself wrapped around the maypole
of infinity waiting just waiting
for thought to
return

54.

themes and variations celebrating *loss*
what else is there to versify to put into words

however inadequate but the intensity of *loss*
does desire arise from malfunction of the optic nerve?
does passion severe the equations of reason from sight?
a whirlpool of emotions the adolescent soul
the *only* soul appropriate for feeling such insanity
and madness it is living on the edge of vertigo
exult mistaking the blade for the cut
become ever lost wandering the place of plight
repeating over and over the *scene* the original one:
dawn unaware breaking through ink-night clouds
blurred contours edges unrefined impalpable being
without relief backdrop of sensuous orange and grey
a body unraveling of its senses becoming *unformed*
as if suspended in the pointillistic distance of sleep
zone of anti-gravity where anything can and does occur
creation undone light returned to its dark matrix
muffled incoherence of pre-linguistic substrata
syllables of sand and shade morphology of longing
at its most primordial dissolving like salt in ice,
so that's what happened
nothing you can really put into *words* a
regret did I ever meet her // misgivings in art
canvas the whole of time in a few brief strokes
lettered alpha to delta somewhere in the back room
a sort of commerce in fugitive glances a priori
wearing a loose summer dress waist band untied
to appear suddenly at the doorway half a smile
soil from the underworld still on her cheek,
themes and variations celebrating *loss,*
that's what she said it was all about
and surrendered her clouds and dust to me
and sent me straight to seventh heaven a vagabond
a stranger to the celestial ways a novice to *existence*
had not heard her name correctly asked for someone else
looked at me as if I were gaga,
there are these abrupt, changes, I stepped out
an airy precipice and below me the 84,000 ells drop
to what the poets call Tartary, pitch black
absolves nothing in a summer, dress untied waistband
loose theme of variations // we are not ourselves
any loss is a regret beyond words to say

(many of these poems first appeared
in something called *Yellow Silk*, where they
projected an eroto-kabbalistic tone to the subject,
she was the red-head in question, the summer dress
waistband untied, who at the doorway suddenly,
and took him down to the infernal parking lot
and undid his trousers, she did)
if we could all play music like *that*
begin to have these weird feelings like someone was,
variations of loss, well let me tell you about,
and launches into a lengthy pointless anecdote
about Eurydice, of all people, without her sombrero
on such a windy day, to die for, and the strong aroma
of opium the perfume, that is, a saga of total and utter
makes you weep, early mornings dawn just breaking
through the mass of inky thunderheads moving slowly
menacingly through the seventh heaven, can we
ever get it back, yellow turns to blank the,
revision of intent, sorrowfully shifting through
the spectra ghostlike pale a cadaver of air, somnolent
// in the art world moved with ease wine glass
in hand her thin vine-like waist undulating, her,
pitch black 84,000 ells deep into the, morass,
the morass, whatever else one can add to these variants
to these, miasma or morass, submerged in dreamy
loss, totally unredeemable qualities suffused her being,
her ghostly, her paler shade of white, her nothingness,
really, a theme non-literary pertaining rather to the mysteries,
rock and sandal and weft, symbolizing heat or its absence,
to the enigmas belongs to, this theme, you know,
the minute you see the one you desire it's lost,
can't own it, can't touch it, becomes a mirage ineffable
mounting an invisible stairway, or in a rapture seized
by the eyeless gods, whether they be thirty three
or three hundred thousand thirty three, repossess *her*
disappear her into the world of the other,
it was all in the imagination a never happened thing, a,
what's to wake up for, dawn issuing forth like a dark wind
a blast of silence and all those voices talking at odds,
a séance perhaps a moving table, chairs of attitude,
mysterious resemblances to, the living

a cry from the maelstrom of sleep, a theme wearing
a single sandal, a sling over one bare shoulder
a summer dress loose fitting waistband untied, when
and if to look back, a glance into the quicksand
as it devours the variation body by body
until only the music a // the world of art

55.

see clearly for a minute into the asphodel fields
an earth of misunderstandings shadow mistaken
for shadow lunacy unspoken in the fixed stare
but why agonize over it   names for the unnamed
careful not to step in the imaginary black pond
nor to pluck the crimson berries hanging overhead
to make one's way through the radiophonic debris
listening intently for the one voice that makes sense
it's not there just the rubble of an immense static
in those garbled strands reports of the recent dead
of those who half way up the stairs lost footing
will we ever know for sure   sight for the unseen
a place where beauty goes afterwards unbidden
where the immense unfinished pours into sand
here and there black stumps echoes of the oracle
not the   sulfuric fission and fusion
how and when to move forward through this meadow
moved by no breeze the stillness the eerie pallor
of moonless night even by day   and there is no
such thing as a poem here no vatic tones
only susurrations and lamenting in the trees
a bracken qualm   something shaking
invisible but palpable a feminine arm cold and
hearing for the unheard and a   drops
filling a cracked basin dark ooze and shivering
in the leaves where a dense physicality survives
asking for its memory back   syntagmata
a disorder of phrases a juxtaposition of images
fragments of a half-forgotten dream of living above
where the grass where the light however spare
but here modulated by isotopes of fear air gathers
itself into tight knots nothing breathes or is it

the very mind struggling to have itself back   AOI
feelings for the unfelt   ruminating on the void
the transience between this life and the next one
fluttering heard only in sleep   vague syllables
constructed of disintegrating cotton filaments
is it a point of departure to say there is no next time
that to wake from this sleep is not a sure thing
that the bodies of the uninhabited do not return
how to write about such matters   signals
perforations in red   speech for the unspoken
not all things here are equally visible a nebulous
patina spreads from hour to hour over the unseen
language itself comes apart in time's invisibility
hoar frost brine salt flats mossy growths sponge
no sure footing nothing holds   no center exists
knowledge for the unknown   vibrations vertigo
falling from whatever went before   an anti-
matter distilled from patches of oblivion   pronouns
not properly employed getting dizzy can't see straight
tongue-tied   misunderstanding the understood
when no yesterday occurs tomorrow has already been
asbestos profligacy winnowing particles of the heard
if I could just once   here is *there*   indistinctly
tied to a post of flame   look! smoke that she imbues
coming round again lifting a finger a symbol of
     regrets to have ever mentioned   longing
for the air above the sense of motion to the touch
not this stagnation this error in immobility peculiar
to the dead who falsely opine this is another world
the other world the asphodel fields the bright memory
echo   spinning spinning in ever darker gyres
the remiss the untold in the telling the ungiven moment
when absolutely nothing happens   are we still going
is the fleet out to sail are the waters at last deepening
sunset is it and what comes afterwards
listening for the song of the stars for the lightning bugs
dancing momentarily in the aperture   camera eye
glimpse of the unpredictable landscape   farewell
the small hands whitening to the point of absence
the once incarnadine mouth ripe as pomegranate
promise for the unpromised   become suddenly pale

parenthetical thoughts unraveling in the descent
come away!   no point in standing there mesmerized
staring at the missing object will not make it reappear
she's gone, man, smoke that imbues *her*   come undone
hair loosened over shoulders of fading ink
a snapshot of her invisibility only reveals light's lack
the great afterworld   sleep for the unslept
dreams for the undreamt   the end-all of it
flowers of asperity and immutability   asphodels

56.

alpha rotates one way
and beta rotates the other way
          my head is empty
but for the big sky floating through it
what you miss in the translation is
the actual sound of the rotations
fused syllables of sand and darkness
the invariably small neighborhood of childhood
encompassed by the wooden stairs to the attic
and the long block with its imposing mysterious hospital
which is the world at large legend and enigma
inexplicable with its endless day
followed by alternating sequences of light
faces that come and go across lawns
spreading infinitely toward unnamed constellations
brightness of night that comes only once
before the transmigrations begin the rebirths
when the undead and the unborn prefigure myth
with a kaleidoscope of stories within a story
bodies exchange bodies in a luxury of detail
no sooner happened than forgotten
mind sends out its amazing triple notched arrow
burning through soundless ether
to its mark the impalpable beauty of the *unformed*
shattering a niche in space forever wounded
I remember virtually everything and nothing about *that*
the undergoing and the ascent
the revolving and the stasis
the waking and the falling from light

corporeal entities as if suspended calling out
as the lover to the beloved for release
while the multiple cosmos spins out of control
dizzying spectra of coming to be and ending

and in a nearby cave could hear a small music
a lute some viols a pan's pipe
for *whom*? a goddess whose fair cheeks shine
as she passes through the oak grove
her white skirts a swirl around her knees
cosmos a whirl around her head
the unborn being summoned by a *fate's* weird voice
gold woven through leaves' faint murmur
silver the archaic taint in passing clouds
a deep red coming up from earth
fully clad in armor ghost heroes of the afternoon
clots of dirt forming where their mouths
a secret hand plies some roping on the sand
it is all so impossible to recollect clearly
salt on the lip soughing air through branches
spilt wine on smooth rock
is it for glabrous gray-eyed Athena
is it for a brother god gleaming like platinum
issuing out of black stone a messenger
things come to a stand-still trees of immobility
heat and passion stifling in monuments of dust
yellowish iridescence shifting through glass
is it for a grammar book reading we live
for the lesson about the stars the wet Pleiades
the zone worn by Orion three bright asterisks
rustling here on this hummock some briars
tufts of worn grass ant-heaps carrion
left over from the last Trojan war
what are the rumors that continue buzzing
or that beautiful soprano voice suddenly bursting
even before morning spills out of its cave
like honey woven into Dawn's broad sash
and the meal worm the grub the midge and termite
who do battle with the invisible by day
and that *canzone* coming forth from the dark
it is to mark longing and its vicissitudes

those unseen alphabets that extend across time
planets heavenly bodies of love dew-inspired
fleeting glimpses streaking across the big empty
and earth is torn apart by rockets
schools turn into blazing swarms of fireflies
mirage of shimmering shields buckling in mid air
noon with its unannounced catastrophes
it is out of the goddess's hand
in dry hills Nymphs in clusters clad in see through skin
jonquil anemone hyacinth like ragged lace in their hair
ululate the destruction of countless cities
distance is victorious and clamorous ardor
where is the eye that sees all this?

and across the street the imposing hospital
constructed entirely of red brick and powder
where we were born and given names
and the whirring of motorized cars rushing night-like
in the broad thoroughfare below
headed straight for Nemesis
and in the darkening heavens a single search light
scours the vast empyrean for a clue
but the mystery remains impermeable
gathered into fragrant bouquets and nose-gays
and behind the hospital gentle slopes
apple orchards and small woods where deer
poke about as the seasons pass unrecorded
we are here doing this and that and the Noise
is all-surrounding like flocks of hummingbirds
silence has been suspended by a thin red cord
and like a flying disk the planet veers out of orbit
nothing but stuttering syllables emitted by the hour
attempts by Hermes to communicate through the din
haze and shimmering images on a ridge
imperceptible as are the words for things
that have gone into deep oblivion
do the children of morning
find in us their bodies?

this is dedicated to Harmony
daughter of Aphrodite and Ares

57.

the ambiguities the unresolved , the
unshaped or coming to be , the unending
deathless counting , because a bigger
thing has , imagined the eye , seeing what
lies inward , what morphology of the ,
shadows , a pool unfathomably deep ,
to remember so far back , to call out a ,
missing since yesterday , her , she , was ,
linking what lies in somber , to what is
implicitly on the other , side , a verger ,
a greensward , eyes the color of honey ,
margins of hair , envelopes of mystery ,
recall a vowel clearly , a moon unlit ,
what is the river's name , how when where
does it , flow , descending , five times ,
knocking an object out of , the air, sky
multiplied , immensely larger than , before
, shifts of organic red , fission , silently
exploding , everywhere , they said , falling
parts of the , body , not since yesterday ,
she , the soprano voice singing , syllables
of sand , remembered the cut of the hill ,
dark illumination slanting , not of the sun ,
not , but here it was , the ant-heap , the war ,
using blades of grass , freshly mown , dew
bright , fading the other , the other , less
than before , some of them crumbling in ,
dust motes suspended in morning , flame ,
mountain valley , murmuring dells , den
darkened the unholy , her , when it , them
, hunters eyeless roaming , weeds rapt, yellow
flush , music sublime first rays , gold gleaming
threads , interwoven mourning , them again ,
volleys of shot , silk , difficulties perceived , a ,
grains of fine , parchments all but , illegible ,
a story therein , a telling a , of a tale yet to , be
told , versions narrated , unheard , who listen ,
who fading in shadow music , who , she was ,
meant to be , mine , falling 84,000 ells , Tartary ,
musk , opium , the way it was first , they gathered

filaments , finely spun rays of light , told , a furious
evaporation , skies neatly folded one , inside , the other
, other , much less understood , hooded figures ,
erased faces , pink , eburneum , blush , patina ,
a skin much like a , song , a voice like honey ,
color of her , remembrance , accompanied as she ,
by a swarm of bees , sacred to , swinging hips ,
walks gently , she , a breeze , the god of the sea ,
who at first , behind her , odor of dried , hills
ready to blaze in , noons one after another , sun
letters , pronounced , sotto voce , details , more
in fine print , the unseen still moving , day's fall ,
twisted a limb , shifting among the reds , a hush
much like azure , clouds moving through the ,
eye , that eye , dreaming , haze , furze , tallow
dripping , pages torn , leaves weeping , an account ,
of , the happening on , crowded thoroughfares ,
cities , tiny , filling the distances , children perhaps ,
a section of time , no larger than , ink , no more
, elegance in her demeanor , her afternoons , piano
lessons with , a mattress on the floor , strangers
at the window , opacity of truth , willing to go ,
taken by surprise , unbidden as love , is , a , Wham!
edges of reality , will you be , mine , ? , certainly ,
not , a slap , a resonating , movie theater empty ,
why , in this artificial night , sobbing , both knees
bent , a sort of god , in her mouth , a , fractions of
light , not of the sun , brimming darkly , horizons
at last , tilting off base , an arrow sent , sweet ,
wounded , her , piece by piece removed , cloth
not of this , world , divine shining , head-dress
like a , pagoda , breasts bared , asking her to ,
please , and then rescinding , envelopes mysteriously ,
period , yes , whenever possible , hair fulminant ,
color of burnt sienna , a , charged with , fury ,
to be there , to have been , there , the moment
of , no witnesses to , the loss , the minute of ,
the hour , not precise , the undergoing , the secret
chambers , the filled with , grasses , longing ,
supernal a deity wearing , only , a deity much
like the music , of Vivaldi , rape , violins , lute ,

to whom pray , to get back , nothing , ochres ,
brown fades , pale suggestions , lips colorless ,
biting air , fusion of darknesses , space at , once ,
all there , is ,

58.
[Orpheus his sea lament]
when the sea is nearby and I hear the murmuring
of marine birds and there is such a longing in the salt
in the air circling above their wings perfectly tilted
in the cut of the light and there are such soft fragrances
rising from the billowing and the waves swooshing
immense whispers in my ear when their cries like
laments piercing am I to remember love then and
infinite syllables of sand criss-crossing shoals
tide incoming sweeping out loud wracked sea-bells
what is that freesong pinwheeling up there that
intense crashing the ear din of surge and sorrow
the incommensurate foam flecked grief wind inky
depths of words unspoken never heard lost tumbled
in surf roar vowels without margin flung in paragraphs
of mist hanging curtains of a day without noon white
embellished by whiter yet eons of spume vanishing
and reappearing in an instant surf sigmas hissing
in the lightless antechamber of oblivion signatures
of water emblems of brine summoning visions of girls
jaunty jibing sea-skirted taunting teasing in penumbra
of the half-known then do I recall love's echo shell
pink with ear-ring pendants hidden inside a coral
signal frills of incoming billows shattered poetry
sent flying like small blank hands into the ocean-rain
horizonless grey perpetual afterglow of mind spent
inside its lantern of fog and distance ospreys kestrels
shrill crying in the unseen girls in sea shanties hiss
of air compressed between lips of the drowned going
under the third time sunless events dim saturations
eternal evenings waiting for the conch to call skirts
taunting last seen bending over breakwater spitting
into the simmering brine do I recollect love's siren
tied to the splintered mast of longing to hollow out

in the cup of blistered hands a swilling potion acrid
bilious like the wine dark/snot-green sea coming to
take by the knees love's buckled cupid shame drenched
ears spouting verdant turpentine brain shaking
sea anemone jelly fish in search of a shape a morning
on the beach strolling death's small girlfriend hair like algae
bracken mouth kiss like the long intake of underwater currents
chill bone freezing cold faces going in and out of the surface
swollen eaten by mollusks eyes the size of dead oriental suns
shifting with the mauve hours beneath an invisible meridian
hopelessly gnarled knotted in thick ropes of saliva shunned
by all who come to admire the ever changing but colorless
sea-scape and hear mispronounced all the names by which
I knew her saucy sticking her tongue out going fffff *at me*
her like some feathered thing taking flight her brief heart
her already ancient hair her eyes the color of absence
the perpetual the sent floating the point of no return the
whatever the moreover the muffled roar of the planet
slip slop slush tap tapping of infinite rain on the glass
which reflects what cannot be brought back oceanic
pulse pounding in the body's sea-channels whiteness
pallor of memory when they came to remove her shadow
pitter pat of distancing footsteps on the washed concrete
when the sea is nearby and I don't have a thumb to speak
murmurmuring water whispers of marine birds pinwheel
freesonging overhead fantail of fading colors sprayed
in mist sheets I remember love a last longing wasn't
it shadowing wavering glassy surface breaking pinpoint
sunless light slanting into fathomless sleeping there
by the cornice white caryatids slowly sinking dream-lace
of surf beating against rotted wooden piers their faces
bent over stone weaving silky liquid in the day fade
water roiling churning spinning maelstrom brink
haunting slurs ocean-frilled dancing on wave-fringes
spume spitting sent high into moonless air thick
with oblivion's errant immobility always and above
swirling in inky ampersands omegas asterisks flung
like an endless song into the air's mourning folds
sodden sand-wet syllables the unheard nostalgia
freeeeeeeeeeeeeeeeeesong freeeeeeeeeeeeeeeeeesong

59.

Trombe, tamburi e voce senza fine,
Che par che il mondo se apra e'l cel roine"
Orlando innamorato, XV, 1

pure yes of form ideas in the ascent
immobile flame put to ether
sounds the trumpet rolls the drum
voice without end world cracks open
and heaven falls to ruin
purity of desire for the unfelt one
is it for the rest of a life time
circumambulating the small temple
setting incense braziers on the altar
is it the second life now
are we still recalling the first one
when the cycle has already closed
glyphs and wedges and cross-strokes
vowels notched into the passing breeze
to make her appear to make her re appear
edges of fruit ripe and dripping
teeth cutting into grape pulp
pure of memory the undead standing
on the rim signal to the still unseen
great are the migrations of winged beings
from afar in the haze of sea-mist a sail
flapping against the machinery of air
to re appear and her feet tiny in their moons
and her knees fair and chaste moving
through summer grass weaving around
can it be the other breath is the next
and we are summoned by the invisible to the dance
lacking a partner who can perform
drill rock and pour honey into stone
ear pierced by a fury of cicadas
it is to be last the one among none
trembling hand on the pivot
eye steadied to fix on the rising planet
a voice as if sent through glass
thunder in the pellucid azure of sky
to measure so much grain in the palm

painting from memory the descent of Achilles
into Hades in burnt ochre and black figures
who does not resemble *that*
there is no imaginary death
and on the other side of the dying
bright globes luminous above the desert waste
laying the old shadow down on the plain hummock
and taking the new shadow from its row
and inserting it into the small niche
where the soul comes out after the threshing
it can be pure and undistilled
as a water extracted from the mill-pond
without bracken or weeds
it can be whiter than whiteness
color of oxen blessed for the sacrifice
standing on the hill of opposites
crepuscular in hue and lowing softly
when there can be no doubt about blood
or the versifying in trance
of the oracle beside the felled oak
this is the day out of time the vacant hour
the instant which is the axis of eternity
unless there is a syllable emitted
out of the pomegranate's mouth
no sound will ever be heard again
hush stealth of heat mirage wavering
in unbidden distances of red
will re appear will not re appear
her hip against the crupper
her thigh bruised by the potter's wheel
a question mark in her eyes
darkening even as the pulse in her throat
                          quickens
purity of the idea of desire
for that which cannot be possessed
the impalpable and ineffable
re appear again by chance on the slope
the shepherd sounding his pipe
argent rills lost in the afternoon of sleep
head reclining on memory's empty quote
only the unformed god dancing in the flame

inviting the purified to join
in endless combustion

60.

the many the varied the countless and the innumerable
what one loves most // the inadequacy of possession
coming up from the stormy dunes barely holding on
sea-wracked numb of consciousness brooding upon the
and by a whole mile left behind all things
chattel fine suits pearl necklaces silk slippers
and looking up into the heavens breaking wide
a wind dark and violent visited the planet and took
from it the mansion with its stables and park
a small consequence is this wound left untended
still bleeding but what is that beside the greater knowledge
we have gained nothing and speak to dumb statues
as if to find the childhood that so suddenly disappeared
we were strolling then through the pleasant grove
and shadows and animals tame came to lick our hands
asking us pray who might we be wearing such costumes
by a pool carved out of basalt and filled with opaque water
a seamstress worked her fingers weaving grass figures
into the pattern of a most comely dress and regal
it was for no one and angrily flung the garment to the ground
how many days spent inside that glass harmonium
sounding melodies chaste and subtle resounding echoes
into the greenery the excellent ministry of the air
when rumors of the war the Trojan one arrived in stitches
undoing the texture of the words with swift strokes
excising vowels unwanted consonant clusters exclamations!
it was a god hidden in the underbrush who lay in wait
for the best of the damsels to pass by and take her and
away with her into the unlit hovel underground
where he and the others would perform the unmentionable
in a single noon in so few given minutes these and other
such events uncountable not to be narrated and the prose
constituting lengthy passages describing the route
around the cape and thence to the larger water where myth
the many layered and richly ornate and misleading
what were we to know in the confusion of names and address

goddesses in a sudden raiment of light and smoke
scampering like antelope or deer uphill into the deep
an entire mountain praised for its temperate clime
and surround by lush forests and dense thickets of legend
trumpeting of elephants and shrill cries of the peacock
paragraphs of incense so overpowering and sandy bodies
collapsed into a single syntactic unit and loud the utterances
a reading of lists of the fallen of women in secret chambers
of the boats in their numbers brought up to shore
and exactly who the eyeless hunters were and whom
they abducted and by what god's whim and whither
all in a trice a flash of lightning a hail storm a summer day
among the wayfarers a set of twins the art of divination
stopped at a place on the heights for prayers and
so much the weeping and wailing the rent vestments the
Euboea Boeotia Achaia Lycia Caria and Paphlagonia
in the woody clefts of Apulia or hard by the grotto
below Paestum who has not witnessed the passing
of Dionysus ivy-girt in his car drawn by Bacchants
ululating IO! IO! IO! beneath a terse colorless sky
steep the climb arduous the effort null and void the result
some deem hazard to be the guide in man's conduct
others to Nemesis ascribe the rise and fall of kings
at each turn encountered still another obstacle
misinterpreting the gravel strewn in the driveway
why the one window was darkened and the other lamplit
passed the evening in the gardens of Villa Borghese
communicating with fireflies about Heraclitus
and moved on to the greater discussion of the imminence
of the world-soul & of the body's tenuous levity of
and from a defile issued forth a thing much like unto Beauty
bereft of her outer dress naked but for her skin
shining like freshly washed stone in the first light of day
who can participate in the Mysteries and who cannot
dense brocade gleaming with gold threads in the twilight
of a murmur coming from the cisterns and earth-urns
scattering barley over the engraved brass plates
each dedicated to a separate deity and from the sky
fell an anvil eight stone in weight and forced entry into the
stood back to let pass the career of chariots swiftly bound for
cities built of river silt and sandstone quivering in the rare

star-flare of early evening when the talk is of
the many sundry matters both random and pertinent
which passed between us as we wended our way from the Wall
to the citadel its multi-fashioned marble glowing in sunset
for I still could not get over the Loss and no amount
you became abstruse and employed a language beyond ken
sanctioned the plural formations of inanimate nouns
we were being *watched* something in the humid stone
could hear a whispering in the dripping eaves a
tumult of distance and rising clouds of yellowish dust
thick making of the sky a vaporous lens difficult to
handed me a rolled volume sealed with a red wax
the imprint from the other world of the testimony of *her* being
which was at once disheartening and a puzzle
were not the many manifestations of the tale already
proof we asked of the circularity of time
let fall small drops of hot oil from the spoon on to the image
could hear roaring the menace of the Cataracts
the mad rush of empty waters into the starry element
the unfixed houses of the empyrean floating like dreams
far beyond the reach of ordinary minds
but we kept to the unpainted rooms and waited for sleep
the many the varied the countless and the innumerable
what one loves most // the inadequacy of possession

61.

birds white parasols mirrors fans garlands cymbals & flutes
borne on brightly painted carts lumbering through the mists

evanescence sweat bursting like blossoms all over the skin
trance-like when will this passage from the world happen again

lay there immobile beneath a weight of inconsolable air
cosmos of circularities and mirrors repetitions and duplications

stories without beginning or end books without pagination
arithmetical problems all resolved with zero plus a red omega

I never wanted in I never wanted out of this dense wood
unless a fire burn the whole and a water drown this earth

I looked to the music and heard nothing but space opening wide
ant-heap and bee-hive made of the summer a constant roaring

sutures in and out of the perfect surface skin a seamless liquid
with no place to penetrate only an endless sable memory

bodies of sand emitting nocturnal cries small echoes of rain
against the cumulated darkness fused to the dreamer's ear

first a hand whiter than light then another one traced in flame
feet at the other end one or two lifting stepping faintly disappearing

into what poem are these conceits poured with their brash assonances
what gilded picture frame embraces this mind's invisible construct

elephant tortoise mourning dove serpent sleek and black a song
immense unformed deity of clouds drawing them to his embrace

suspended a city as shiny and perishable as dawn making noise
fanfare and parade of sleep's two thousand million painted cars

I am a hotel a deranged radiator belt a fission of prussic acid
blue and red lotuses hang like skulls around my impatient neck

the rock upon which seated I derive the sublime code of notes
is nothing if not emptiness the abyss the end-all of uncounted time

the minute I saw her she was dead a perfect entity a maze
had I looked any longer I too would be *there* an unborn thought

swarms of winged things minute and deadly as the month of august
nest in the hair of anguish and it is forever in the anticipation

how many thousands of years do we keep circulating this ode
this paean to undead love that has never been nor will ever be

this is what never happens when I go to the umbratile other world
she gets it from behind and a truant wearing Pluto's day mask mourns

they tell me it never was they tell me to write another song to
whatever they want to hear on the radio night and day sobbing

she is a jasmine behold! she is a lightning bolt lo! if she is not water
she is a dark fish darting through the goddess's incandescent eyes

that is my song that is my poem for today and it is noon even
before the hour is struck and all semblances lose their shadows

62.
"Solitario bosco ombroso"

her name is cloud
her name is absence
her name is the thing you keep hidden
    between books no one ever looks at
her name is Lala the free-for-all
her name is not what you think it is
her name is written on her broad brow *Δικαιοσυνη*
her name her name what's her name
a pocket full of memories
a reverie in dark despond
a situation of sky and fire
it isn't last summer it's right now
the last days of the burning month
when her name loses register in the smoke
that does not return
her name is vacant room to let
her name is migratory bird
her name is violin solo
her name is I forget
her name is written in phosphorous
her name is asbestos
her name is Abydos or Skira or
wherever one travels in dreams
losing the body losing all earthly rights
go mad for that
go crazy looking for the photo you kept
of her in the beehive hair-do
between the pages of a Provençal lexicon
her name is migraine
her name is *"Solitario bosco ombroso"*
her name is dancing skeleton

her name is the detail in Red
her name is the uncounted
her name is sand
her name is the ungiven
her name is the Thrice-Holy
her name is corporeal evanescence
her name is RAGAZZA
"hey, Girl!"
her name is κόρη
her name is whatever cannot be explicated
syllables in reverse on a broken tape loop
ghost vowels left out of a vedic utterance
or coming to light on the last day
the face outlined in an Etruscan mirror
her name is breath
her name is her name is her name is Ω
her name is unwholesome
her name is empty parking lot
her name is grace without heaven
her name keeps being hidden mispronounced
easily confused with what other name
it is going rather than coming through time
her name is lack of presence
her name is Revulsion
her name is her name is her name is unutterable
her is ineffable cursed exiled banned
her cannot come home again
taken abused submerged dissolved in the underland
white face on white face pale invisibility
of who she used to be
you know what's her name
the ineluctable moment of no return
her name is instant recognition
her name is the unsounded note
her name is boomerang
her name is rope-dancer
her name is Our Lady of the Serpents
her name isn't what it should be
legend of the moon's backside
the thing barking at the crossroads at midnight
the Hag who eats placenta

one should beware of saying her name
it is broken glass inserted in the wound
green turpentine spewing from the ear
the ominous syllable of the deadless
her name is Sweetums
her name cannot be reversed
her name is ochre twilight
her name is not affordable
her name is endlessly monotone
communication of cicadas in grass forests
swarm song of flying insects hummmmmmmming
rachitic devouring gnashing of ant hordes
mmmmmmmmmmmmmmmmmmmmmmmmmmmm
what none can understand
hissing hushing zzzzing ping ping ping!
it is not rationale to think of her
who has undergone all the nothingness of ether
betrayed by the simplest of vocables
left to list in a glass limbo
seeing and not being seen
hearing and not being heard
dreaming and not being dreamed
her name is Hapax Legomenon
her name is wave length
her name is phonetic decay
her name has no alphabet
her name is indecent exposure
she is speaking hermetic hieroglyphs
she is a wasted symbol left to ruin on the water
the Ionians called her Mu!
her name is the first thing the Persians learned
about the occident
her name is a flood of diacritics
her name is phenomenal
woof woof woof
! ?
her name is ultimately why
passage of light in dark exposure
a camera eye gone blind
shuttered down
nightshade

her name is Mystery
her name is Mystery
her name is Mystery

63.

it explains nothing new to me
between this water and the other water
the uncountable one there is this depth
this gap between eons between cycles and universes
fallen through the interstices a vast darkness
to wake on that other side as if nothing
only the innumerable grasses the violent suns
flaring at daybreak the millions of gasses escaping
through the unpronounced word and the many small houses
rutilating in the abyss like unassailable promises
whitening shining disappearing no sooner manifest
nothing new to me waking on the broken ledge
beside the fate anointed one the shadowy crepuscular
who is without body unless it is what imagination supplies
the fluctuating undulating supple formlessness
it is what poetry can come to be a rupture in silence
or a thought breathtaking and sinuous as film
unwinding on its infinite spool showing not what is
but what could never be incongruencies and alpha notations
mind in all its wild directions passing into nebulae
if only to catch a snatch of that breakwater sound
of those innumerable waters rushing underneath the mattress
where is it all going what immense possibilities
of lightning and desiccation revolved and evolving
around the deity's putative thumbnail
to grasp even a grain of the hurtling sand masses
called consciousness or history and to wake again
here or here or even here in the great insubstantial
nullity of void Tartary of the hiatus of evanescent space
levels and levels undermined collapsing sinking silently
holding on to what whose small hand gripping the light
photo fade of the all in the swift passage to Hades
talking rapidly in a subterfuge hill dialect to Achilles
as his body takes leave and inky darkness wraps its night
around his beautiful shape and again death shakes its wand
a day and still another day bright for a few seconds and the blooms

variopinto lush swarming on Gaia's illusory surface
was that a memory or something I read?
poetry with its bound feet winsome but clipped wings
abundant curly locks adolescently darkening
over one eye while the other rapt and intent on beauty
opens wide to the oceans of sky flooding the glass
which reflects again and again the *other* caught in flagrante
trying on one pair of shoes after another declaiming
white sonatas serenades of irreversible meaning
shot through by the triple notched arrows of the Love god
hearts on fire fueled by enormous epic verses rolling hexameters
like the waves of the unfounded middle sea seething in its noon
apocalyptic and funereal against a painted backdrop
of arcadias where shepherds and blinded giants recite
their roles rehearsed countless times in the Cave
and the multiple sun of the second death and the shield
which gathers its light and splendors of wastelands
how many times must we suffer this?
it is what poetry says to do surrounded by black swarms
of bees says to do wearing a celestial thing around its loins
barking at the fullness of Selene shimmering says to do
wavering on cliff's edge declaring marginless words
to the empire of winds and surf the stormy tempestuous
afternoons when lighting a single unending cigarette and the girls
who have come all fulminant in their wet tresses and torn
to do says poetry is what matching sea spout with rock drill
in the tossed sleep of the mothers bemoaning their offspring
who have given away their minds to become *divine*
taking with them the girls undone towards the famous abysses
where everything and nothing happens in a trice
a once in a lifetime the only one and it's over again
death takes their skirts and flings them to the stars
constellations of mythical entities exploding multiply
in the inspiration and havoc of creation yellow red azure gold
threaded through the tenuous and evaporating skin
is it a song a melody a whispering in the deep
a *the barely perceptible rockslide*

64.
*"La vida es un engaño demasiado serio
para que tú lo entiendas, Chinchibirín!"*

what a cheat being born given light breath
awareness of the self and the other all at once
then inserted like a shadow into the mind's eye
death spreads its amorous dark wings throughout
lulling inveigling being with the child the child itself
posing for a life-size portrait in a devastated sun
growing up with that right next to the walking thing
death winking in the marigold and summering
on great antique lawns called Nostalgia and Longing
who will be the first to go is always the question
watching from a falsified distance one after another
the bodies disappear careening into a crevice
not far from the schoolyard where Eurydice and Maya
and Euphrosyne and the girls all frolicked singing
round after round of nonsense carols love flirts
and look again and one of them is missing which
you ask and turning a shoulder bump into the wall
the invisible one erected overnight to keep out the nameless
it goes like that twenty years pass in the time it takes
to pluck a blade of grass and tease a freckled face

ex abrupto the files open and close the flowers
with all the pretty names folded to fade and wither
the missing teen last seen wearing a parrot green jumper
with her hair cut in bangs was walking home from school
with some classmates when she responded to a call from
someone in a mouse colored vehicle of foreign make
in no time flat the car with its prey was speeding down
sunset boulevard creating a dense choking smoke screen
the teen's parents reportedly deities of a lesser order
have offered an immense earthly reward to anyone
knowing the whereabouts of the missing girl or the identity
of her abductor infernal or otherwise obviously distraught
the mother was heard to hurl epithets at the paparazzi
who trampled the carefully manicured palace lawn and
at one point all but fainting uttered this imprecation
Magni Di! Tibi sint mortes multae semperque uraris!
foaming at the mouth eyes rolled back falling into the arms
of her husband who equally dispossessed of his wits railed
like a brahma bull lashing out left and right at bystanders
demanding his Pulcinella back referring to his teen daughter

as nothing less than a **Kumari** *a goddess of the realm*
police investigating the case are less kindly disposed and
suspect that the teen may have been in collusion with her
predator as witnesses the nymphs in attendance implied
a willingness on her part et cetera et cetera hummingbirds
jasmine red coral blue lotus petals pampas grass wind tufts
by moonlight floating backwards down the Godavari
how many hundreds of thousands of steamy years ago   ?

how much time do I have left *mi corazón* what do I have to do
silently rushing through the high grasses the sleek jaguar
a god no less an infinite portion of the sun's long career
if I put these books up for sale and if I pawn my grammar
and listen carefully to the instructions on the back of the box
and hang from the invisible branches of the Bo tree these ideas
and section lovingly the areas meant for immediate disposal
who can say I am not mastering the art of dying then the red
sort the uncanny ear that listens to the threads inserted hard by
the dry well and the yes I believe it is so she is preparing herself
stepping into the mouse colored vehicle of foreign make Whoosh!
leafing through these old comic books who doesn't feel heroic
on top of it ready as never before to walk into the antechamber
where the Minister of Horrors spits into the mirror and ejects
from the planet the many mercurial decision makers Aghast!
to get over this deception talking to the birthright about what
happens in the great fiction of the afternoon fever hot fainting
hush of dense heat face down in the fertile soil of the Delta
swarming with empires of carpenter ants excavating galleries
lengthy discussions on the porch eating flame and admitting
defeat admitting total defeat a rout of the senses a disinclination
to come around to the vagaries of truth do I have left *mi corazón*
maybe less than fifteen years and consult the Delphic and
seriously give up intentions to learn the language of the Buddha
stare for years at the same stone lengthening the shadow by an inch
lying down through tall grasses a god the sleek predator
who took her away in his mouse colored vehicle to some backroom
where sharing the same cigarette a host of gods toss the dice
to have at her ignoring the appeal of a huge earthly reward
who know of her whereabouts and contact the radio and sign off

it *is* twenty years later and they are no closer to the truth
mysterious disappearance of the teen that fateful afternoon
has never been solved though many claim to have seen

a girl in a parrot green jumper with hair cut in bangs
strolling nonchalantly through the great 21st century malls
smoking strange foreign cigarettes and no sooner is she spotted
then she vanishes Poof just like that and her classmates
each has written an account and published it become best sellers
made into movies defied gravity with the weight of it all
born dead they say never had a chance to grow up
was a bride only until dawn when the fierce sun eats its own horses
and the charioteer mad to have a go plunges flaming to his end

65.

recollection mistake and doubt
much of what else is left simply fades
a world away and childhood a mourning
for things unnamed and lost forever
leaves that number green emptiness
forlorn as the divide between man and woman
divinity is what joins the two in sleep
fused metals faintly rocking membranes
if one is called *memory* the other is *oblivion*
passages of unremembered summers deep
in a corollary that seeps slowly into rock
nothing comes back but the incision made
by a diamond needle on a vinyl recording
hundreds of years ago in musical history
orphic and descending ever into darkness

diapason of eternity followed by small notes
flute and hummingbird immobile in the air
shadows the color of water spreading across
the length of a spear of grass in the afternoon
silent wheel of the hours passing through glass
sand in enormous shapes like ink erasing
sleep's inevitable back rooms slowly slowly
until dawn the return again of light unpromised
the ampersand of dwindling time suspended
just inches above the music's treble fray
chords of minute effluvia echoing in soil
& vibrating in spatial mansions until silence
uncoiled from its remote celestial drum prevails

poetry is the again of recollection of a light
a blade inserted by chance in the waking mind
a shift in temporal spheres moving the ear
around to its precipitous fall into chaos divine
a rain of words flame colored or stained deep
shattering the immobility of reason with echoes
of something heard in the water beside the
repetitions the fantastic the ineffable the sublime
the at once forgotten for being so terribly beautiful
arches of verse linking ether to ether in a paean
to the struggle between the soul and its *other*
mistake and doubt whether to move or rooted
to the spot cease dreaming flinging an anchor
into the inky pool that exists levitating above earth
where electric fish weave currents in and out
of the Eye which imagines its own vast remoteness
circling the impending stars painted on the immense
but fading background which is the act of creation

that's when I told you about it that's when
sitting on the rock in your shepherdess smock
grass stained and lit by a lamp other than the sun
otherworldy as you were pale the shade of a girl
you listened not attentive to the notes in my voice
garlands of perspiration on your broad brow
but intent on something behind those notes
something massive brooding incisive cutting
the air like glass into neat hemispheres when
I repeated to you about it and the levels of sand
rising imperceptibly in what you saw which was
not me but some other "me" reciting in an echo voice
the legend of the myth of the tale of the story about
and everything came together in one dark point
brought to us by the wind shaking the narrow willow
and shivering the skin pellucid in that yellowish
flare of antiquity which invested us that afternoon
counting the hours as if they were seconds strung
on an invisible rosary watching the pulse in your
throat the fine blue veins just underneath the song
that was about to scatter its music all around
tumbled you into the field the long rent grasses

and the terrible circular heat face down dark
rushing the unseen animal its menacing growl
to not know what happened then to fall asleep
unexpectedly one arm still in the air to forget

66.

does one begin by giving air a shape
pronouncing one by one the syllables
that gather like sandy cumulus clouds
in the small verger of a summer sleep
to revive from certain claustrophobia
love's archaic but fading perennial bud

dogwood primrose snowball violet lavender
aster anemone sunflower hollyhock daisy
eglantine lotus rose jasmine hyacinth
narcissus crocus lilac peony tulip amaryllis
magnolia delphinium dahlia zinnia iris
chrysanthemum pansy gladiola hydrangea

sallied from the hedge the black charger
not a moment too late the lorn damsel
hair unkempt eyes wild garment rent
white petals everywhere bestrewn fate
to live a blank existence between blades
of itinerant grass in the heavy july air

how then comb the trace whither gone
through dense reeds marshlands heath
stones upturned rocks riddled heather trod
was it here or there or which the hidden path
nocturnal sedge wickerwork palaces smoke
something lying in wait a stifled breath

meadows like awnings spread beneath
an alabaster sky truculent deities weapons
poised to strike unwary traveler of the soul
through dense wood and sylvan glade dark
shadowy figures barely cognizant alive
for the brief second it takes to undo a tress

is it for this the poem in medias res takes
deep measures distant rolling seas verdure
in lush abundance wrapped around the spear
verses unraveled describing the never been
glass palaces bee swarms dizzying heights
heroes nameless and great who spurned die

and the poet in solitude grieving hours spent
by little light his song in hand the lyric draft
recites again and anon to no one but the lady
of never seen whose dwelling is a salty wave
somewhere beyond the hill of love unknown
where mingle dreams and visions still unkenned

was and cannot and would but never did a
thing denied a singing in the stone a water rushing
who is where a what then such a life a light of breath
this is that and Thou art too much is why the which
is come and naught but fares a single way a dark
a frayed a wood a puzzle will but never be and

O there is great a working here a sorrowing an ever
floral games and deceit shoes to be flung evening is
a sheet lavender deeply dyed spreading over the all
maintain then the greater arch the letters carved in stone
that to the world proclaim the secret is and was remains
did never lasting breath so short a light believed to be

with a whisk brush the marble dust away the white
the more than white pale the pallid albescent rumor
was this a statue once with human voice grieving
a vowel with feminine grace in the winds dissolved
why mire the troubled head in futile grammar rules
bestir the empty crowd of consonants a life betrayed

is why here I sit on this gilded tomb a fading gram
a picture I never took a section of air more pure
shaped by my absent hands into the form sublime
ask to question no more the passing shadow where
if solid rock its hive distills a honey sweeter yet than
she whom I sing a yellow darkening into deepest rose

color obscure the image evening fiercely burnishes
hair in envelopes arrive and cold under the voice
breathing soft between parentheses and sudden night
snatches the idle mind's self devouring breath from time
alas the wink her eye it flashes once a closer thought
remembrances a season out of order burning bright

but once alone and not again the effort to justify
most lonely the remote adverbs so perfectly round
sequences of circularity that repeatedly embrace
the, no, our milky way revolving our sleeping fits
into steeper crises of consciousness so wake! poor
wandering *animula* and these wasted lands desert

is it for grief only we nominate these flowers
enumerating their myriad blooms counting ecstasy
among the teeming varieties a hastening of hue
arousing from the unshaped air as yet the single most
the one required by love's entelechy to evolve
a flame derived from the moon of deathless passion

mere words hobbled phrases vain desires put to flight
put out syntax a blight on mind's once pure emptiness
there in the small diagram to the lower left in all
its lunar particular she was there she was the idiom
of hill and spectrum dying with the sun in its gauze
daughter of the Pleiades watery evanescence *night*

67.
αοιδε!
partake no more of the shale grey light
move thence to sundered rock the salty air abounds
where once they hauled their broken ships to rest
              and darkness its veil
does only a voice move through like a drill
reciting from a dream fragments of epic verse
ask of the ghost who walks the walls
what of those who waking on sleep's other shore
where are they today
who have tasted the bitter lees as characters

in a literary memory
am I of them?
such as the fragrance of almond and cherry
in the chinese breeze
      so are we specters tantalized
by light's brief recollection kept shifting
though gyres that circle earth's former grace
or plummet unconscious through a grape skin of time
was it for whom?
is this the study of stolen love
shadow cut in half by jewel sized knife
her naked form at the window bent
to seize from the passing air a cry
like a peacock's indigo vowels shot into the sky
      for her the shaft with its bright flowers
sent straight to the breast and there interred
to linger making bitter the day's long hours
Kama the love god sent me it says incised
in tiny devanagari script
      I saw Helen with grammar book in hand
striding atop Mount Kailas around her loins
a panther's pelt and her small feet like dust
moving across the unfelt ether
function of limbo to maintain bodies
afloat in the concrete atmosphere more like twilight
than any other time of day though it's broad noon
and the gate diagonally sliced by shade
partly open to reveal still another cosmos
evolving with shapes of gold and ivory
fauna soft-eyed barely conscious stirring
      are there others we should recognize
whom Circe in her spell has transformed
to spend the remainder of their existences
in this ochre stained hill country roaming
      aimlessly
    αοιδε!
neat sections of the hymn fade off the margins
words become inaudible
      the unheard floods the ear
bodies of those who rowed tirelessly
and ate of the cattle of the sun

unburied who lay in levels of air and
unattended lost their names and wasted
after the last Trojan row
where argent threads weave into crepuscular
    and the Fair Angelica I saw
raving on the moon's far side
for a glass of pure water for what
cannot reflect back for what is opposed
to the motionless wave
we plunged our shadows unknowingly
into the liquid murk color of late autumn
russet blending into carmine incarnadine
like blood or the pulp of the pomegranate
her we left unbidden at an entrance
        cars drawn by unicorns passed
their wheels left no mark and a din
arose   a goddess for sure
the tip of her heel roseate and wet
swept by with her hundred nymphs
scattered in the dense light
      thick sandalwood incense
in choirs of smoke rising from the leveled stone
one of us was *marked*
am I of that number?
the one bruised by Kama's sweet shaft
herself has multiplied and we see her mirrored
everywhere impalpable and unique
   as the door turns
        as the rock removed from its space
she is as mysterious at a dozen windows at once
and nowhere the minute you look up
   a bite sized stain on her perfect skin
memory has left its echo there
plum branch and dew fall
   a shiver
        before being returned to the dormer
chasm of black glass just inches below
     diminished and faint the figures
of former humans exchanging shapes
a distant animal cry in the night
who draw smoke and love's waning incandescence

integers green and wild dancing
and it is Eurydice at last I saw
moon cicatrix and pumice stone coloring
her voice with a soft lavender brush up and down
the infernal walkway in expectation numb
reversed of memory her wide pleated skirts
as if a breath in them moved
function of limbo to maintain stasis
irrecoverable remembrance of bodies
hues tawny and dull like the hides of beasts
have lost their enchantment
mauve and wan blush
powders vanishing into the soft
other worlds just glimpsed
slipping through silk into
a deep underside
faint whorls
damp skin
αοιδε!

68.

is the mind in a constant re-creation of itself
does it exist inside or outside of itself
is it contiguous or coterminous with what it perceives
in the photograph version is it a mere dialect continuum
is it seated on a jeweled throne wearing on its head
a heavy miter made of pure elephant ivory
does it go into a new formation with each awakening
being on the outside of the myth it is creating
to become that myth itself diapason and drum of breath
what occurs to the mind is a reflection of itself
moving mysteriously through constructs of galaxies
and the myriad personae within who are talking talking
arguing for this or that theory of heat and collision
for why the godhead is in the shape of a tortoise
or the guiding principle of ether manifest in lightning bolts
naming and unnaming all the refractions and inconstancies
that are fused then become undone to the interior
where everything is happening at a molecular rate
and nothing is happening except for the immense silence

gazing on the whole manifest of always becoming
everything I see is what I am asserts the mythiform dreamer
who arousing his brother *shadow* performs on the lawn
his great music opus number one for two violins cello
organ and theorbo and the world is at once gratified
rock stone sand and grass are at peace and the congeries
of beast fowl and fish assume in their ecstasy pure immobility
to return to such a state of grace is the impossible
as much so as to run water backwards to its source
for mind is *that* and not any other unless it is Thou
the immense *unformed* that is continually retelling itself
by day what by night was chaotic and multi-directional
now fixed and full of longing for what might have been
seeing and being seen in the glass of its totality a refraction
bending in the slanted light of the sun in its daily error
and coming around to nothing holding on to pinpoints
of air or billowing wind currents where fragments of color
fly shaping at will the mirage of the Beloved in her movie
of sheer intangibility skin and hair and cosmetics
fictions that make of loss a greater hurt an irretrievability
mind revolving in and of itself the why did it go wrong
where or when if *everything I see is what I am* lies the blame
did I not in making assumptions about the *other* realize
there is no *other* but in the mirror of the persona
back and forth identities conjure their willing opposites
tropical storms whirlpools sunbursts impending catastrophes
brought on by the fortune teller's mercurial flights
into a future that cannot possibly exist as yesterday
is the only tomorrow rhythm and debility of the mental
which is it I chose to be then why am I running around
in this confused parking lot drinking bootleg alcohol
in the redundant passion to find what I never possessed
unless as a wall-sized poster of the femme fatale
peroxide blond dumb from the waist up stupefying
with her glassy tantric stare intimating a pornography
of the most sublime order the mind at its worst
creating realities that implode with a clockwork regularity
every time it thinks consummation is at hand the devastating
wasting perplex of bringing together forged possibilities
that at best are the sandy distances of a sleep disorder
OK that's it never again not the next time or any other

I swear to lay off not touch it put it aside do penances
for a thousand years standing on one foot only
putting out of *mind* the idea of the substantive Eros
love's illusions everywhere struggling with its own hiatus
mind is its own inside out creating newer plural selves
as if the older ones no longer mattered glass splinters
or moon shards scattered across an increasing darkness
claustrophobia of dying with an intensity of masturbation
magnifying the eclipsed second of the original Big Bang
all pervasive self destructive instant of eternal retrospection
because it thought it was so and that girl strutting down the street
Uma or RAGAZZA heading for that big peninsula of gas
or creating no selves at all becoming No-Mind
while flying 30,000 feet over a teakwood forest for years
mind thundering echoes of itself until a million light eons pass
in a trice and the same street shows the same girl strutting
a kaleidoscopic version of mind trying to outthink itself
colors that she radiates into the magnesium tinted atmosphere
it is being there all the time thrilled with the orgiastic red
emanating from the centerpiece of her mouth ripe pomegranate
to be devoured underground only waiting waiting for
death's dizzying sequence of cycles to come full circle
me that's me fixing to get her back sometime soon
because *everything I see is what I am*
love's illusions everywhere

                69.
mystery and fragment alone that remain of the *seen*
whenever that was and however it occurred
distance as a plausibility a chance mirage
fragrances budding white and tender in the eaves
where thought notched in boles of air wavers disappearing
a time it was in and out of rock formations
lustrous afternoons bathed in light and the verdure
of earth's new romance language a series of vowels
etched in sand singing somehow into the leaves

where is the ideal city gone? stone fractures
signature and effacement   that remain
the hour when the sea's shadow turns deep indigo

mountains reclaim evening nothing but hush
azure immemorial   unformed beings
that enter dreams betimes and haunt the ear
with incantations in an unknown tongue
to wake again if ever and address the brother
whose airy flight so unexpectedly
and the republic its imprint faint on brass sheets

of the *seen* rustling and whispers in a blur of sound
names fall away from their object
statues eyeless formed in a vague circle *watch*
for the unheard moment to approach when noon
multiple and circular with heat evaporates forever
from any recollection earthly or otherwise a
figment of law   winds bruised by a marine flare
ruins all that remain on history's burnished rump
Κλειώ her nose amputated her thumbs broken
her stone peplos folded in battle with the unseen
those numerous and illiterate deities   clouds
ruddy and mysteriously moving over the water
the dark

breath and food the body make who is invited to
die beside the great irrigation canals and who to
write the psalms being fanned beneath the impenetrable
the enigmatic swoon fallen into the shifting slowly from
red into indigo depths a mirrored sleep an instance
woman of word by day flower by night female
margins go blank erased histories of megalith period
Herodotus to the contrary elevated peacock throne
white such   cadaverous skies drifting asleep
remains fragments of voice stone markings chalk
circles feet counting meter   prosody a
death a section of meat a hazard dangerous rocks
engines by color and the planets by number who
is to count them and who lay aside the ledgers and who
beside the great reed beds write on wax tablets
early versions of lyric poetry   being scanned

starlight   recollecting the *seen*   O
syzygy   muse of lyre playing a

by dim lamplight the   crawling across the floor
soiled garments   russet   ochre   depths
long and short syllables some sandier than the others
in rows the students lined up to recite hesitantly
one after the other   incomprehensible
a language no longer spoken unless by
      marble   chalk on their fingertips
wearing a bird's nest in her hair
      immense gray eyes solemn
hoisted Anchises up on his son's stout shoulders
before the flame reach them
      the inevitable
'til smoke return
    sudden flurry of little speak   ruins
        edges of the invisible

70.

uncanny resemblance to the *other*
what were you wearing last night
what were you doing dancing like *that*
holy like a temple whore and yet
it was paradise it was salvation from rebirth
going on and on about the price of silk
about the Boxer Rebellion about foaming
at the mouth ecstatic I knew you were lost
you who said *"love only lasts the night"*
weaving between your unspoken words a
sound unworldly a ululation and echo
I knew you were gone for sure before dawn
and in vain I searched the rooftops
the bars that were still open at four AM
the streets wet with the rain of distance
I saw doors yawn open entrances to hell
and watched mangy dogs eat human offal
and heard yes heard the gods of intoxication
revile their mortal lovers for insufficiency
wherever I ranged the futility augmented
traces of red on deteriorating latrine walls
jazz slums littered with broken glass names
small houses unlit and sinking into miasma

signatures in burnt neon flashing in the air
here was Nestor set to rest in deathless sand
and these blistered fragments Cassandra's
oracular catastrophes turned to ashes
and I knew you were forever missing there
where night draws evanescent demarcations
engraving hours of forced lunar migraines
you dancing with what were you wearing
skin frozen to its own skin shining loud!
pale the fashion of ivory darkened against
whiteness that borders on blank beyond blank
forever the nuptials of instantaneity on hold
noon will never come with its brimming wine
because I almost touched you I am exalted
turning three times on the coin of irreverence
flush with base ignominy of the profaned
being and not being at the same time a void
I Orpheus locked inside my vehicle roaming
quarries mortuaries lime-pits and crematoria
for some trace of you for the jasmine scent
mingled with that nocturnal purulence that
signaled your presence wherever in the house
the golden-eyed fish of the celestial waters
it is never in eternity today and morning
with its great undersea lanterns blinking
will never come again since you are nowhere
knocking on petrified gates of gas and ether
stepping deftly on peninsulas of mercury
avoiding the lair of the three-headed dog
carrying in my one hand your former hair
and in the other the shadow of your forenoon
insane to have a kiss in your absent totality
jungle wracked hoodoo baby-doll tattoo
I am come to the bottom rung to the inkstone
beneath which a planet rots fermenting
small lights flicker on the right paper margin
dit dot codes in Sumerian Braille on the left
immense fogs obliterate the remains
of that tortured prehistoric epigraphy
where myth fades into enigmatic grasses
++++++++++++++++++++++++++++++++

did not find you in the sumps east of here
big diesel rigs hauling frozen meat overhead
searchlights in defiance of the curfew scouring
the fixed heaven where sacrificed animals go
did not find you at all
hotels with lights blazing 24 hours a day
embalmers desk clerks with green baize eyes
simply stared into the artificial meridian
memory of you dancing hips swaying
tin-foil tassels smeared black eye mascara
hectic blush like death-flame on your cheeks
that wasn't you at all that wasn't you
sitting there in the tanner's yard, Homer
some semblance of you some nightshade
flower or memory of being a flower
transposed heads marigold and daffodil
shorn by a shadow's sudden movement
air cut by the slant of a slender leaf
evening immersed in liquid azure
darkening not you at all
            all of space for a home
"love only lasts the night"

                    71.
        "Je me félicite de n'être plus dans la vie"
              Jean Cocteau, Orphée
between the sleeping water and the waking water
the five palpitations of your deceitful senses
you sit meditating considering what was the first thought
sky was the first thought fog is your breath
your eyes are what you want them to see
inwards you are the cliff of insubstantial earth
your organs keep rhythm with the distant sea
outwards you are not perceived but as the *other*
walking coming to dominate what cannot be possessed
your tongue is the argument and the quarreling
strife comes about because your mind is not quiet
if you touch you think you can own
lie down in the sanctified grasses of the dawn
with eyes shut see the procession of ruddy kine

the ever glorious clouds that enhance the heavens
where undetected cunning and jealous the thousand gods
watch your every move as you proceed through the hours
a day is not enough and exhausted you think to sleep
someone else is dreaming you cutting you up into slices
and each slice is a part of the cosmos wet and starry
though you consider yourself whole you are but a page
a flapping paper in the oriental wind unnumbered
and you shuttle about among animals domestic and wild
and out of anger strangle even the slightest fly
winged demons enter your left ear possessing you
with feverish desires and lust and imagined fornications
you spill your seed on the immense thigh of a powder
whatever a woman is you cannot define that
it is within you as well the swelling unwholesome thing
how is it you can talk about the holy
with a sacrificial knife in hand to decide wars
it is the savage beast you must slay to become a god
so you think processing various herbs and formulae
and raving because you have eaten the mushroom
see things beyond the visible hear things beyond the audible
in a faint and lethargic you re enter the old body
transmuted talking nonsense lips bleeding a flint
shaping on your skin fantastic designs of galactic origin
yet you persist being *you* the outline in the mirror
unwilling to surrender the contents inside your skin
someone else is dreaming you a thousand gods watch
your every move up and down the stair daily
in your veins there is an azure bird beating time
in your heart a parrot asks which came first
the sunflower or the sun illusion of sun and another sun
words fruit saliva smell your nose is the south
your lips are the west your teeth the far east
biting into grape pulp or chewing the blue lotus
and a vision comes to you and the sea raises its arm
the large awning of the northern waters
and deities porous and gushing amber liquids step forth
and take from you the cattle you have stolen
and take from you the First Bride leaving you desolate
with the four hundred five remaining wives
what will you do with them how will you settle with them

when you wake on that dun colored ridge below time
what is it you think you are and what are you doing
the four hundred five wives are nowhere
in the wind there is a dry chattering
it is the monkeys who have come to watch and mock
it is a wasteland you inhabit the sole resident
mourning the loss of so many wives turned to yellow dust
you remember drinking wine with them at noon
when a messenger came bearing a history
an intricate monogram an incision in baked clay
which you puzzled over before your siesta
and when you woke it was the same again evening
an almanac of futile stellar predictions
the sounds of battle at the gate chariots and horses
waves of besieging darkness black armored warriors
seized you from sleep and set you up as a puppet
playing with liana grass and burnt ivy on a stage
on an island floating somewhere above planet earth
all of this the mirage of your five deceitful senses
insects devour your insensate mind
red and black ants make a terminus of your body
swarms of bees reassemble your hair
imagine in their buzzing that they are the four hundred five wives
and you keep asking what was the first thought
sky was the first thought

72.

and here in the 21st century everyone and his brother
chattering chattering away on these hand-held gadgets
oblivious of their neighbor or the girlfriend walking next to them
and for this they no longer recognize the sky nor that
Akbar the emperor of Hindustan is marching upcountry
with all his silks radiant in the glare of day nor
that the mountain rat who has deceived him lives trembling
in unimaginably dark and dense woods waiting
just waiting for the fatal moment when
or playing with their fingers tapping messages constantly
about the petty diurnal sections of time they employ futilely
to unseen others equally employed and the world is a vast disk
sent spinning out of control with so much electricity and flame

heat makes ever greater demands on the atmosphere
and there is a terrible circularity burning invisibly
less than a generation ago there was much less of a buzz
air stood still slanting in the ripples of primavera's birth
breath was still a measure of music the stately sarabande
eye was heard ear was seen so much left unspoken
but isn't it apparent that death is all around today and that
my Eurydice with her gesso white face and silken black tresses
no longer treads the small grass with her dewy feet
where has she gone but south the direction of the dead
this place really belongs to them this is their broadway
this is their palace with its thousand columns & hundred doors
this is not a zone for the living or even for those resembling the living
these are ash trees asphodel fields marshes of blue lotus
but my Eurydice what is she to these wastelands what is she
but *She-who-is* walking as a shadow figment through marble
so why are all these global minions in their look-alike see though
parading like zombies with their electronic digitalized minds
throughout this vast expanse below the duplicate sky of death
they cannot possibly see the immense circling invisibility
that menaces the very cosmos with extinction within minutes
and my Eurydice is somewhere else in the southland of the dead
being led through fragrances of pepper and turmeric
to the throne room where the hoary Judge sits in icy stupor
this is the house of mirrors this is the glassware of time
yet she is nowhere visible in the funambulistic array of images
++

this is 21st the century of zero equation banality dumb down
everywhere people are communicating without knowledge
winds are rife with disembodied voices appealing to nothing
directions become confused a robotic sense of implication
and false awareness govern the states of mind of the hoi polloi
love passes as an advertisement for a new application or a bank loan
and in the narrow circumference it says *everybody can be a poet*
but isn't it apparent that death is all around today and that
my own Eurydice has been suddenly snatched by the eyeless hunter
nobody witnessed this act which happened in broad daylight
storefront lottery games were in full session television sets
suspended forty floors above the earth broadcast the event
but nobody saw it happen no one heard the cries for help
there was a sequence of red dots flashing in the air
mythiform figures in neon raiment passed out leaflets

announcing a séance at midnight in the hall of Uranus
a drum beat solemnly at an unidentified distance
and in the great southland which is a vast sandy necropolis
syllables compose decompose and recompose her name
vowels are sifted through radiators and tumblers echoing
a music recorded before the universe had its present shape
and *She-who-is* walks in a trance through marble
when will it ever be again? when will the nightingale singing
amidst ivy girt columns reappear her wings flashing gold
and fly swooping gracefully through   leaves
+++
grass adds to grass
                        light in variation becomes more light
mystery
                        what cannot be explained
                remains unknown

73.

what is other if not the inexplicable which is never
a far remove from the waking state
the shadow woven into the mirror of the hollow
where a murmuring persists in the grasses
where shivering you lost a finger and for the remainder
of your life not conscious of it went about
at a loss for the meaning of blood and all about
the mysterious houses of the ancestors with their porches
that abutted into a summer night sky
and the siren song of the crickets and the fatal
flight of white moths into the burning lamp
well what can I tell you if I know next to nothing
wandering here on the only shore of the cosmos
not understanding what is passing before my eyes
whether it is morning among the crocus and amaryllis
or whether it is only the dewfall in your eyes
honey-colored and fixed on the distances of Orion
or some other remote myth now become a gnarl
of lost words sections of syllables removed from the sand
intimations darker than usual in the dreams
that have entered your right ear recently and
what can I tell you if anything at all about the poetry

inscribed in the moving current of air that takes your hair
and shapes it into an afternoon spent beside a water
next to the intricate glassware of antiquity
imperceptible shadings of russet and ochre and burnt sienna
a world of hills that of themselves move secretly
into a crepuscular hemisphere defined forever as *longing*
of what memory are you a casualty?
is there a permanence to oblivion?
what invisible hand descending from the clouds smote you
carefully on the left temple giving you the wound of *life*?
in that instant you became a stranger
you raved to the darker side and prophesied dimensions
of no return amidst spectra of light ever brighter
what can I say about that falling into the loom
what do I possibly know about the depths beneath
where unlit your mind carries you around like a small bundle
far from the precipice where madness
of course you couldn't understand any more than I could explain
just exactly what and who and why and wherefore all the doings
painted upside down and in miniature the loves divine
so much more chaotic than human despite the similarity
of the positions and the passions all indigo and green
like the time you woke after the collapse from grace
a wagon was carrying parts of your shadow away
you kept looking around for the traces of recognition
ruts in the red clay country road one hot noon
the air more circular than ever involving us
speaking to each other in absentia about the quarters of sky
diminishing rapidly because we could not keep count the times
day came and went flashing seconds indistinguishable
what did the world look like before the gods
what were the original shapes of things
we looked down into the place where grasses grow
multiple and dark the swarming of mind
creating and dividing and loosening and forgetting
the first thoughts were they only about storm clouds
or about coitus and sleep and dreams
everything turns around an unseen axis of flame
from Asia Minor rumors of divorce laws and conscription
came on two-wheeled chariots drawn by fiery steeds
that was the time they burned the islands

scorching the sea bed and the palaces of oblivion
I had to turn your face from the disaster
great pearls of sweat broke out on your brow you wept
how could I tell you it could be no other way
you *had* to disappear becoming formless
the sun was in the stone and the moon in an amber bead
of the three faces you exchanged before going
only the second the resemblance to Aphrodite remained
glowing in the soft turf of the fading hour
then you were gone a mass of blazing hair
bracelets jangling silvery echo and the one slender anklet
gift of Diana the disembodied

for lack of memory cities of vast antiquity
porous dehiscent vibrating in a dusty chaos
cattle raids and endless hymns to the dawns
innumerable references to the enigmatic one
to the dark clause buried deep within the phrases
meant to illumine the passage of things
back to their primordial forms the misunderstood
a falling away from conceived geometries
from arbitrary ciphers attached to the planets
rotating at mind-breaking speeds from the whole
and ultimately the silences plural and ancient
as sleep all for lack of memory the devastating
formlessness of dew and water and space

74.

Κύθηρα

which is the one which is the two
delving diving into the dark recesses
worms the color of silver coin
the cytherean deity clean washed
rising from her foaming re birth
whiter than alabaster her skin
does she turn her back on the lot
word woes simplex effervescence
longing is equidistant from sorrow
and Lo the peacock a god for sure
winged aloft for a second only his

shrill cry indigo hued reverberating
it is the hour past the other day
sand sifted through the small vowel
it is never certain to spend this minute
in hell or in Elysium's fretwork bliss
the broken lyre the mysterious note
unsounded for the nth time a verse
recited plangent voices repeating
echoed syllables drifting in the waves
by the breakwater flung into unknown
waters resounding in the sleeper's
other ear like molten gold poured
into the brain's uncanny childhood
sieve and rock crystal honey hive
sun born of stone and orange rising
sing we then the ivy-sprouting oar
plowing the loam-dark sea field
praise kingfisher kestrel and gull
disembarked on the rocky isle
oblations to the ceaselessly dead
count a wooden ladle and cup
two carts a gold necklace five stones
an antelope horn and a red bull hide
and there stood as if enchanted
in the mauve blending into tawny
lamp flare of late afternoon hearing
as if for the first time the sultry surf
pounding at the reef whispering secrets
into the wind-tressed rock pile
going in and around the magic
and thereupon arose the flute sound
issuing as from a cave somewhere
to the south where the crocodile
'neath it they lay the body to pray
and no wind but the blast of heat
oppressive and circular taking mind
off its course to list in the noon glare
nothing moving but the eye's symbol
like a new sun embossed in metal
reflecting on the shield a shadow slant
in the osiers hear a slight rustling

padded feet of a wild beast transformed
hold still the breath and uneven numbers
that make a plinth and hammer set up
an altar first and around it sprinkled
dark wine walking counter clockwise
to appease the god of false starts
and to the east pointing a broken staff
fingers raised and crossed thumb and index
and broke from the clear empyrean
a Noise so startling the leaves shook off
and on the ground a circle appeared
perfect in form and the magic again
everyone in a trance seeing from within
which animal they were and what
resemblance was to be fastened
to the already alternating shadows
hard by the fresh spring to drink
mistaking that for the source
whence mysteries make obscure the west
evoking mountains of dun colored stuff
and to every man of us the large skin
wrapped tight around the shoulders
spotted pelt of the leopard or wild cat
a growling in the bushes behind
where the north takes its escape route
knowing nothing of the passage back
to the skiff tilting in the spare shoals
our captain immersed in opiate
or already beheaded by the turk
wild eyed the oracle began hissing
night took us totally unawares
and the palace of multiple planets
its doors shut tight to seal off the air
now just a dream or a smoky mirage
which is the one which is the two
if the difference can ever be known
or the two can be one or none at all
to sing like the chirring cicadas
to dart into a section of air a firefly
perfecting its minute existence
to be as the blade of grass halved

by the passing afternoon's shadow
possibilities shivered in the gloaming
to define what is constantly changing
and is totally without boundaries
just so we become unconscious
slipping from one life form into another
dazzled in the island's ebbing glow
thus it happened and in confusion
and calling out noticed our voices
were not the same as before
but a mixture of bellowing roaring
whining chirping unh unh unh

75.

lost the thread of the tale
and walking down the second street
brother recognized not brother and
here she said slipping the envelope under the door
this is the perfect counterpoint music
the sonatas opus one of Archangelo Corelli
through walls of mist a different consciousness
can the universe exist without a mind to perceive it?
on the opposite shore erected a massive hospital
not so much brother but the shadow of a brother
passing through the glass shop windows of second street
inveigled by trinkets and toys glittering there
an edifice so imposing of fourteen stories brick and glass
on the windshield a sticker label said *Beloved*
in the history of what went before the various chapters
dovetailed into one another like hours
sifting slowly through the compass of days
each with a different fable to tell about the same
in a void the parts are tumbled and names
surface attached incongruously to bodies at birth
and one begins saying yes *this is me* that I am
it is out of that building hospital if you will
that we set forth each with our own story unwinding
blood-red thread twining in and through stone
sun bursts at the right moment and the flower
turns a fragile head in its error

a rhythm like breath or the wrist's blue pulse
can this music ever be surpassed in sublimity
in the envelope one had to guess its contents
most said it was merely hair as an offering to the Nile
but why and the medical practitioners only smiled
making gestures like shadow puppets on the wall
we acted as if nothing turning the soil over
every spring under grandmother's watchful eye
beneath the immense canopy of azure
here and there shoots sprang up tender green
learned to both use and break up the words given to us
to learn to speak of the unheard and the unseen
leaving the unspoken for a later grief
the second street broad and evenly asphalted
stretched as far west into the mysterious hills as possible
should we ever go so far then we would *know*
what lies underneath where we once heard a voice sobbing
to grow up and be mindful of the myth
the one illustrated in coppery brass tints in the book
the stranger with one sandal left on the doorstep
that was when as children we assumed everything was one
connected by the slightest application of the button
maps unfurled on the green baize floor
as easily walk in and out of them as through a gate
garden of language breezes with oracular syllables
one had but to listen intently with the right ear
just before falling asleep the
rope-walking across the slender but profound Lethe
took turns and on the far side of the cosmos
hailed one another as the same vertiginous beings
a paragraph left out some phrases excised
left to chance other structures occurred
narratives of pure thought verging on sand
the extent of time was no greater than the next wave
we lay there inert dumb beasts waiting for the bell
something in the upper portion *moved*
tasting like salt faintly and the dark hive appeared
with its immense noise and winged accents
for the first time *black* shapeless and endless
from which the labyrinth came to be and the girl
whose waist is an ampersand of light

to guide the wary guest out of unwritten danger
such and many were the fictions unfolding
all things in one the inception of the epic in the midst
of seething seas raging gods dominatrix of mountain born
who was when where they were all speeding in chariots
with axles of melting butter careening out of
and lying in bed reading this one constantly unwoven tale
how many poems did it become how and which
phonetic symbols aggravated on the margins
a thought that the street could go around the world
that behind the hills a still greater enigma
a sphinx or a sibyl encased in amber an oracle
leaves of indecipherable notations a sudden wind
mixing up the thousand and three leaves
scattering etymologies and musical scales
rock formations sea-loom spectra bloodless and
everything demanding its piece and eerie light
not recognize brother his shadow and led into an orchard
surrounded by tamed animals with wheat colored eyes
seated on a stony abutment and his other sandal dangling
an air played he on the seven stringed instrument
how did swoon the Nymphs come from heaven
just to listen and variable and speckled the air
lost the thread of the
                what was I saying
staring into the opaque distance where
a bare white arm signals
it's time to go
underground
again

       76.
on the one side the Zoroastrians on their desert plateau
setting up numerous fire altars below the bare heavens
and on the other the court of emperor Akbar of Hindustan
gathering together muslim hindu and parsee to *learn*
studying the Sanskrit with its copious declensions and conjugations
and the Greeks come forth in their miters and beards
with the mysteries if we would but listen to the Musick
hours of hymns and incense hooded mummers in ashcloth

cataclysm in a sunflower seed deluge in a cup of ceremonial tea
what is in the rock has not always been in the rock
what is in the air has not always been in the air
a drop of honey on the cusp of infinity
a blade of grass is the total length of time
the domain of the body is shadow
the domain of the body is shadow
and wherever it walks carries with it grief
and wherever it walks carries with it grief
but the domain of the soul is light
and wherever it dwells there are no margins
and wherever it exists darkness is expelled
but the domain of the soul is light
and I saw as many as a thousand angels descending into water
and the sound of their wings was deafeningly sweet
the followers of Mani assert an everlasting struggle
between light and the forces of darkness
whose skin was flayed and filled with grass
but the mysteries according to Orpheus declare no such thing
and that the distance between this life and any other one
is an approximation of breath a matter of forgetting
and reawakening on the other shore to wander
never remembering what the house was like
only that the Beloved dwelled in one of the twenty eight chambers
in descending order space ether fire water inert matter
it is in the last where we are born and live
and if ever we hear the song of the Nightingale
are we then reminded of the celestial spheres
of the congregations of stellar bodies circling in the Noosphere
but for the most part we are as sand-bags moving
through aimless warfare of the elements claiming
this or that part of the earth to be the better portion
enslaving and corrupting and smoking and fornicating
with all the abandon of witless beasts
calling the summation of so many pointless deeds *history*
but in harmony and nobility of features the stag is superior
and the elephant crocodile or tortoise too have their pedigree
which sets them up as beings to be revered
and whoever steps on the least of the ants killing it
according to the Jains is sent straight forth to a *Naraka*
to be consumed in an eon of burning penances

how better to explain the mind's agonizing ricochet
of againbite that plays havoc with consciousness
for there is no sure step in ascending the ladder to heaven
even Orpheus in the end misstepped to be savaged by Bacchants
wailing their shrill threnody in one dark movement after another
it is the body's gravity that sends it plummeting
to its earthly reward a castle and a good pension
before submerging it again in the lethal flows of oblivion
do we then keep nattering like devils of conscience
arguing the this and the that of salvation
is it not plain that in the end no umbrella holds
++
be-bop doo wop jazz-a my soul
abracadabra hobson jobson dialectic
this my good sir is the automobile for you
lives on pure sugar run-run-running through all-space
the light-show of consciousness in a delivery system
that works like a camera shutter
now you see it now you don't
great the chiaroscuro of the completed painting
showing by degrees of perspective and hues
the Jerusalem which is the habitat of the soul
a magnificent thing of a hundred thousand palaces
suspended by elastic bands from the seventh heaven
wherein see the fleeting midges termites gnats
with their complex human names exulting
because they think to have seen the light
in immense shafts entering through the multiple chinks
in the hive-like structure where they live condemned
to belief systems where black equals white
and the myriad levels of births have no end
unless in the vortex of unconscious bliss
how many others have their sight confounded
and the unheard take flight with wings of sound
manifold buzzzzzzzing in swarms of formless entities
animus and anima shifts of red and blue lotus
waters assuming all the spectra of the galaxies
everything folds in on itself and silence
reduced to the infinitesimal point of no return
seeps itself into the sleeper's enormous ear-root
              NOX PERPETUA

didn't you hear me call
    a blur a smudge of ink you were
echo fade of a photograph
no matter how much I tried to write you
the words slipped from grip the
    vowels turned to sand the
how you suffered from phonetic decay
from a worsening of the syntax
    nothing held   nor the vibrations
nor the miniscule parentheses
meant to contain you when you got loud
    vociferations much like music
no matter how strongly I forced the pen
the plume the embossed wax intaglio
    which was supposed to be your name
a red seal on yellowing parchment
nilotic blue at the edges a surreal
    bee swarm your fantastic hair
no matter how much I rewrote you
syllable by syllable pronouncing you
to make sure the tourists would understand
    that this was the legend of salt
this was the pallid mirror reflection
this was the mimesis of the burr
    caught in the throat of a god
you were the hemline at the edge
of a very dense paragraph describing
water in its infinite varieties
shh sounding hmm hissing steam
evaporating through the azure duct
    where the circumflex is kept waiting
you I mean the you of the hologram
the you of the ecstatic verse sung
to the Muse of the missing day
    the time you were supposed
to manifest rubicund dehiscent
amorphous and dactylic at the same time
hemistich and iambic stammered
in long hexameters parsed in a grammar
    the trope and the type of a

girl in unwinding sentences phrases
snatched out of the dust in an alley
the long ago of the archaic goddess
the white-out on a blank sheet
erasing the invisible orthography
    of a pronoun long fallen from use
the sort of you when on the tip
of the tongue just burns ssssss
sigmatic aorist verb formation
employed for deictic exposition
a grapheme in elegant alphabetical
    order smart chic brief
gone before the sound is out of the mouth
tongue-tied restless and aphasic
a linguistic conundrum in velvet
no matter how often I stenciled
your monogram you didn't respond
    ta-ta-ta you used to say
in that dream speak of yours so
idiomatic so incomprehensible
as you always were ineffable one
pressing your lips for a prehistoric
kiss yes yes always yes on your mind
if only you would have just once
said it I mean spelled out the tonic
accent before it spilled from the
    ledgers sewn in linen and
tanned and bound and rewound
long versions of chinese characters
variously meaning horse or mother
ideogram cuneiform wedge rune
listening to the you of the tape recording
the you of the berlitz lesson
the you of the office dictaphone
    was your etymology wrong
did the code for your part of the
dramatic monologue in which
you were meant to represent
the southern hemisphere slip
did the diamond needle wear out
did the vinyl disk run out of sound

acoustic flaw you must be then
missed echogram of Mnemosyne
   how I regret never saying
it right saying you right writing
you right in the small red book
where I kept all your phone numbers
you never answered any way
being somehow content with distance
being the little fragment of a text
to puzzle over for years
after your disappearance the
what remains of you the ruin
in a consonant cluster
the the the
never
you
Εὐρυδίκη

     78.
before the eyes there is nothing
behind the eyes a spark begins to flare
when was that what wind fanned that flare
and behind that the ninety and nine rivers
were loosed and the winged mountains
much was there great in the first movements
desire came before breath and the region
now inhabited by gods was a shining waste
then came the dawns the multitudinous
red-hued on their cloud-steeds ruminants
devouring air and the huge breaks of rain
that covered the mist-felled lands below
before the eyes there is nothing
but behind the eyes stirs the entire cosmos
in columns of pyrite and hematite
hurtling stone upon stone in a brazen air
desire comes before breath and loosed
beyond the first pinnacle the ninety and nine rivers
flooding the massive plain between the straits
the shining wasteland before the gods
who in number are but three thousand six hundred and one

and after the gods straight away their region was lifted
by levers of prime gold and named heaven
or some such unattainable and full of endless light
where no meat bleeds nor do they ever die
but jealous of men they descend constantly
to wreak enmity lust and wanton desires
among puny mortals just learning to wear pelts
and moving mysteriously more like shadows
than creatures of breath and blood
until suddenly a breakwater crashes behind the eyes
and political units are formed and princelings
and women covered in sheen and see-through
tempting on their boldly shaped rocks
and with a stiletto a man carves his name
the first ever and says *"I made this"*

then do I resemble what lies before the eyes
or what comes behind them in a fiery rush
when was the time of the twined osier bed
of the dense silt and the mud that reflected heaven
is it that coming forth from the orient
I am most myself at dawn when mist covers mist
and the smell of salt is strong and the distant cry of a bird
and I dip the damp oar into the brine embarking
unknown into the unknown in search of longing
and trembling a feeling overcomes me a sweat
before my eyes sheets of nothing
and behind them an immense column of fire
in which I can make out a script letters moving
smoke involves the turrets of the sky
a great noise moves out of the airy ramparts
it is as if coming to be I begin to exist *conscious*
of the every and slightest stirring in the immobility
afterwards when the light alters its shape darkening
and I wake on the other shore attended by a Nymph
then do things begin to become unclear and I am invested
with a vast bewilderment as to where on earth I am
and what I am doing and inconsolable she takes me
and delivers me to the underground Palace
in the midst of specters just as I who speak
but say nothing and I am given dreams to remember

but none brings anything to mind
crystal sounds and a sweet ringing in the ear
thus I pass from this life to the next
bearing little weight but that of an anxious thought
a foggy unwinding toward the new light

these are the mysteries secrets of dying and renewal
buried in the rock the flaring spark immersed in water
the thunderbolt and the god who determines it
in shivering air all around the hidden names
waiting to be affixed to moving and unmoving objects
everything is contained in the kernel of the instant
which is the axis of eternity the irretrievable moment
the flashing swirling brilliance of light and sound
life! the inexorable within an indivisible stasis
I am the promontory and you are the wind that
circulates around it giving it form and luster
the beyond is inside germinating flowering
becoming opaque and crystalline both
the variable and the invariable of mind
intent on its thousandfold paths through light
where nothing explicable occurs only madness
and dark unreason which give birth to illusion
whence all beings join in the round-dance
maelstrom of consciousness and the other
lip to lip lover and beloved consume each
their imagined counterparts swooning
as birds in flight suddenly taken by storm

the sheer monotony of it
the seemingly endless row of identical days
what did you do yesterday I don't remember
but I'll be doing the same thing tomorrow
sunrise sunset noon in between the moon's up
stars are out for a date someone whispers an antidote
green turpentine flushed into the ear
keeps you from falling in love ever again
what the eye sees in front is nothing
what the eye sees in back is the image of a flare
everything burns in that heraclitean flame
you don't have to remember anything

not even the time she said *OK take me*
you go back to the same books count the number
of the same gods live in a vacuum of letters
re read the first efforts at this or that
sleep on it sleep into the rock
indivisible immobility
numbing taxonomy of weekday names
irretrievable minutes of sand
vowels becoming more and more faint
a large voice reading from the text
incomprehensible passages of shipwreck and
porous sunlight slanting through the classroom window
dust motes whirling in the chalky air
NIL POTEST SINE TE VENUS

79.

daughters of wells and woods and of sacred streams
how much further have to go pushing against rock
sleep in sands of misarticulation waiting for the big
dusky vehicle to arrive that will take from the body
its memory to deposit it on the other bank of the river
loud sounds the voice of departure louder still
the ensuing silence in leaves of distant summer trees
will have little recall of being here of stepping lightly
over the small pebbles shining brightly in the moonlight
looking for the place where you were abducted
what its name was which island floating drifted away
from the main how it was you succumbed to a tease
to a small gift held in the goddess's precise white hand
a fruit a sweet nothing which in tasting dissolved you
keep repeating the details of that myth re writing
the elaborate particulars of hue and place and depth
time circulates in a swath of heat and the color red
supreme for a few instants and animals come to lick
the salt block their eyes damp and disarmingly human
come to know and just as soon to forget the outlines
discernible in the passing sky yellowish cloud landscapes
remote peninsulas of gas and thunder and the roaring
the inevitable storm that occurs in the medias res
of the poem being developed around us around our

recollection pushing still deeper into the hinterland
into the fringes of a bosky bower where like bells
the laughter of unseen daughters vibrates in shadows
and the zing of darts or shafts sent flying into the soft
the unheard is a great hush around what is remembered
about us in the unfolding verses of the tawny afternoon
talk of fate of transgressions of some unconscious act
amorphous at first we slowly take shape within the poem
as in a dream we keep repeating with slight variations
our brief encounter and adjectives begin to dress us
not the thing in itself but the substance of the thing
and the verbs which are our acts perfect their conjugations
dividing the world between marine and terrestrial
and we keep being written in recension after recension
despite scribes' errors typographic misconstructs
poor translations from one unknown dialect to another
our conjoined myth becomes more and more fabulous
have you become an angel have I become the inventor
of language itself the itinerant minstrel who transforms
stone into water because sorrow is the transcendent art
it is all spent in a magma of misuse and hyperbole
yet we remain authorless a sequence of personae
not one or two but multiple in the untraced mind
that goes on developing and unwinding the thread
of the unconscious against the loom of language
making of the constellations a fabulous syllabary
the backdrop of our shadowy and romantic tale
of something once told many times in a waterfall
by a heap of glyphs employed by Nereids in sport
spurting the vowels of your name into the indigo
and expending the simple mouth of my origins
in a flagrant untruth that outlasts its dark origins
being and not being in legendary iterations of
fragments we ultimately become pieced and shaped
enigmas to fret over lost rhyme schemes implausible
connections between vast lacunae illegible margin notes
a lost and unplucked string hung out to dry off key
a song reconstructed out of bits of sand and ivy
an oar tossed off the Ionian coast a hymn surviving
in the dried algae of a Rhodian beach hummed softly
by the daughters of wells woods and sacred streams

80.

between the sphere above and the sphere below
the temple the size of ink dedicated to Artemis the chaste
who keeps summers for herself in the damp hours
when by the passing stream the body comes to reflect
on its transitory nature and leaning to sip from
the cool waters in itself drowns to memory and daytime
just so it was between the two opposing spheres
when the radiant and circular blow of heat
struck you on the brow and looking at me
no longer recognized me for who I was because you
were no longer yourself but the possessed of the goddess
could summer be so brief less than an hour
the length of time it takes a blade of grass to spend
its eternity the whirlwind of an instant the color of sand
in which everything and nothing take place blossoming
in the fervent exchange of lovers who have forgotten all
in order to expend their identities in cloistered ivy
suffocating in that glorious instant of self abyss
surrounded by an all-encompassing green nightfall

Artemis twin sister of Apollo! what is a year many years
to you who take to the wilds hunting heedless of time
yours the glass ankles the unheard clarion call the wax
embedded in the mind that keeps the divine impress fresh
yet you hear not my appeal sister of the Far-Shooter!
things are amiss here there is great confusion and sorrow
summer has been cut short by a year and the hours
sifting through the eye of the needle dissolve in mercury
promised a month of endless light and a bed of sacred grass
what I received was a pointillistic sequence of black dots
the immersion of consciousness in a thimble of water
and the sensational shot of breath in the ear the word
that was supposed to mean Forever but which in a trice
left me deaf and in a swoon attended by swarms of bees
and the remote feeling that I was becoming a mountain
darker and more distant than an evening in Hesperia

heat the words for heat what heat means ants red and black
battling over a spear of fallen grass a blade of heat choking
dust whorls of heat heat so thick the city goes lost in it

an entire summer of heat reduced to opaque crystal wavering
in mid air just above the pool where Narcissus lost it
echoes of heat Nymphs bathed in heat naked all over
plunging the selves into water which is a reflection of heat
heat the color of sand heat verging on infra-red yellow heat
out of proportion to the immense towering furnaces where
Hephaistos manufactures bellows and volcanoes menacing
heat in turbines heat like the brazen breath of bulls storming
the shadows of men heat prostrated heat smitten lovers in heat
coupling on white hot side-irons heat oozing from mulch
heat that begins to rot stench of heat carcasses of heat
cicadas' deafening song of heat months stifled by heat
the body overloaded with perspiration gnats and midges
exploding with heat skin heat-singed heat the size of Miami
heat the shape of the sky clouds of heat billowing steam
heat becoming dense circular rotating over the myths
forests lit up by heat voices asphyxiated by heat calling
out to the other to abide by the stream lest heat fell that too
hymns to heat to the gods of heat and flame paeans to Agni
prayers for rain petitions to no avail Dionysus is dead!
skins and pelts of wild beasts dear to Artemis soaked in heat
heat revolving in galactic formations heat in the Big Bang
let is lie down then on these sheets of heat beneath sun's
errant and burning eye let us join our mouths in heat
while July and August smother us in carpets of heat
and witlessly coupling in the mire of everlasting sweat
out do ourselves in memory of these blazing fields
where adolescents we surrendered to heat's endless light

between the sphere above and the sphere below
long did I mourn the loss of that heavenly noon
what was it in my head what circling gyres of flame
what did I see if not all around the nagging sprites
condemning me for my grave mistake when looking
back when looking back when   moon sphere
disappearing like a firefly in stone
when looking back and powders of miasma and whiteness
more white than   a section of time
sheer as a cliff fell off into the dense
only the nymph Echo now and then comes around
with her small book of missing pages

tells me something whispering in the rock
some shade is gone
some shade
(z)

81.

vagina   insects   fragments
figments   fictions   an ant-heap
gateway to the underworld   teeming
with the unheard who   vagrants
wingless   drifters   who in afterlife
is anything more possible   poetry
whatever that is   a broken harp   labia
sumptuous memory   long hours
in the   a single blade of grass is more
intricate   its shadow   how much
the bus that passes   is   a ghost
song   dust and gas   labyrinth of
air   steeples that penetrate   sleeping

how high it   exactly goes frays
sessions in Mu   logic sideswiped   Ω
space re oriented   death throes   swift as
feathered   small precise and white
her hand   unsighted   longing for more
minora disjecta   eyelashes   literary
nothings   smooth entrance   meta-
omicron   followed by fiery   traces
air disintegrated   indigo cry   breathing
for the last   or dream   yes,
it is a   *the* in isolation   heat wave simul-
mapped a current   watery steps
virgin   termites resembling   masks

oedipal and   stasis   of joy
emphatic and sexual   mercurochrome Oh
wavering   shimmering   to strangle a
firefly   the unseen who   inhabit our
earthly   burning tenements   cloud inspired
distances   like the finger missing   grasses

wound around the   a small suture   device
can it   however much a knife   abacus
calculating   eyes like roses   not probable
sighing and   spirit messenger   You
who travel across space   who embark on
who   dimensionless   yet transitory
as a phone call   from   down under

demon of the right   who governs   the ear
listening   steam hissing   heavenly
brigades   sent me   this just once
grotto shade   dripping in the   shhh
trembling lips   pudenda   *ora pro nobis*
sectioned off   the,   willing done a
distinct   her was a   thrill in red con-
but is one of them   either is to the left   shifting
from azure to   dolmens and lingams   stone
artifice of love   shale slipping of   other ear
entrance to   there saw Achilles   or his
shadowy likeness   others and   substitutes for
eating of the   forbidden   her ripe soft

coitus interruptus   in flagrante   animula
vagula blandula   habeas corpus   the rest is
history   wanton and lewd   directly to the
animal and   leading the string through   what
is poetry if not   *that*   somnolent weeds
drifting face down   in sedge green water a
why?   another why   more intense than the
playing the lyre   inside the stone   music
manual evisceration   did she have a name   did
never occurred to   damp brow   sun's error
turning   graphic and moreover   filmic attri-
running to the   shore where   masts broken
listing rotting   timbers   at least twenty names!

so they go out to sea, a madness to re live
who wants that   undergo nausea   heat
in thick strata   rough hewn oars   washed
the grizzled face   no reflection   tumbled down
kept repeating   the devil was in it   glassy

turbulence	mysterious		whispers
will have no more of		it	spinal
splash	disjunct	unstrung	the bow
sacred to Artemis		other small artifacts	
found	could piece none of it		together
their shadows		darkened ivy	crepuscular
as are	the days, of man		*I sing*
and arms	whoosh		frrrrrrr

82.
"la vida entera es recuerdo de la muerte!"
John M. Bennett

the shape of the wind // they battered my hand
could no longer hold on // to re write the constitution
and of it make a whirlpool // arias of haunting beauty
woven into the idea of time // loosely fitting brush sabotaged
hills raven-colored disappearing // one sun after another
behind which flits undressed // the spirit of poetry her
soft impress on the inner thigh // damp whorls of echo
or hair curled by sperm // in a dead faint her voice
lives in the last house // third corner from the left
where the demon is said to // employing verse schemes
lofty triangles of rhetoric // it all darkens worsening
chill hour of the mandragola // is that a serpent?
sepia tinted motion picture cuts // splice of life and edges
molding frayed under losing all // from this distance a blur
a faint without trace of breath // a lingering isn't it a real
listening for the code word // red enlarged to the size
of the moon or its partner // reluctant backside shivering
feet scurrying under dust // small yellow recension of text
placing words in a different order // they shattered my wrist
replacing whole phrases with powder // at first white then alba
greenish apparitions where once // stood the tree of life
heaven has its roots in the eastern // what did she do to deserve
that fate was a question of meter // philology of abracadabra
longing for lawns and a summer // moving their mysterious cars
through shadowland some of the gods // others bent over the balcony
laugh at mortal despair // in caves grottos and hillsides bare
dressed as shepherds troubadours // rebec or tambourine in hand
imitate of yore great Orpheus // his lady lost in a year of days

white spent in diminishing ovals // worm swimming in the eye
out of context and unredressed // indigo the cry of the peahen
azure the reply of its mate // constantly becoming unclad
image of beauty in forlorn skin // an instance of oblivion
in the key of delta minor // is it teen age violence
is it gun patrol wasteland // nothing is familiar in the afterwards
syntax breaks down into fractions // thought implodes in figments
fragments are the rule // puzzles and enigmas in the mall
exploring the lover's broken vow // indicting the decimal rule
foregone the lyric trembling // eerie cuprous sunset
before the moon was formed // the great disorder of trees
in which hotel does night perform // they hammered my ankle
doubled over with angel the pain // substitute her for poems
white on endless white what more // demand nothing at the gate
on knees implore for one mouthful // the god she devoured
as if it were a coca cola // death pursues death willy nilly
up and down the peggity board // a herculean task in ink
nowhere does it say *Beloved* // space leaking at the seams
all the gas out of proportion // on a peninsula or belvedere
looking out on the circular ruins // of heat and its secrets
how few are the remaining // how lesser still the fiction
the soul is in that envelope *there* // saffron colored and oblique
case grammar functions as witness // twelve kinds of aphasia
either knee endowed with desire // on all fours barking at Σελήνη
temple the shape of a cloud // offerings of black ram and millet
chronicle of a breakdown // left hemisphere alone at work
soon it will be noon again // the beast panting in the reeds
a pyramid and a song after it // enormous body of sand
shifting leeward the mind's salt // waves like hours
the drowning the attitude the alpha // this week is forever
multiple as the memory of death // a minute at a time
until here and here dit dot // criss cross the eternal
with an oar sprouting ivy // and the singular cry of Pan
(08-16-14; Madonna's birthday//Elvis' deathday)

                         83.
[fragment   s]   a second too late   issue
         (I won't say how many   )
              the body is that *darkness*
a vocabulary that consists of   birds of prey

booty ransom omens oaths   a fierce struggling
in a night shot with gold infusions
        knee deep in quicksand the heroes
who listens   striking the lyre alone midnight
Artemis!   arrow sent through pith
what is that agony but the body's weight
pulling down from the thought of heaven
and the countless reds that color memory
dense red of roses contrasted by Daphne's pale hue
do not discount   membrum virile erect
as a stag's horn and   [Ω] -s
followed the path out to where the sadhus
naked but for the tattooed left arm
        insignia of the god   silent letters
vowels that when uttered give shape to a deity
raiment of shining light the   mysterious whole
distinctions between paints applied to stone
whether to heighten the idol's intent or   to
shadow over the pool shadow over shadow
in the rock a sun is lit   for what purpose
and go circling the   deeper red of
blood sacrificial in the moon's ivory glare
to make of this a myth framed in   words
listed in small columns reading from right to left
urns full of golden flakes   dung in heaps
sections of space hewn   and falling
making a great Noise   breaking a string
out of tune the   turned then his grey eyes
into the sandy waste to discern there a figure
a faint outline   there is no sky to observe
when the sea mists come rolling in thick
could that be the ghost of Κρέων   who
Thebes did rule   magnified   [-tion]
the eye which breathes a fiery light
    magma   listless on the tow path the small
irreverence stumbling on the crushed gravel
twenty kilometers of bad unpaved road
and Lo the entrance to Hades neon flashing   and
[-gments of the Pythian   ]   mauve over ochre shade
a river bank   unh   bent over to stare
motionless a head of water in grandeur like unto nothing

hoary and vast as if brought down from the skies
a shifting   a paralysis   speech acts of the dead
hiatus in which we are born   ! a sort of red
in confusions of more reds like her hair   once
flung to the side a flare   of passion
longing   hour before sun-tide   a burst
trying to return the soul to its seed-bed
the silvery messenger barking into   sands
a place of disorder   *Saṃsāra*   descending
(orphism platonism jainism)   of wandering
from the center   [-ive   o]
could be a mirror image a   reflection
obverse   consonants
moving mysteriously through woods glades hills
the rebirths seeking   among gnarled roots
soil in upheaval worms things have lost their wings
blind larvae struggling to recall their former names
fragile syllables embedded in rock an unlit sun a
fused to the moon's unseen side and speaking low
pushing aside shadows of substance of lost motion
and ask for sense and meaning manifold in a spectrum
of reds violets yellows indigos paler hues shimmering
cold essences removed from language from thought
a sphere darkening in the steep shale underfoot who
that was sleeping in the image of water
who that was dreaming the reverse of matter the
archaic portions of grammar before
differentiation how the female ordains and how
the male submits listening to the insect in the ear
burrowing through histories of ore black dense
is there a deliverance from this   ?
sitting at the other end of the bar the woman
speaking to me through the glass
is reincarnation only this exchange of bodies
this confusion of names?
a rustling in the leaves something dripping
in the dark a   [frag   -micron]
drawing closer we   our mouths inside one another
fragrance of rotting pine needles   a fiction
of music   in her eyes electric fish darting
back and forth between the universes

colliding   the small pond opening up
issuing forth a   ἐλέησον
her head of unkempt hair became a lamp
lit from within like the sun in the stone
a single spark   dusky globes swirling
color of spun honey evening in the hills
languid   marginless   softening vapors
when I can your unfastened shape reveal &

love the unformed thing passing through
substance of rock crystal into the archaic
shadow over shadow opalescent pale
fading   f-f-f-f-fading
          ἐλέησον

          84.
a score of words no more all implying
something of the moon struck the lorn the
smitten of heart whom chaste Diana pursues
not let up the whip the shaft the swing of the
curses raining down from the cloud belt
making one's way through fields of tall maize
toward the motel ere the hail storm descend
battering all manner of things tin and glass
from the remote hold espy fleeting figures
white ants gnawing at the bow string
furiously by day so night-fall finds the slain
headless in the ditch booty for ravenous dogs
and hard by the ant-heap the Nymph shivering
in her skin thin raiment drenched and cold
witless her gaze intent on the unending
such scattered detail and the immobility
like a painting fixed in the sleeping brain
discuss later the remnant of the dialogue with
and penetrating darkness a small flare
that is to say a lifetime spent in one afternoon
heat in its tremendous circularity beside
the body exploring in its dream the *other*
intransigent disintegrating in the labyrinth
perspiration swollen lips and the small cut

across the brow was considering setting out
by mid-day in memory's verdant bay
whom chaste Diana and her hounds hunts
shadow against ivy wall blackening hours
in a glass catching the day's errant glint
the many fallen on the road-side
hands that have yet to meet or
faces erased and turned to stubble
someone calling from afar the voice
of the Master of Secrets bidding one to wake
spiritual dawn hidden in unhewn stone
who will evade the burning dart and come
to the opposite shore of Phlegethon intact
to harbor mysteries dense and endless
dew on the blade of grass marks infinity
and Light once the gift of the gods a loss
buried like death in the sun's black spot
+++++++++++++++++++++++++++++++++
why am I here you as well do know when
you dropped from all things visible into
Tartary's spoiled rock garden darksome
envelopes of fire vowels of gritty smoke
instinct was to chase you through the cliff
to follow spiraling downwards in quartz
burning the memory of what was once
the seen and heard of you all Pale one
nuance and detail of the sand-clock
am I turning round on the inflection
of the verb to be without even existing?
am I to last half of eternity without you
and the other half go on being *nowhere?*
+++++++++++++++++++++++++++++++++
this is not poetry on hire by a literary agency
this is not a lyric suite to dappled clouds
an elegy inspired by time's broken vase
nor is it an epic fragment of a greek lyre
tuned to the music of crystalline spheres
in the nowhere of an imagined mirror
where tarnished heroes are sent plummeting
by a slight wound to shadowy Hades
remnants of this and that and the cycle

of avatars numbly circulating in a heat wave
nothing but an orphic rant against stone
lament and revulsion against unending
this is not a pretty selection for The anthology
nor the insertion of an interpretation
of what was originally intended last summer
when the oracle manifested in ruin:
if death is the pupil of the eye what
is blindness but the seeing of nothingness

85.

this is all happening thirty centuries ago today
we are no longer becoming but are absent in hearing
that the most beautiful part of our lives is ending
tomorrow when the lawns will have yellowed
and the small painted furniture turned to dusk
evening's once and future envelope filled with ants
and the voiceless monotony of night's stellar symphony
what will harmony be and the cessation of light
worms crawling through acres of years old star dust
will you turning to me recognize in the mutilated form
of rock the eternity of song I used to be imploring
for just a minute of your shadow a single second
of the persistent and enervating sound of your name
which it took all this time to survive perambulating
galaxies of ghost worlds a mythology of infinite numbers
and I returning your stone smitten gaze a sort of ivy
growing inside the left eye and the right one all pulse
beating a rhythm of insect terror paralyzing the brain
will I then see you for what you always were a cicada
drenched in a summer of pointless sun storms burning
Echo and its water in the small lunar crescent
we used to call love the ill begotten the unfolding tomb
sand vowels consonants of riveting mercury a poetry
revolving labyrinths of ether being drawn from the ear
and made to sound like cymbals before the sphinx
enigmatic pharaonic riddle syntax of distant dust
to exhaust the mind with petroglyphs and ciphers
the total history of the dream reduced to gravel
is it I am you and you are nobody returning soul

from the endlessness of the after-time looking for
the place where you first descended those eons ago
which is today on the rewind of cinematic tape loop
conversations we were having in july and continuing
in june all around us the new grass in its cycle of light
before going under by the suggestion of Persephone's
small right hand scattering daisies for a nosegay
what it was we were/are saying a fierce toothsome debate
whether red is the color of constancy or does all dissolve
in the indigo tinted breath of the peacock dancing now
on the thunder stone threnody of cloud work tempest
it all passes by like a flashing arrow entering the hind's
delicate thigh and hills roll away as the flesh opens up
and we hear dozens of voices making noise at once
and the troubled air becomes dense with the meridian
silence slowly burning the last of its uncounted hours
your head drops into earth's moldering dark lap
it is white suddenly a bright entrance to otherness
the most beautiful part of our lives is ending

86.

such as it was life was that brilliant dalliance
spark in the grass that dries unwinding hair
in the involvement of light that invests statues
with a mythology of speech dreaming acts

but held up to the mirror those qualities
those colors and shapes that surf billowing and
heightened joy were clearly an error of perspective
the glass only reflected back a crepuscular stain

one and two and three which are we going to be
the thing on the other side that remains nameless
the thing somewhere in between shapeless and dark
or the thing no one has ever seen Echo itself

of the countless gods and among them marble Apollo
and ivied Dionysus which has ever kept the promise
to keep us together when the stark Queen took you
and I was bidden to strike the unstrung lyre

soil stone fire air earth ether sea's tormented wave
what does it matter which element strives to destroy
the end is always the same a single pointless dot
undifferentiated in a swarm of haunting bees

accompanied by a girl the often invisible one
I spent the only summer of my distant manhood
either she was merged in the dancing sun rays
or an aerial turbulence took her by the hair

whatever the meteorological circumstance
her existence was reduced to a red hiatus
mirage hovering inches above dense pink clover
faint pollen cloud immersed in oceans of heat

alphas spent in a dozen migraines yellowing out
fusion of crocus and narcissus downstream go
wending in hypnotic whirlpools inky steep
nevermore to return indigo to its velvet rain

how little mind we pay to the world of before
when loss sustains a grammar of broken plurals
withered the sigma and the omicron pale
more pallid yet heaven's unreal omegas rent

myth of dots and signs emerging from the leaf
symbols of salt and dew embracing in the eye
ruptures of sand and massy brass in the passing sky
clouds the shape of water surround the sleeping ant

ampersands and viaducts convey unheard traffic
the din of goddesses rioting inside their skin
blood seams genetic codes fistulas and aneurisms
unseemly plants of gorgeous color taint the brain

where do we fit in the order of flies midges and termites
when did we lose our wings when did unconsciousness
take from us the seashore of our lunar holiday
why do we never remember what was meant forever

shakes a hold bitter's sweet undying flame a smoke
devolves sleep's underside a thickening quilt of dark
anomie ennui despair decline in masses of dense hair
hers was the dormant case of angels unrevived

when was the poetry ever lesser than its role
when was the divide between breath and accent
ever so intense the ambergris the faltering cliff
antidotes to life's unwanted underthings

heather domain underfoot whisperings shifts
from azure dun to hills of ochre Umbrian
whenever it will be again is never known
dust in piles of yearly gone the fading out

books derail sentence long dervish drum-rolls
hispid waters roiling high an angered tidal spat
can never be as was my love the hive of your mouth
the honeyed darker sounds of moaning after

'tis to choose from a frame of many longings
painterly kisses sealed in woebegone bed sheets
golden stirs evening's last breezy mists afar
silvery memory argent plaints of finishing

splish splash languid dying on your lips' recall
ginger on the tongue a temple full of wooden
lessons late afternoons declining aspirin moons
how can I ever get her back the bronze of tarnish

the eglantine the ant-heaps by which we lay
I garlanded her tresses in hibiscus jasmine sweet
and ambrosia's rosy trickled down her cheek
as dead we lay for weeks in etruria's dry fane

nor linger then more the breath of life disdain
was bright such dalliance of light heightened touch
a finger lost a forest of tiny grasses smothering
the month's supply of days until the holy dust

Ye gods! by number more than stars can count
where have you her assailed and 'neath what rock
does she smoldering turn to vapid fumes while I
thoughtless bard solid earth betray her memory

a wild beast is my heart turning on its violence
trees and innocent bushes the greening things
uprooted I go ravaging 'til bacchants & maenads
alike an end put to my mind's fleshly discontent

AOI silent flashings understreams small fishes ply
bone-white thoughts polished by eons of dying
smidgens of flower petals bittered torn and lost
every afterwards is here and gone a long away

                    87.
            whence this ghostly swirling where
no idea to burn it goes turning on its empty gyre
            saw it first a day or so ago on the sands
            making vowels to winding quires of sheets it was
            a moan so resonant a reddish consonant
pronounced hard by the lower lip and bled
            do teeth make so deep a mark reclining
peevish twists into a darker coil returning a
            maddened and wanting a go at the furry
does sleep such tricks play on the jesting fool
            a soul marks the air not even so much as
an ink spout a gingerbread chrome something
            sizzles in the waning what gold it stains
she was ne'er so nearly pure as the river's
            and tempting bodies with such brief allure
a flare a fume a smoking nerve ending a story
            before it scarce begins drawing dusty
spires and columns of the unending cloud stuff
            miles before we meet again and the cold
can't explain why and the mold under the pale
            wainscoting where the mourning doves
they do every such thing before daybreak
            sounding like rusty winches freeze framed
dried out on the linen line flapping sorely

can ships go so far in the winter drear
mist bound scuttled and overturned by bile
not recognize that face again its basement
contours coal soot and bottled darkness rank
never said why and collars removed seams
stitching totally undone show a fine blank thigh
curse to a man looking like that ivy twined
around a throat to speak's so hard that kissing
tongue's curled around the nether tone
unaccented the words keep coming out like steam
hissing clanking and ringing the dead to sleep
iron in their fist tight dream of the other land
ahoy mizzen masts half cracked a darn
scattered to the winds all this indigo parley-vous
polite for French in the canning factory
where the girls keep to worms and sodden tins
waiting for five of the clock and histing skirts
making mirth of the clark checking pistol guard
waist deep in hives of honey dancing loll
and furthermore comes meridian a second time
fanning dust spray in the liveried eye
who can see to tell the toll it takes to give a while
especially when underwards the ointment
cracks and insects take to night to learn to die
they've made away with my li'l Eurydice
as well and brighten nothing with their foul
come on don't take it so hard the oil
that runs round metal foil and poem's big bang
they come singing through the ancient grass
the rusted yellow the tinted glass the embossed hide
roaring it is with memory of being hooved
a satyr on the hills cheeking sweet his clarion
sky's the wood to knock on clouds are torn
to be made again in different shapes and temple fold
don't be so gassed revive the pulse within
go greening swiftly through the lair with bone drawn
wasn't it just yesterday the car broke down
the horses ran either way hauling the main frame
you just stood there worse for the spool
a webbing of taffeta and soil your face a mark
talking like you was just out of bed alive

but for the ruin the circular powder the oliphant
       begad a sight you was lovelorn undone a cloth
to be pitied for the wear and nothing else but skin
       the livid spoils of archaic recollect in white
Artemis it was did you in with her unerring aim
       ha! joss house and stable yard a flock of weeds
withering in olden times with mill stone wheeling
       like your mind going daft in gyres ever deep
to pull out of the orient an earwig's flossy stain
       writing hymns of madness to the lunar deity
aspirin solves a legend in despond revolving shots
       you can't go back the shift's gone red to blue
all space is pocked with gutty stuff scarce shining
       and lightning strikes the peacock's bole
shrill cries alarms the call to thunder's arms
       no time for back trekking life's run its thing
albescent horizons thin fading paler most than
       whitened hoar and cast aside the skull
pranks no more the shadow play and silent
       what can no more say the why you were
the evanescent puling by the shore appalling
       driftwood hove into the clearing ere night
its murky sword cut off the main and islands sink
       you with the detritus algae strangled lore
alas the vast is wider still spacious undying realm
       to write these things to reminisce the swell
she was the tender how can you call her back
       mmmmmmmmmmmmmmmmmmmmm

       88.
       "Well since my Baby left me
       I found a new place to dwell
       It's down at the end of Lonely Street
       At Heartbreak Hotel"
deriving from India speaking what hill dialect
does new born god Dionysus spring ivy girt
and noon drunk in search of a bark to lift him
to the Ionian sea   wild his tongue hymns
and praises in any number of languages high
Anatolian Hurrian Hittite and especially Doric

half naked twirling a strange sort of whip with bells
and the girls and boys both eager to follow him
singing singing singing and swilling the cold booze
his right eye is a signal from on high that things
starting today will be different a form of catharsis
through intoxication and from his left eye radiates
a flame a secret burning that can cleanse the soul
practicing strange rites and concealing old mysteries
alike and psalms and threnodies both in his sweet
tenor voice who can understand any of it all those
words recently shaped from light as it were and
a cascade of smoking water from an invisible cloud
who will be the first to succumb and mingle
in his veins the porphyry of this young deity?

code switching from mother tongue to lingua franca
tuning his instrument carved from a tortoise shell
Orpheus seated third from left in the class photo
who would guess his career in enigma and hermeneutics
diffident shy held back pale morose secretive shadowy
not popular almost never dated voice trembled easily
when addressing even a crowd of three who would infer
not sure that like a god he was ever born appearing
initially among rocks and crags wearing a strange pelt
tawny or amber and an affinity for floral games
designs drawn in the heated air and humming always
tunes in a minor key sad melancholy gesturing to
the unheard and unseen to the ones hidden in leaves
distant as heaven to those nearest him a total cipher
a shadow in the woods white flowers where nothing
used to grow mirage of cities inhabited by the undead
where the thousand syllables thrive in a single voice
stepping as it were from and through rock crystal
to fix the shape of water in its archaic tripartite form
making this the moment when all things stand still
animal junction in the midst of burning globes
wings paws fins bright scrutinizing eyes gone blind
breath the all or nothing that lies secretly in stone
where the sun's pulse beats quietly for all eternity

with some trepidation he walked into the Sun Studios

on a day radiant with heat Sam Philips took one look
at him androgynous moony brooding and saw the Future
hummingbird and lizard both in the casual leather
of his demeanor a forest of vowels disassembled in
the nervous diapason of his voice querulous and
commanding at once and looking around the dark
gathered itself in tight flaring knots one could hear
the fierce breathing of an invisible panther prepared
to leap into the amazed silence and the startling noise
of a myriad black birds in oracular flight to the sun
sat down in the small recording booth to start singing
"train I ride sixteen coaches long..."

89.
"Well that long black train got my baby and gone"
is it by the many headaches we come to create
by the solvents and irregular verb charts and the midafternoon
cocktail hostesses in pink filigree flirting with history
is it by the irrepressible love affair with an invisible goddess
whose mile long tresses have their end in the Euphrates
and whose infrequent visitations cause black migraines
the power she is *shakti* to create preserve and destroy
at a whim is it by letting up on the lawnmower and
simply daydreaming beneath the family willow tree
in the everlasting shade of a mythology more real
than the fabricated text books about the Roman Empire
here's the thing I won't take anything back
the road is beyond aspirin and mere dolorous complaints
windows fly open upon hitherto unperceived galaxies
this is not about financial concussions and poverty gaps
nor about the quotidian maelstrom of religious differences at war
not about who does what to whom before hitting the red carpet
nor afternoons squandered in a motel with a faceless mistress
it is about from nihil creating absolutely nothing
until *nothing* sounds more beautiful than the *Follie d'Espagne*!
it is the survival by twin of the manifest unholy
splitting things in half rejoining them renaming them
after the numberless unseen gods residing in the membrane
that separates breath from light and what does it matter
if nothing makes sense if evening precedes every other thursday

if the piano in the bathroom cannot be moved but by levers
upwards into the noosphere where it can resound eternally
in a performance of the Hammerklavier sonata
and I myself am reduced to rubble an inherent nervous ploy
reciting ad infinitum and backwards the various epics
about the seven city states of Etruria and their destruction
rock fitted doom oriented with my thirty seven paramours
who in order of age can only number from alpha to zed
and striking the Hour with my glass finger Behold a
rush of water with its cows syllables and girls--the world created!
I am felled stunned knocked backwards unconscious
aware only of the insect blindly making its way through
the vegetal pleats of stone only to encounter even more worlds
and on and on it goes this insane chicanery of illusion and art
always on the verge never near the center losing balance
holding to the body's precarious gravity looping through
intense cycles of heat and summer and the strange sensation
of loss and longing accompanied by the sirens of distance
ever more faint paling in the sad and crepuscular hill
guarding the remains of what was once palpable
human a barely illumined heap of ash and prayers recited
and the long sequence of lives and rebirths on the wheel

90.

when was it ever over the disregard and ennui
earths of a separate paradigm the stifling afternoons
shunted by an unseen thread back and forth over the chasm
who is you who is who who is me in this repeat version
of the afterlife of a twin produced and presented
by the makers of the holy intuitive process and its other
breaks down all sad the oak shade around its base and
nereids hamadryads and the like pining and moping
waiting for the great hulking three wheeled carts
to take them back past the water over the black demesne
forests of night where croupiers whisper to weavers
non stop wagering on the one way trip with no stopovers
to the palace of no reruns whiteside up under the turf
but no matters do get worse *in the course of things!*
as if everyone could just go on living and gossiping and
going to the museums for lunch and bicarbonate of soda

and the anvil in the window and the chaff and mulch
and the next day with one more book to read another language
to learn another kite to fly into the mansion of the gods and
Artemis with her silver glow lurking in the wings making
like she don't care and *whing zing*! there goes another one
only this time it had to be you moon-cursed and paler
than the day you lost your finger in the grass and something
opened up in the air a hole full of the unused faces of the unborn
darkness with its riveting winds and speeches loosed
in the tumult that for a second seemed to last an eternity
back home again without you and the flares guttering out
like gold threads fraying in the miasma and the place a mess
unswept dust laden mythic shadows pantomiming the walls
Punch and Judy Rama and Sita Orpheus and Euryidice
shibboleth of vowels pronounced like sand in a bottle
who can ever be so late who can exchange roles who would
in the middle of a dream cross over to the other bank of the Lethe
and standing there in the all alone of moon drift freeze
for centuries in the alluvial of oblivion

how little is spent on what we should know
and even less on what we should love
the garden is neither here nor there
sheer rock confronts us unpolished stone
despair seeks its entry in sleeping sand
nowhere the small light of rosy dawn
just the vast and murky distances
endless waters of the pure unknown
for us no fable satisfies no sweet tale
for us not even the great greek restaurant
open Sunday afternoons for the elect of heart
for those in whom the coin of passion
was never spent

91.

abstruse inarticulate incomprehensible
was that what they said about my poem
I was only being elusive enigmatic sublime
and if I said it all before I'll probably
say it all again but in filigree and lace

a dryad from a shady wood sprung
some say she was but what matter
her loss the ever grief to me remains

stopping by a sylvan spring to quench
what spied I in the liquid glass but me
a pronoun out of joint an inflexion tort
strange over quires of distant heat
a flush of indigo in the battered breath
quick I fell into the sublime pitted pool
next unknown a hundred and eight ends
seemed though none my death approached
and sudden spoke from deep without
an inner me to cast darkness in the light
of day no trace remained and where
what was it saying more like a barking
beast this outer me his skin a thing
of riddles and nothing kind to behold
I am to you what you thought you never
were and in a maiden's dress your mind
now frets its uncomely tress and plaint
a wavering dwindled thing a shy a
what most troubles me is what's more
inside than can ever proceed to be again
an afterbirth a renewed life a simply
mythic harmony to seek myriad forms
in parentheses meanings of unzipped night
you cast aspersions on this revolving
thread this shape of water called Eurydice
whose many books of plaited leaves
whose sundered coils pleading voices bleed
contain me no more this tight veil
this *membranum subtile* of hellebore
can nothing revive this pleasure sore
that of yore the greatest thrill am I
so plunged from the rock that me bore
and to this ill plagued land a waste
whence roots tangled a syntax circumflex
no understanding but what summer steals
away and grasses where legend shivers
its insane monotony of love and like dew

too soon vanishes in the sun's errant haze

so there you have it confession and seal
a signature of airy ink that drains the light
and puts an end to this brief written hell
to grammars now and rusty lynch pins
all words are surfeit of the unheard voice
surface terror sleeping below the bole
a section only of the greatest sleep
go then ENVOI and me decline in dark

92.

how does it get so out of focus
one day you're in high school marching
in step with the band wearing a red monkey suit
with gold shoulder braid and blowing into a big brass horn
and the next day writing and re writing a book
you give it up throw it out the window stare
straight into the sun's private maelstrom
daring yourself to go blind because of why
a myth of a whim a psychological imbalance
you don't care you walk out of the mansion looking
for Hermes you want to curse him curse any one
of the gods all thirty three thousand one hundred and six
and as for the embellishments of language and the
breakdown of syntax you go berserk tying knots
at either end of the perfect sentence and like a dog
on its hind legs go howling wildly at that bitch Σελήνη
but then what does it matter a page five million pages
in that backwards Etruscan hand-script you so carefully
cultivated in the mirror all those years to prove
a point what point you can't even articulate it
running willy nilly to the local bar for a shot of Grappa
snarling at the glass tossing your head back as if to
bare fangs bristling at the human touch longing
for the rocks crags cliffs heaths of your unbegotten childhood
all around you they stare they begin to marvel at your
superhuman nature at your intense indwelling madness
coming to the surface manifesting on the skin
like a song about endlessness and the antipodes

you reverse everything revulsion is your primary emotion
you lose one by one the signals that alerted you to the world
is it simplicity you crave is it the ability to annihilate
the self in a storm of nonsense verbiage ultrasound vowels
catapulting consonant clusters into the attic
where your infancy sleeps beneath imagined constellations
is it that lacking focus you also lose gravity can no longer
walk a straight line feel constantly inebriated
can't find the door key walking into the wrong house
fucking the wrong wife mid afternoon go speeding
on a purloined motor scooter a vespa to be sure bzzzzzzzz
rounding the corner at 90 rpm like a phonograph record
about to lose tempo with itself the diamond needle
abrasive and exulting on your brain and if they arrest you
you don't know who you are you can't remember a thing
not even what you had for breakfast today something
else tells you that having lost focus you no longer matter
you take your shoes off and instinctively make for the hills
those mysterious dun colored ochre backdrops
where evening is the only time of day lingering melancholy
chilling with its tall solitary conifers as if pointing at a moon
that is about to rise if only the page would turn
and Bang the similitude of this to everything else proves
you're beyond the pale all exits are the same entrance
there is a light above your head there is a demon in your pulse
there is in your left eye a map developing of the lunar craters
and in your right eye a small flare is lit and it reveals Troy
in the tenth level of its historic midden heap Sing Muse!

                        93.
do I still endure though the better part of me
has escaped this century's degrading strife?
when sky's faint ruddy glow announces things anew
for me the past stains the inky clouds motionless
that embrace the present tense and no more flower
as did the hollyhocks beside the graveled roadway
where once we walked in a light more light than day
but such a brief moment was caught like a butterfly
on the breeze to be transported to climes unknown
wings dust laden in the planet's trembling turn

am I expected to continue my song to tune my instrument?
what soul does omega represent among the many uncounted?
in which of these shapeless rocks is the sun hidden?
is life more than just a literary device?
is *poetry* only an arbitrary error in syntax meant to remove

do the words *opalescent sublime pith* and *arbor* mean
anything more than an elevation or annihilation
of the senses a departure from the ordinary
is *poetry* nothing other than a *memento mori*
the hash-house of death embellished by the Muse's mind
to resemble the

what is the plural of love but the waters underneath
invisible that rushing bear away thoughtless moments
what is this   arbitrary scheme of syllables
to climb sky's unseen ladder into the mansion
where demons wearing the masks of gods plot men's lives
woof and weft and fascicles of multiple personae
all dwelling within a single mind—Mine!
madness is just the beginning of the circle
never the end of the circle never the end of the circle
never the end of the circle madness is just the beginning
and on the hill side I number the variable sheep
whose utter whiteness makes them uncountable indistinguishable
and I make a music on the pipe and foment the solitary rock
and out tumbles the fresh rivulet of a limpid stream
it is worrisome to be green to be fingerless in a dream
to wonder what has happened why has it never happened before?

talk talk talk about these things to an audience of the unheard
redressing the instant of cognition with a stupefying drug
and find oneself crawling up Vallejo street four in the morning
knowing this is the backside of the clouds and not asphalt
an initial form of the rite that correctly performed
and Bang it all goes away desire and the imperturbable
wholeness to be other forever

so it is with me every turn of the century witless
watching warriors of sand pitch themselves against vowels

credited with the invention of language Orpheus
after whom countless theaters are named remains dumb
stricken with the twelve varieties of aphasia known
and who is seen retiring from a life of shadows and doubt
to the more familiar recesses of the Thessalian outback
a virgin to the ways of commerce and globalization
to pen with a peacock quill his unending lamentations
the mysteries of birth and rebirth and deathlessness

must endure the rest of my sojourn on planet Gaia
lacking the better half of what I deemed to be myself
poetry is that redundant sense of loss and longing
that sustains me in the drifting waters of consciousness
for I am without myself as any mirror can contest
a virtual wanderer a mirage passing through stone
a grief a dormant spill a small pool an eye a leaf
there is no bone that clings to me no sinew however

there are sounds I hear more like the colors of the amaryllis
sprouting on a lost hill sounds more like indigo hues
more like the sheen on the side of a brass ornament
echoes of red that pass through my ears when I least

crocus ranunculus nasturtium narcissus hyacinth
in me drown your fainting stains a pale meandering
the wane of endless day

94.

in the world before the world
that was the time before you moved to town
when the unborn gods walked as shadows
that awful undifferentiated season of waste
not sure that their physicality was permanent
when the hills maintained their dusky distance
when the suggestion of light was dangerous
and the temples fallen to ruin   but
in the world before this one happened
what a chance encounter that was on the field
when the unborn gods were at war with their doubles
picking your assortment of variopinto flowers

the demons whose various masquerades
and I chanced by on my imaginary route
set fires up waters rushing and skies to emerge
to the palace of mirages with my invisible music
then this world happened material illusion
a song you stopped to listen falling from your hands
levitating between gravity and anti-matter
a whole array of colors indigo violet red hues
what memory is there of the previous world
tones of burnished longing archaic and fluted
what recollections of that globe suspended
did it matter if I stu-stu-stuttered for lack of words
between paradigms of space and the mirror
did you care if I was only half visible and half rock
that reflects the emptiness of unrecorded time
shadow upon shadow covered the script
how do we come to be walking so many fine lines
the joy I felt and the concomitant despair
maddening corruptions of an imagined purity
of the foreboding I had et cetera

the gaze of the self into the nethermost tracts
where a single water the shape of space
contains all the speculative colors of the mind
unreleased with its centumfoliate personae
aggregates of man and woman combined
white blossom opening within a whiter liquid
a voice issuing from the vegetal recesses
echoing and re echoing the plethora of syllables
cascading like sand falling through the interstices
of a light whose source is beyond determination

hemispheres apart in the world after this one
the following summer we reconnected on a porch
when the unborn gods have ceased being physical
lit up by fireflies your face was a map of distance
succumbing to the doctrine of impermanence
I reached out to touch the phantom proportion
and their doubles the demons have deteriorated
as blithely as water runs under the door jamb
into imps commandeered by the chief sprite death

your presence slipped away into uncounted night
lissome and elusive firefly that she is

there in that peninsula of gas and morphine where
white on white palest lavender a shadow only
dreams go to dry out where desires become eliminated
beside the slender blade of grass a body of dew
the rest of fickle you lies in abandoned waste
shimmering for a moment only evanescent forever
a voice nothing more than a wan handful of vowels
to name the parts of speech to enter into discourse
repercussions of the language of sand tossed
with the gods the unborn ones the incorporeal ones
carelessly to the winds those dark heaving breaths
where in the world to find the entrance to those
and heat in its vast concentric units descends
shining mansions to those mountain girt rooms
to dissolve the portion of time and space
what is an entreaty a prayer an appeal a hymn
which were allotted to the under realm of Pluto
barely visible spirals of bluish smoke wafting high
erasing all memory all trace all permeability
night's deep indigo canopy flutters over the whole
of you that wavering indistinct embolism of water
shivers whispers the sound of feet fleeing sighs
vanishing simply vanishing into the nameless void

95.

the shape of an idea
the force of a form
so goes the translation:
        sublime forte pianissmo gravitas absolutely
in medias res naufragrantibusque ad infinitum swimming
rudderless at the helm grey-eyed Pallas Athena in the guise
of a great-winged sea bird a man's voice pace humana undarum-
que salsedine ventorum *fiammeggiante* end to history to tales
of heroes demons warlords bloodthirsty sanguine dedito ditto
participated in the massacre of thousands of millions of asuras
devas theoi dei hunka munka hunka munka tom-tom voodoo
hell frame falling out of the sky's greater eyelid tuono e lampo

in a flash of an instant of a millimeter of a second it all between
the ears *my god* I was deafened by the roar in mare tantae naves
usque ad litora flammantes fumoque nigro aquaque rubra AOI
spectra dimly walking mists whose feet are denied the touch of earth
tactuque Gaiae et brachia alba circum collum deae wisp of a thing
her underchosies her lachrimans ore aureque what a devil may care
sub terra in solio aureo sedens Maiestas Proserpinae shadowy
billows shuddering vagueness of all mortal emotions pending a
rude hanging from the Lucerna how many other frivolous things
escaped from that box and flitting stinging biting bloodsuckers
wearing girls' faces pinafores all white and full of Zephyrus
visus eius sine forma meant by that a person in the shape of the sky
intravit domumque cremavit et cras quid facies Tu! abhorrent
lying face down in the tufa Umbrian letters engraved on brass
may you by the Gratia Mariae find consolation in his verbis
sit you down on this grass ere evening clears the heavens and
full fireworks of the stars Ursa Minor burning the mind's back
fanged and hissing that basilisk in the corner IO! IO! Euge Phormio
e culina abi! other recensions indicate inebriation of the hand
and the postpositions so amply employed in the Hindustani have
little correspondence tactile and umbratile alike selva oscura
serpentine weaving between the little feet of prosody spondee
and trochaic versatility of the wave pausing between sea salts
mersit in humo manum and out came the worms from the clod
many with voices like those of boys punished for killing flies
in the margins rosy crosses skulls and bones grinning Lear his
filiae uxores Charontis and the magma raining from dark clouds
this saddest day of my life I must pen you the drear news your
dear I am afraid to finish the phrase is dead Lugete Veneres!
(pause)
from Delos sailed we then   ex cursu   cerulean winds
in a little cove put the skiff and all but dead we set foot
burning sands   dry stuff   everything in a blazing
white haze   whose voice cut from the leaf   and slanting
the preternatural light of the fourth hour   meridian
sank slowly into the   like a tapestry opened up
tawny maned the singular beast with honey colored eyes
a maiden's voice   swarms of bees accompanied from Hybla
her hair   a grammar book voice chalky and
twilight   waning everything waning pale absent
lavender and violet shadows   trepidation
the self   the fourth way   light dimension
bodies exchanged   mysteries

96.

"she came through and saved us once again
replacing the unbearable dead fish stench with
heavenly aromas and we waited all morning
our souls in our mouths and about noon
the old man came out on the beach
and as he approached we lay our sturdy hands
to wrestle with him but he did not forget
his wily ways and one by one transformed
himself into a lion a dragon a leopard and
a mighty wild goat he became running water
and a leafy tree but finally with bravery in
our loins we overcame him and he asked what
god has sent us to trap him in his lair"

many the mix of marvels the sleight of hand
the prestidigitation and shifts of thought
that turn the mind from the world of appearances
to that of ideas and the spheres of perfection
the music that issues from no known source
the at last   I am exhausted
and have little more to offer you
hints of sacrificial rites notations mantras
libations to be poured over what smooth rock
juxtapositions in the order of names to call
down the deities from their various houses
that rotate invisibly in the heavens
lay me down here on this bed of mown grass
the head is heavy worn from heaving
artifices into the realm of the senses
you know I am just decibels from the last
and the multiple perceptions of passing time
where is my room the one in which I studied
first the concepts of language and space
did no one ever know to return me there
finding me half dead from love's failure
in the darkening leaf of the hour
am I the lark aloft in flight or the tortoise

bearing its burden out to sea a final time
when the first full moon of autumn draws near
and the scent of jasmine is strong in the night

"and the old man answered that we must take
to the tempestuous waters again and set sail
to the mouths of the Nile in Egypt where
the lotus-eaters have their abode
and as he spoke the blood froze in our veins"

not once but several times indeed in the season
of rain and mistrust when the fields wither up
full of stubble and blasted
and I amidst this map of rock and barren stone
recalling nothing of the
              fiercely beneath the empty moon
in the center where the dedication offering
was laid garlands of brightly colored blooms
and the promise of an ascent to some
where shining the portals to heaven
how could there be an answer to the mysteries
in these small white pebbles in this eerie
a voice out of nowhere came moaning

bad dream loving you, Baby

              97.
to name and number the times echoing
hues of waning to sleep gone the lasting one
buried in the stone of sentiment a drop
nothing eased in the wasting a flame dying
colored faint streaks of gold in night's tapestry
folding down over hills where no one goes
shot through burning clouds of distance
longing shadows that pass through blank walls
cries in the sundered ear the physic of omega
shafts burnished red slowly becoming darker
a nether world just beneath the icy sheets
would not gather the sense to return whole
or fix the body with invisible darts passing

from one world to the next falling steeply
into error carved from solid elephantine
umber halls mirrored in the evening's dune
where a deserted fane pulls in its ghosts
rocking faintly the shuttles of communication
have not been there will not go near there
white tapers against shattered white cornices
curtains of words lost in the wintery mists
sound of bodies many tossed to the briny depths
this error of passage weaving blindly between
endless darkness and darkness unending
lose count threading memory's thin flue
through the bric-a-brac of numbing illusions
painted here and there a deep ochre or mauve
lumbering through muds of night one-wheeled
carts bearing carcasses urns of ashes timber
rotting stumps by the side voices issuing
from tangled foliage with autumnal syllables
everyone being nowhere in mattresses of space
bleeding sound into the thick gasoline turf
until nothing resounds no vowel of sand
no consonants once rich with liquid gold
syntax riddled with mistaken propositions
brown services the aging brass tarnished
when doors hanging by a hinge swing violently
in the mental tempest of an isolating rage
it isn't the colors blending into an untoward surf
nor the winds rushing with their nations of cinder
but something else falling asleep

pile rock upon rock
pile rock upon *cursed* rock
SHIBBOLETH!
it is the mid seventeenth century
and we are looking for new musical forms
stone contradicts stone
stone contradicts *cursed* stone
is δικαιοσύνη only to be found
where the stately sarabande
the ground the chaconne and passacaglia
are measured to the thrill of the running bass

counterpoint! life the uncountable
scansioned in beats and strophes and breathings
pile sand upon sand
pile sand upon *cursed* sand
SHIBBOLETH!
and of Αρετη what of its nature
who is to qualify its density and width
its proportions of air to water
and what of life the uncountable
moving as a serpent through the shoals
of consciousness one after another
the births and rebirths
which am I and which is you?
is it possible to count higher than three
without getting bewildered?
is that what civilization is – the higher numbers?
SHIBBOLETH!
fix sleep upon sleep
fix sleep upon *cursed* sleep
this error of passage weaving blindly between
endless darkness and darkness unending

98.

the long descending curtain call of Hellenism
the body of the wound inarticulate invisible
hemispheres of sand and distance divided among satraps
my girlfriend in a trance dancing on the body
and greeklings Seleucids and Ptolemies astronomers
disquisitions about the soul and where it goes
and Babylonian star gazers writing mini-epics
wearing her pony tail and Nile-blue boots
about the duration of the sky and the length of time
comatose in a small puddle by the time I got to her
in Bactria and Gandhara encounter with avatars of Vishnu
can there be more than one Jupiter I kept asking
Buddhas turned into greek statues mouthing orphic riddles
amorphous as the sky the soul's impalpable presence
papyri of mythological poetry in pure Attic dialect
a thing with frayed edges azure fringes soundlessly
devolving from origins in stone the unending variation

in wispy indigo hues like a last breath ascending
of the seer's life caught between enlightenment and oblivion
and in the temple outskirts where the ruddy stream flows
between inter-dimensional travel and utter damnation
where the yellow crocus and darting goldfish play
fed to maenads and bacchants in aspiration to godhead
conjugating verbs of inaction and languorous submission
and the unutterable secrets of eternal love
anklets small ear pendants and thirty ivory bracelets
experiments in atomic theory and the steam engine
reed beds flattened nasturtiums hyacinth jonquil
bucolic idylls and the hymn to Mithra
lay the head to rest beneath this silent verse
wasp-waisted Isis doing pyramid math sacred cats monsters
introduction to the afterlife in a slender blade of grass
with crocodile heads Thoth the double of Hermes
or a sun hidden in this mass of unhewn marble
Berenice's Lock the Almagest and various Phainoumena
the heavens themselves swept from view under the eyelid
celestial warnings cataloged in the Library of Alexandria
are we merely dead or are we past the point of survival?
what have the Achaemenids bequeathed us? soteriology?
one hieroglyph after another issuing from her mouth
magic dark untruths floral juxtapositions papillae
vowels the shape of the new moon diphthongs hiatus
passing from Transoxiana to the Hindu Kush feverishly
as if a forest of languages were burning in a single moment
heard nothing but the hollow echoes of remote tympana
nothing sanctioned nothing inhibited nothing revealed
on dromedaries carrying burdens of thought and number
the slender blood-red thread tied around her left wrist
and in exchange brought back intricately sculpted temples
and if we are not merely dead but without salvation?
mother-goddesses with fifty breasts sweating magnificently
and if I could not keep my promise about rebirth?
the beat of the tom-tom the soles of their feet brightly painted
if there is no edge to things then there is no center
swirling far into the night inebriated and exultant
hush in the stone within the stone silence all about
skirts shed like snake skins thighs lustrously gleaming
nor will I offer my life as the price for any other life

erected Sancta Sanctorum in the very desert
though divine I am not the god you prefer
and from bare walls ivy sprung entwining minds
I am but the chaos indwelling the ferment of the East
arithmetic syllabaries prescriptions for opium and Bang
she has died unto me a hundred million times over
Vita Alexandri mum mum mum hash eaters assassins
and if there is no center how can anything be measured
small café near the Hellespont over a cup of Turkish coffee
moving out through the dream portals into sleep's
discussed the etymologies of the many Nereids and Nymphs
             unending   *-lessness*
wearing a leopard's skin the pseudo Herakles entered
talking talking talking
the emperor Nero
         QUALIS ARTIFEX PEREO

         99.
         "Now surely Phoebus knocketh at the door
            with his beautiful foot"
               Callimachus
mothers, I have come this long stony path
scarce remembering the day I set forth the light
the formlessness of the sky and all that I witnessed
without shape nameless haunting things in stone
or in rocky recesses along the way, mothers
there were flowers in profusion on hillslopes
peonies hydrangeas dogwood hyacinth jasmine
and bees in dense swarms marking the air
where did I think I was where in what world
was I meant to make a passage from the other
time to this one, mothers, I do not know any
other way any other light any other sky above
the shape of light and the extent of sky flowers
what is destiny to me what is another life
beside this one the one I did not choose but
which some wayward deity has signaled out
for me, mothers, do not recall clearly why
it was I set out on this rocky meandering path
to give birth to language and to music fair

to give to things without form shape and name
and in passing to catch in the air some beauty
a visage sudden in appearance and forthwith
her espy stepping forth from a water fresh
as the morning rose dappled with otherness
singing some paean to the goddess her hand
intent on removing the briar from the *wound*
and, mothers, how smitten was I then in her
gaze that chance to alight upon me a shadow
a mere transitory being coming to daylight
to know between stubble and towering cliff
the edgeless spheres of thought incommensurate
dimensions of longing as if the fields that drink
summer had this creature yielded from a depth
and together for some brief moments dallied
plucking from the hawthorn a bloom to put
in her spreading chestnut hair a whiteness
dazzling in the, but, mothers, too soon does
this shining turn to dull and by a sudden wince
go lost in the dun colored hills of distance
dust dissolved in the fiery breath of the south
wind whence this consternation and dizziness
this unsure footing on the sharp rocky ledge
am I to fall would it be any sweeter for grief
than this instant pivoting on the eternal
directionless and unfathomable wherever I
but, mothers, what is it to you I make this
plaint this sorrowing noise strung on my lyre
for neither you nor any one of the unseen
gods can restore that phantom pallid presence
smoke returns no sooner to its source than
love unbidden and were I to descend to the
realms of the Queen of Hell what would that
avail me this solitary passenger on the path
mothers, *nameless haunting things in stone*

100.
Eurydice, her afterlife

seashells small roseate found on some mountain path

bees on a dry stump

                              iridescent the hummingbird
air ablaze

            indigo cry of the peahen

      echo of a hive

         thunder in the ivy

invisible flames
              of longing

vowels of sand

                 a voice the shape of ink

grass trodden by invisible feet

                   unheard prayer to Artemis
claustrophobia

seashells small roseate found on some mountain path

101.
"Orpheus, son of the Thracian King Oeagrus and the Muse Calliope
was the most famous poet and musician who ever lived."
Robert Graves, The Greek myths

the afternoon of the *Pastoral Symphony*
      on the map it is no time at all
hills redolent of sage thyme and oleander
      mingling in the dense foggy marine layer
who set the maenads on him
      and cast his head still singing
into the waters to float to Lesbos
    ire and jealousy
      for instituting the mysteries of Apollo

Hecate and Subterranean Demeter
        has angered Aphrodite as well
rocks moved by pity weep
    hard stone drifting sands salty buttes
the world is nothing but echo
    a distant shiver a night shade drawing
its fatal curtain over the demesne of fireflies
    did pass by here at day's end
words variations mills ford by river's
    edge the eddying waters of
        phrasing deep green vowels liquid
transparent but meaningless
    unless from the looming shape of
darkness other worlds stir a
    tempo in the gathering leaves in
the unbidden voice of the grass of
    a finger lost to evening's peril
how indistinct memory becomes in sand
    dissolving its light in the descending foam
a bird a broad winged kestrel
    mewing in the invisibility
waves surging darker still on to the shore
    the head drifting in the wine-tinted waters
singing the incomprehension of it all

        exit Orpheus

Berkeley CA, 06/03/14-08/29/14

IVAN ARGÜELLES' *ORPHIC CANTOS*

"The ghost may represent a refusal to let go, as in classical accounts of melancholia, but this may also lead to new attachments and solidarities... Instead of shutting down the past, the ghost in [James Joyce] occupies a transitional zone in which traumatic memory has the potential to act as a resource of hope, providing glimpses of a way forward, even in the darkest of times."— Luke Gibbons, *The Irish Times.*

As we age we discover to our dismay that relationships we had expected to last a lifetime disappear: loved ones—even the marvelous ones—die. In an age of skepticism, in which the heaven stories carry little weight, how do we deal with this immensely disturbing situation? Ivan Argüelles' *Orphic Cantos* is an exploration of this situation—intensified here (a) by the fact that the loved one is an identical twin, the famous New Age prophet José Argüelles and (b) by the poet's own sensibility, which has passed beyond Surrealism into a language-haunted, "syntagmatic" assertion of imaginative chaos, multiplicity, a depth he refers to as "enormous enigma / unformed." "Tell all the truth but tell it slant," advised Emily Dickinson: "The Truth must dazzle gradually / Or every man be blind." Here is Argüelles:

> **the sea with faces of a hundred thousand suns**
> **the woman with eyes the color of salt**
> **the black wind that never goes backwards**
> **the protean egress through funnels of ink**

Orphic Cantos supplies hope and depth to inchoate feelings that cling to the very substance of daily living. "How little," the poet observes,

> **how little we have traversed all these years**
> **leaning over into the abyss**
> **to see in eternity's opaque mirror**
> **what semblances we are to the recent dead**

—Jack Foley

Beneath the phenomena of Ivan Arguelles' Orphic Cantos there remains this hidden respiration that expands and contracts via nutation, nutation that implies something other than human complication "with its consonants of oblivion and decay." One feels a concussive roar that has in its midst the contraction and expansion common to all phenomena, but with this difference, this being the germinating power known to all planes and possibilities. —Will Alexander

Heretical and erudite; passionate, aphoristic narrative ...the single thread is Ivan Arguelles, his mixed tape... his heterogeneous landscape of classical allusion, care and the torment of those have gone through hell, from Orpheus to Dante to Homer. Eat your cookies on the banks of the Styx, since you cannot forget love's loss. —Peter Sherburn-Zimmer

There is a wonderful lyricism in Orphic Cantos that seems to come from a rich sonorousness infused with equally rich imagery. This collection has a poignant beauty enhancing the reader's experience of each poem. A sense of loss pervades the poems, but it is part of a fully realized broader whole. Here is more evidence that Ivan Argüelles is contemporary America's most brilliant poet. These are poems worth savoring. —Fred Bauman